The Design and Practice of Joinery

Joinery in a house at Whitchurch, Oxfordshire, designed by the authors, 1957

John Eastwick-Field, B.A.Arch.(Hons.), A.R.I.B.A.,

John Stillman, Dipl. London, A.R.I.B.A.

The Design and Practice of Joinery

Foreword by Robert H. Matthew, C.B.E., M.A., F.R.I.B.A.

Drawings by Robert Maguire, A.A. Dipl. Hons., A.R.I.B.A.

THE ARCHITECTURAL PRESS LONDON

Made in Great Britain. Printed by the Shenval Press, London, Hertford and Harlow;

and bound by G. & J. Kitcat Ltd

Table of Contents

List of Illustrations

Acknowledgments

NOTE *This book was first suggested by the* R.I.B.A. *Text and Reference Books Committee (Chairman, W. A. Allen), and the authors were greatly assisted by the grant of the* R.I.B.A. *Alfred Bossom Research Fellowship made to them jointly in 1954 by the Royal Institute of British Architects.*

We are grateful for the help given by many individuals, firms, associations and research bodies in the collection of material for this book. As far as possible the information has been obtained direct, rather than from other books, and most of the photographs have been specially taken.

During the last three years we have visited joinery manufacturers in London and the Home Counties who have readily answered our questions and allowed us to take photographs at their works; in particular D. Burkle and Sons Ltd, Ebdon's, Samuel

Elliott and Sons (Reading) Ltd, H. Newsum and Co Ltd, Rippers Ltd, John Sadd and Sons Ltd, Tomo Trading Co Ltd, John P. White and Sons Ltd. Also the joinery departments of Dove Brothers Ltd and G. E. Wallis and Sons Ltd.

Messrs William Mallinson and Sons Ltd gave us similar assistance for the chapter on the timber trade, Messrs Adams and Co (West Drayton) Ltd for veneering, and Hampton and Sons Ltd for polishing.

Many individuals gave their help and encouragement and we would like to thank particularly William Allen, B.ARCH., A.R.I.B.A., Chairman R.I.B.A. Text and Reference Books Committee, Charles Allman, R. H. Hordern, F.I.M.WOOD T., Lecturer, Liverpool College of Building, David Medd, A.R.I.B.A., W. B. Metcalf, A.I.O.B., J. H. Napper, M.A., F.R.I.B.A., A.M.T.P.I., Norman Potter, C. C. Spence, B.A., A.R.I.B.A., Harry Trinick, F.R.I.C.S.

Of the research bodies and trade associations, mention must be made of the detailed information on timbers supplied by Dr W. P. K. Findlay, D.SC., and Mr W. C. Stevens of the Forest Products Research Laboratory, Department of Scientific and Industrial Research, and advice on many matters received from P. O. Reece, A.M.I.C.E., M.I.STRUCT.E., A.M.I.MECH.E., the Director of the Timber Development Association. The Joinery Managers' Association made a valuable contribution by reading and criticising the original drafts. We are also indebted for advice and loan of photographs to the British Wood Preserving Association, The Kiln Owners' Association, The Fibre Building Board Development Organization Ltd, and The Furniture Development Council.

For valuable information on finishes we thank Mr A. J. Evans of Hadfields (Merton) Ltd, and also the paints division of the I.C.I.; and for technical and trade information on other specialized subjects we acknowledge the help given by G. B. Crow of Beves and Co Ltd, J. Gliksten and Son Ltd, W. W. Howard Bros and Co Ltd, and The Phoenix Timber Co Ltd; C. F. Anderson and Sons Ltd, Flexo Plywood Industries Ltd, Thomas de la Rue and Co Ltd, Thames Plywood Manufacturers Ltd, Veneercraft Ltd, Warerite Ltd, and John Wright (Veneers) Ltd, and K. S. Meakin of Aero Research Ltd.

PHOTOGRAPHS. Messrs John Sadd and Sons Ltd kindly allowed us to reproduce some of a series of photographs taken at their works by John Maltby: Figs. 3, 20, 81, 99, 126 and 128. John Goldup, Esq., allowed a photograph of his new house to be the frontispiece. Other photographs were lent by F.I.D.O.R.: Figs., 216 and 217; J. A. Hewetson and Co Ltd: Fig. 25; Interwood Ltd: Fig. 264; D. Meredew Ltd: Fig. 197; Frank Newby, Esq.: Fig. 198; British Plimber Ltd: Fig. 234; Thomas de la Rue & Co Ltd: Fig. 247; Stenners of Tiverton Ltd: Figs. 18, 73 and 129; The Vere Engineering Co Ltd: Figs. 218, 219, 232, 233 and 244; Wadkin Ltd: Figs. 75, 76 and 80; and Warerite Ltd: Figs. 245, 246 and 248. Many of the photographs were specially taken by W. J. Toomey of the *Architects' Journal*.

BIBLIOGRAPHY. The R.I.B.A. library made valuable suggestions and with the N.B.L. checked the final bibliography. The British Standards Institution helped compile the list of BS joinery specifications and kindly gave permission for extracts of BS 1186 Part I to be reproduced.

Finally, the authors consider themselves fortunate in having had the assistance of Robert Maguire, A.R.I.B.A., who, besides helping in the research, produced all the line drawings and the book jacket; and in having had the closest co-operation with Colin Boyne and Lance Wright of the *Architects' Journal*, in which periodical the bulk of the material in this book originally appeared, and with Raymond Philp and Tom Colverson of the Architectural Press during the various stages of the book's production.

November 1957

JOHN EASTWICK-FIELD
JOHN STILLMAN

Foreword by Robert H. Matthew

In recent years joinery has received scant attention among architectural text-books. The days of the nineteenth-century Joiners' Handbooks, sometimes illustrated with a precision and clarity that might well be the envy of students today, have been forgotten; I doubt if the craftsmen's vademecum, however well produced, has ever been considered suitable for a 'professional' curriculum. Nevertheless, joinery remains one of the most important elements in building; timber for finishings, both inside and out, has, after a period of some neglect, not only regained its popularity, but has increased greatly in range. If there is one common characteristic among progressive architects, it is a renewed appreciation of the qualities of this most traditional of materials.

When I look through the fragmentary sections on joinery in the text-books of my own student days, it is not hard to appreciate why the practising notabilities of the day sometimes took a slightly cold view of formal education. For their part, they carried the knowledge in their heads (so it was said), but they successfully kept it there, much to the detriment of the schools.

When sections of this book appeared in serial form, a year or two ago, in the *Architects' Journal*, it was evident that a new standard in text-book writing was about to be attained. This promise has been amply fulfilled. The book is a comparatively short one: the subject obviously far from simple. But within eight chapters, the authors have brought together a logical presentation of the essential facts: essential, that is, from the point of view of the architect who, as designer, must know what is possible, must make his precise intentions clear, and, not least, must then be able to judge whether, in fact, he (and his client!) is getting what he wants.

In my view, one of the most valuable characteristics of this book is the consistent examination of the limitations of the material considered against a wide background of possible use. The mechanization of the joinery trade, and the development of plywoods, boards and veneers might well have induced in the young designer a belief that the limitations inherent in traditional joinery have virtually disappeared. The chapters on the nature of timber, and particularly on movement in timber, are a sharp reminder that wood is a natural organic substance still highly sensitive, after all its processing, to the atmosphere. I have not read anywhere a more useful description of the factors governing movement in timber. The tables (Fig. 25) of comparative moisture movement values, taken along with the graphs of equilibrium moisture contents for different relative humidities

(Fig. 26), are a most valuable guide to the selection of appropriate timbers.

The analysis of construction (with its illuminating division of requirements into *skeleton frames* or *flat areas*), and the following full discussion of the design and machining of sections and joints are dealt with in terms of basic principles, illuminated at all points by well chosen examples. Throughout the book, the illustrations, by drawing or photograph, are clear and intelligible: the drawings, particularly, are a model of their kind.

I find the whole approach of the authors to this eminently practical subject both new and stimulating. New, because of the degree of common sense and logic applied to the analysis of intricate processes against a wide general background. Stimulating, because, while the subject must for convenience be divided into recognizable sections, the book as a whole has a sense of unity. Requirements and performance are linked at all times, and clear reasons are given for all recommendations.

Chapters VI (Plywoods, Boards and Veneers) and VII (Transparent Finishes) cover much new ground. Chapter VIII (Specification and Practice) should be read by every practising architect, and I have no doubt will be. This volume is more than a school text-book: its value to architects has already been demonstrated from the preview already mentioned: its value to the joiners and manufacturers of joinery as an indication of the way that the mind of the architect works in relation to their trade will, it is hoped, be greatly appreciated. I hope that students will not be daunted by the number of British Standards Specifications applicable to joinery listed in Appendix III: they might be especially grateful for the specification check list suggested on p. 185.

I commend this volume to all interested in good joinery, and also, may I be permitted to add, to potential producers of architectural text-books.

ROBERT H. MATTHEW

Department of Architecture
University of Edinburgh

Introduction

This book is about joinery; that is, about all the woodwork which is exposed to view in a finished building. It deals with the architect's work in his office, at the joinery works, and on the site; with what he has to do, in fact, to design and supervise the production of joinery.

It may be argued that joinery has become a specialized industry and that reliance can be placed on manufacturers for technical knowledge, making it unnecessary for an architect to have more than a superficial knowledge of the subject. Many architects in fact do no more than draw the profiles and leave the construction to the joinery trade. We think that there are at least two good reasons why this procedure is unsatisfactory and why, therefore, this book is necessary: one, that without some knowledge the architect can be thoroughly misled, and will not know whether what is being made for him is being well done or badly done; and two, that since it is not always possible to go to firms whose standing is such that it is in their own interest to produce only the best, he must be able to specify what he requires in sufficient detail to ensure that he obtains work of the standard which he has in mind, and his specification and drawings must contain sufficient information to permit fair tendering.

Of course, in practice, an architect has to consider everything at once! But a book must for convenience be divided into chapters, so the subject matter of each chapter in this book and the order of the chapters have been arranged to correspond roughly with the stages in the actual production of joinery.

Quite apart from the two reasons we give above for writing the book, we feel that much joinery which is produced today is inferior in quality and in design—though the best is as good as ever it was—and that a book which sets out the principles of design will be helpful in raising the general standard.

The factors which we think have contributed to a deterioration in the quality of joinery are:

Bad timber: most defective work is blamed on the poor quality of timber available, particularly since the last war, but it is by no means the only factor and it has been much exaggerated. Exploitation and bad afforestation have certainly resulted in the loss of most of the larger trees, particularly in respect of softwood: also many of the sources of supply for both hardwoods and softwoods are now denied us as a result of economic conditions. Best quality timbers from the Baltic ports have not been imported for some time, and since the last war the principal familiar and well tried hardwoods, particularly Honduras mahogany, Burma teak and good quality English oak, have been either prohibitively expensive or difficult to obtain. Despite the excellent work of the Forest Products Research Laboratory and of the Timber Development Association in publishing reliable information about the behaviour of the unfamiliar species of hardwood now imported in large quantities and varieties, the timbers themselves are not all reliable and the trade has not yet had time to build up a working knowledge of all the varieties it may encounter.

Seasoning: old methods of air seasoning are now largely being replaced by kiln seasoning and although the latter is in theory no less satisfactory than air seasoning, it requires considerable skill in operation, and in practice this is not invariably given. Many practical joiners are doubtful about its efficiency, and from experience claim that it makes their work less reliable. There is, however, no question but that kiln seasoning is necessary if only to obtain dry enough timber for use in centrally heated buildings. Central heating is in fact probably the cause of more trouble in joinery than anything else, because the low moisture content which it demands is so often ignored.

Cheapness and the tendering system: we now accept a standard of workmanship which would not have been accepted in the nineteenth century. Because of the demand for cheap standard joinery, techniques have changed and machine production has greatly increased. In a competitive market it is understandable that there is a temptation to employ relatively unskilled labour and allow very rough work to pass. New materials, such as plywood, chipboards and hardboard, which, when intelligently used, are of great advantage, are often abused.

The development of competitive tendering has made it more difficult for the architect to work closely with the joiner. He is expected to complete his details before the contractor or joiner is appointed: thus he does not have the opportunity of discussing his proposals in detail with the joiner when he is working out the design.

Labour: in common with most building crafts, there is a shortage of men who are really highly skilled, and the present wages are based rather on quantity of production than on skill in workmanship. The number of manufacturers, therefore, who are qualified and willing to take the trouble to produce good joinery is probably less than it was in the past.

Architects' education: when architects were trained in offices they learnt their joinery by the experience of detailing. Joinery was a very important part of architectural design and if they were lucky they will have benefited from the knowledge of their principals in whose offices there may well have been a strong tradition.

Today most architects are trained in schools where a multitude of subjects is taught over a relatively short period, and joinery, which in any event does not lend itself readily to theoretical teaching, is often given insufficient attention.

Departure from established practice: formerly there was more timber used in any one building than there is generally today, and fairly elaborate

16

joinery such as folding shutters, cornices, porches, panelling and so on held an important place even in humble domestic work. To architects, joinery was of importance as a means of aesthetic expression since it contributed greatly to the character of buildings: and to the craftsman it provided a test of skill. The incentive to produce good work was strong, and there was a correspondingly greater need for expert knowledge.

Because the components commonly used in the eighteenth and nineteenth centuries are both too elaborate and too expensive for general use today and belong to a different aesthetic, it has become more necessary to invent new designs for joinery. The architect will, however, not find books on the subject which do more than repeat the traditional patterns—sash window, battened door, panelled door, etc.—showing sizes and shapes of sections, but giving little guidance on the principles on which they were originally designed.

THE INDUSTRY

We now propose to say something about the various people who make joinery and about their factories and workshops because we feel that to know something of them will enable the architect to avoid impracticable details and waste of time and material, and will also enable him to take proper advantage of the widely differing kinds of joinery works of which the industry is composed. For example, a particular design for a handrail terminal for a housing estate which the architect might think would be simple to make but which has not only to be put many times through a machine but also to be finished with a spokeshave by hand, would not be taking advantage of the machine production desirable for this class of work.

When one comes to consider what kind of firm shall undertake any particular work, one finds that, very broadly speaking, there are at present three classes of joinery works, each of which is best fitted to do certain kinds of work: the small builders' shop, the independent joinery works together with shopfitters and joinery works belonging to large firms of building contractors, and finally works organized for mass production.

The small builders' joinery shop, traditionally a part of every builder's organization, is mainly used nowadays to carry out small scale work in which there is no great quantity, and for repairs. The quality of the work is variable and depends to what extent the builder has retained a traditional organization, employing skilled craftsmen and having some system for obtaining properly seasoned timber. Within limits of quantity and for the class of work which they are equipped to undertake, it is possible for such shops to turn out work equal in quality to that of large factories with elaborate machinery, and to do so very economically. They have, however, little capacity for working out the construction from a design drawing and are unlikely to produce work satisfactorily which relies on modern techniques. On the other hand, although they would possibly not learn much from the architect about traditional forms of joinery such as double hung sash windows, they would nevertheless welcome and expect to receive full size details, particularly for anything which departs at all from the conventional. They will normally produce their best work if the architect discusses the job with the actual joiner who undertakes the work and who is, incidentally, in all probability the same man who will later fix the joinery in the building, and with whom the architect will inevitably come into contact on the site. Nowadays, however, by no means all builders have their own joiners' shops, and it is likely that the number who do will decrease. Builders find it difficult to provide a steady flow of work for their shops, particularly since doors and windows can be purchased more cheaply from factories where they are mass produced to standard designs.

In the second class, there are the independent joinery works, which may vary considerably in size but which are generally bigger and more fully equipped with machinery than the average builder's shop. They now supply the bulk of the joinery for the building industry—acting as sub-contractors, sometimes nominated by the architect but quite often they are approached by the builder direct. Because of the volume of work which they handle they are able to work more efficiently and economically and to take advantage of more elaborate and expensive machinery than the small builder could afford. Sometimes they are able to maintain their own timber stocks and kilns and in our opinion this gives them an obvious advantage. The best and some of the worst joinery is produced in these independent joinery works, and it behoves the architect to find out any particular firm's reputation before entrusting his work to it or allowing his builder to do so. Most of the large contracting firms maintain joinery works, under separate management, which, whilst being a part of the concern, are in no way comparable to the small builders' shops, and do in fact supply joinery on a large scale to the trade in general, as well as to their own firms. They can therefore be considered in the same category as the independent firms and are accustomed to giving estimates in competition with them. Within the general category of 'independent' firms there are some which specialize in very high class and complicated joinery both for modern buildings and for restorations, where much of the work may have to be carried out by hand, if not actually carved. It often happens too that the work which these firms undertake extends to furniture and cabinet making—and the furniture may range from individual designs by architects to mass produced articles such as wireless cabinets. A number of the larger firms, some of which are owned by the principal furnishing stores, have gained reputations for work requiring special knowledge, such as the interior fitting of ships, hotels and board rooms, and are able to call upon associated departments to enable them to carry out the whole of the interior furnishing, including, if necessary, its design. Slightly different in character are the 'shopfitters', since such firms employ craftsmen in many trades in addition to joiners. The different trades work together in the same building to produce the often intricate fittings which are used in shops, and which incorporate glass and metals and plastics, as well as timber. These firms and others similarly organized carry out exhibition stands and often design them themselves. The standard of workmanship is

18

usually high, and for work involving the combination of several materials and the use of new techniques such as might be required in a showcase or counter, it would be appropriate for the architect to ask them to undertake the work, although because of the organization and labour which they have to maintain they may be more expensive than other joiners.

Finally, in the third class there are firms who are specially organized for the manufacture of standard articles by methods of mass production. Since the demand for standard joinery components is mainly confined to doors, windows, skirtings, staircases and cupboard fittings made to British Standard and English Joinery Manufacturers' Association specifications and these are largely needed for housing estates, such factories aim at producing the components as cheaply as possible.

MACHINE PRODUCTION

Having mentioned machines in connection with mass production we must avoid giving the impression that only in works of this kind are machines used extensively. In fact all joinery works and shops—except the smallest of local builders—are equipped with machines which perform a number of basic functions (sawing, planing, moulding, joint making) and, in the main, the large machines for mass production are designed to perform the same functions, but to perform them more quickly.

It can be taken that under today's conditions, timber sections are always prepared by machinery: that is to say, they are cut from the logs, thicknessed, planed, moulded and sanded by machine. Having obtained the required section, the joints are also nearly always cut by machinery. Incidentally, the joints which the machine makes are, with few exceptions, almost identical with those traditionally made by hand, and their design is, broadly speaking, conditioned by the timber and not by the tools.

After the joints have been cut, however, their fitting together, gluing, wedging, cramping and finishing is almost invariably done by hand. Only in certain works where mass production is fully exploited, as in the manufacture of flush doors (and very rarely in casement windows), are there machines which do the whole operation, so that this general pattern of work is departed from.

With the increase in mechanization there has come about a distinct division of trades into 'woodworking machinist' and 'carpenter and joiner', even to the extent of allegiance to different unions. The craftsman joiner, who used to carry out the whole operation, now receives the sections fully prepared with the joints cut by the machinist, and his work is thus restricted to the putting together and finishing.

1: The Timber Yard

Tradition is still strong in the timber trade which seems to retain a nineteenth century atmosphere to a greater degree than do most other sections of the building industry. The trade is still linked closely with water transport; the logs are often floated down river, shipped port to port, and frequently even today brought by barge to the timber yard or joinery works. One notices that most large joinery works are sited beside rivers or canals for this reason.

The trade requires a high degree of personal experience and knowledge. No two logs are alike and their selection and grading before conversion call for great skill. The reputable importers and merchants are in a position to give advice to their customers both as to the most suitable choice of timber for a particular purpose and also as to the selection of the actual pieces to be used. It is in their interest that the various timbers be used to their best advantage and their customers satisfied; and they are therefore always pleased when architects discuss their problems with them and visit the timber yards. At the very least they like their customers in ordering timber to state the way in which it is to be used.

The timber trade also has its highly competitive and often less scrupulous side. Dozens of varieties of hardwoods have been sold under the names of well-known woods such as mahogany, oak, teak and walnut. The publication of British Standards 881 and 589, *Nomenclature of Commercial Timbers*, has provided a solution to this problem, but even in compiling this standard some of the misleading names in general use had to be retained. For instance, woods known by the standard names Tasmanian oak, Rhodesian teak and African walnut have no botanical relationship with oak, teak or walnut. In spite of the British Standard, loose descriptions of timber are still accepted, and an order for 'mahogany' might easily produce gaboon, which is not a mahogany at all, or sapele or West African mahogany, both of which belong to the mahogany family (*Meliaceae*) but which are a different genus from the true mahogany (genus: *swietenia*). It is indeed unlikely that one would get the latter, which is now available from Central America, unless it was asked for specifically.

Apart from the obvious fact that the wood supplied may not behave in the way expected, accurate description is essential where competitive tenders are being sought for joinery contracts which might run into several thousand pounds. On many small jobs it may matter little if the architect specifies 'mahogany' and gets sapele, or if he notes on the drawing merely 'hardwood top' and gets what the joiner happens to have in his shop, but if the value of joinery in a building amounts to, say, £30,000, and this goes to tender, an accurate description of the species and grade of timber is essential. One way out of this difficulty, which we discuss in Chapter 8, is to include in the specification a prime cost sum for the cost of the timber (per cubic foot), but, unless this is accurate, the accepted estimate does not give a true indication of the final cost of the work, and the advantages some joiners may have in purchasing timber are lost.

Putting aside the need to be able to specify accurately so as to obtain prices which give a fair comparison, there are other good reasons for an architect's knowing more about timber than merely the superficial characteristics of a sample in the office, or of the prepared material in the joiner's shop. Some general knowledge of the sources of timbers commonly used, the systems of supply, methods of conversion, stacking, kilning and grading is most helpful as a background to all that one may have to do with joinery.

On the practical side such a knowledge will enable one to realize the limits in size of different kinds of timber, and to avoid designing sections which are wasteful to produce; it will also help to clarify the bewildering number of timbers and to gain a working knowledge of those which are most useful. * The ability to talk the same language as merchants and joiners increases the mutual respect and confidence between the various parties and leads to greater co-operation when a particular job of work is carried out. Furthermore the sight of wood in the log or in planks at a timber yard impresses itself on the memory more vividly than a small sample; and a discussion about the characteristics of any particular species of a timber is likely to be remembered more than reference to a book.

This knowledge increases one's feeling for the particular values of the material from which designs are to be realized. Timbers vary enormously and their different characters should be recognized and expressed by the designs in the same way that the technique of the stone mason is varied according to the hardness and texture of the stone or marble being cut. By talking with people in the trade one quickly learns that many species of timber have definite 'personalities'. By tradition certain woods have become associated in the craftsman's mind with particular uses, and fashions for woods have like other things changed with different periods of history. English oak was for centuries regarded as the best joinery wood, and was once used almost exclusively in work of high quality; a tradition which remains in ecclesiastical work. It is still usually wax polished and the joints are often pinned in a way which derives from early techniques. By contrast, Cuban mahogany, often known as Spanish mahogany, was, until the forests were exhausted at about the time of the 1914–18 war, the joinery wood *par excellence* for the highly polished panelling and sophisticated work so admired in the nineteenth century.

These traditional associations are more often than not quite logical. English oak, for instance, is a strong tough virile wood subject to movement and splitting. It looks well treated simply, but has lost much of its reputation by

* See Appendix I, p. 188, for selected list of joinery timbers and their characteristics.

its ubiquitous use for panelling work, veneered plywood and cellulosed light oak furniture and fittings, mainly of course in Japanese and other foreign varieties which, being more regular, look anaemic beside true English oak. Another famous wood, teak, won its reputation by being remarkably stable in external work such as ship decks, for which it is ideal. It is, however, rather open-grained and inclined to splinter. It is also difficult to work and quickly blunts tools. It follows that it is best used in simple sections and not in highly moulded work.

For finely moulded work, panelling or cabinet making, timbers of medium strength with straight close grain are wanted and mahogany, both American and African, satisfies these requirements. It has a good colour and takes a high polish. Woods with irregular grain are also used for this type of work where a more interesting appearance is required and their beauty of figure justifies the additional labour. Walnut, yew and cherry are common examples but there are in this category many beautiful and rarely used woods such as purpleheart, Indian rosewood, zebrano and thuya.

Although nowadays the expression 'high class work' when used in the trade seems to imply the use of hardwood, there was a time when fine joinery, in windows and doors and panelling and even in carving, was commonly done in selected softwoods such as Archangel 1st (BS redwood) and Canadian white pine (BS yellow pine) and was usually painted. Such joinery is found in Georgian houses throughout the country, and was made possible because of the existence of very large trees in virgin forests from which clear straight grained wood was produced: a situation which no longer exists.

Timber supplies
The few species of common softwoods grow in relatively compact areas in Russia, Scandinavia and North America, and in answer to the demands of western civilization the sources have been heavily depleted. Although there are still plentiful supplies, particularly of the lesser used species such as western hemlock and red pine (both from North America), there is never-theless a tendency to use more hardwood from tropical forests, many of which have hitherto been unexploited. This tendency has been accentuated by the economic conditions caused by two world wars; latterly by the need to avoid purchasing Canadian softwoods with dollars. In 1938 the total soft-wood imported was nearly 2,000,000 standards and hardwood 33,000,000 cu. ft., but in 1951 the totals were 1,700,000 standards of softwood and nearly 60,000,000 cu. ft. of hardwood.

SOFTWOODS
The terms deal, pine and fir by which softwoods are commonly known are most misleading since they can refer to a number of species, and are used differently in different countries. For instance 'Pinus sylvestris', which is the most commonly used softwood in this country and is now known by the British Standard name of 'redwood', is called, amongst thirteen other

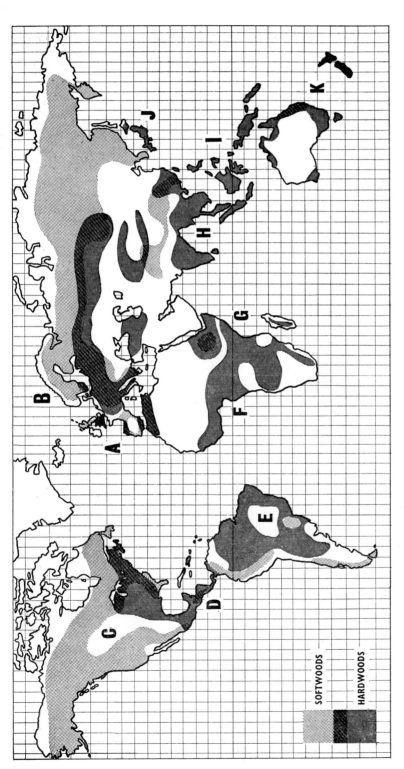

Fig. 1. TIMBERS SUITABLE FOR JOINERY PURPOSES
(*Note: Hardwoods are shown in italic type*)

A. GREAT BRITAIN AND CONTINENTAL EUROPE: *ash, beech, birch, sweet chestnut, elm, hornbeam, lime, oak, poplar, sycamore, walnut,* silver fir, European larch, Corsican pine, redwood, whitewood, yew.

B. SCANDINAVIA: *beech, birch, oak,* redwood, whitewood.

C. NORTH AMERICA: *beech, birch, maple, oak, black walnut,* western red cedar, yellow cedar, Douglas fir, hemlock, jack pine, longleaf pitch pine, ponderosa pine, red pine, western white pine, yellow pine, redwood, Canadian spruce, Sitka spruce.

D. CENTRAL AMERICA: *C. American mahogany, Cuban mahogany, Cuban santa maria, C. American cedar,* Brit. Honduras pitch pine.

E. SOUTH AMERICA: *S. American cedar, crabwood, freijo, jequitiba,*

Chilean laurel, Ecuador laurel, mahogany, white paroba, rauli, santa maria, 'Parana pine', mario.

F. WEST AFRICA: *abura, afara, afara, 'African walnut', afrormosia, afzelia, agba, avodiré, celtis, dahoma, danta, ekki, gaboon, gedu nohor, guarea, idigbo, iroko, African mahogany, makoré, mansonia, nyankom, obeche, okwen, opepe, sapele,* podo.

G. EAST AFRICA: *East African camphorwood, celtis, dahoma, gedu nohor, iroko, African mahogany, muninga,* African pencil cedar, podo.

H. INDIA AND BURMA: *gurjun, krabak, padauk, teak.*

I. EAST INDIES AND MALAYA: *Borneo camphorwood, gurjun (yang), keruing, meranti, seraya, teak.*

J. JAPAN: *beech, oak, Japanese ash.*

K. AUSTRALIA AND NEW ZEALAND: *jarrah, karri, 'Tasmanian oak', 'Queensland walnut', rimu, matai.*

names, red deal, yellow deal, Archangel fir, Swedish pine and Scots pine.

Although there are only about six commonly used softwoods, their differences, though sometimes important, are not so easily recognized as in hardwoods, and the names are so confusing that it is difficult to distinguish one from the other. It is doubtful whether many architects or builders could always be sure what they were using.

The most satisfactory solution to this problem would be the general adoption of the British Standard names printed in BSS 881 and 589, *Nomenclature of Commercial Timbers*.

B.S. 1186, *Quality of Timber and Workmanship in Joinery, Pt. I: quality of timber*, lists softwoods suitable for joinery, as follows:

Swedish	Redwood or whitewood	Better shipments of unsorted
Finnish	Redwood or whitewood	Better shipments of unsorted
Polish	Redwood or whitewood	Best shipments of unsorted
Norwegian	Whitewood	Best shipments of unsorted planed boards
Russian	Redwood or whitewood	Unsorted White Sea or unsorted Kara Sea
North American	Douglas fir	Clears and door stock Select merchantable
	Western hemlock	Clears and door stock Select merchantable
	Sitka (silver spruce)	Clears and select merchantable
	Western white pine	First, second, third and log run (clears in, culls out)
	Western red cedar	Clears and select merchantable
South American	Parana pine	Prime (80 per cent first, 20 per cent second export grade)

It is obvious from this list that the bulk of the softwood comes from countries in the northern latitudes and mostly from countries where the ports are icebound in winter months. For this reason the trade, unlike that of hardwoods, is seasonal. The logs are converted in the country of origin: that is to say, they are sawn into square sections, the ends of which are stencilled with the shippers' or importers' marks, and they are sold through agents to importing firms in this and other countries. The system of purchasing is similar for hardwoods and softwoods, but the hardwood trade is more specialized and intricate because of the great number of different kinds and grades of wood.

The marks which are a familiar sight on the ends of stacked softwood used at one time to be sufficiently limited in number to be of value to architects in selecting timber, and lists were given in reference books. One can still obtain a full list in *Shipping Marks on Timber*,* but the system has become too complex (there are some hundred marks) to be of much value to architects. All one can say today is that Norwegian timber is stencilled in blue, Swedish in red (lower qualities in blue), Russian timber is hammer branded, and Canadian timber is stencilled: 'Astexo—Canada' or 'Cantim',

* Published by Benn Bros Ltd (£2 10s. 0d.).

Fig. 2

Fig. 2. West African hardwoods stored 'in the log' before conversion. The ends of the logs have been painted, and marked by the various concerns which have handled them before their arrival at the consumer's yard. These logs show large shakes, or cracks, which make economical conversion a difficult and highly skilled job. Fig. 3. 'Boules' (or logs cut through-and-through) of elm. This method of conversion is the most common.

Fig. 3

Fig. 4

Fig. 5

Fig. 6

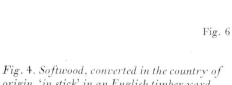

Fig. 7

Fig. 4. *Softwood, converted in the country of origin, 'in stick' in an English timber yard. The shipping marks can be clearly seen.*
Fig. 5. *Square edged boards of coigue. The boards are of varying widths, from 4 to 12 in., but the nominal thickness should be constant. This is an unusually bad parcel of timber, showing shakes, warp, and twist, and emphasizes the importance of careful specification.*
The sizes of timber available vary widely with different species. Fig. 6. *Boards of mahogany (swietenia), some of them 4 ft. 6 in. wide, and in lengths up to 25 ft.*
Fig. 7. *Kingwood, showing a typical log, only 9 in. in diameter. This is an expensive and highly decorative timber.*

26

or with the mark of the export or import concern. US timber is stamped or stencilled with the marks of individual concerns.

Timber, like other materials, is sold in grades, and European softwoods are known as firsts, seconds, thirds, etc.: the first five grades being used for joinery. Since the war firsts have been unobtainable, and the usual classification is 'unsorted', which is wood of all grades except those lower than fourths. * This does not, of course, preclude merchants regrading 'unsorted' timber themselves, which they often do into 'joinery' and 'carcassing'; indeed, unless this is done the specification 'unsorted' has little meaning. The grading of North American timbers is different, and there are two grades imported to this country for joinery, the best being known as 'clears and door stock', and the other 'select merchantable'. 'Clears and door stock' has been difficult to obtain, and 'select merchantable' is equivalent to European 'unsorted'.

In principle, the best method of specifying is to rely on definite requirements of quality as incorporated in BS 1186, Part I, which requires that the timber shall meet certain standards of appearance, structure and freedom from defects irrespective of its species or grade.†

Softwood sizes
The timber is cut in the sawmills in the producing country either into baulks (i.e. squared up logs) or into a range of smaller sizes which from experience are found to meet the demand in this country. The different sizes have names such as battens, boards, deals, planks and scantlings, but these definitions, which are different in meaning in this context from their usual meaning, are rarely used, and the timber is generally referred to by its dimensions. Since it is obviously desirable to design to suit these common dimensions, making allowance for the preparation of the timber, it is useful to know what they are. The trade has not in fact been able to agree on standard sizes, but inquiries show that the sizes shown in the accompanying table (Fig. 8, page 28) are generally available.

Softwoods dry more quickly than hardwoods and they are converted before shipment into small sections. For these reasons the natural drying which takes place during the time from their conversion to their ultimate use is generally sufficient to reduce the moisture content to a figure of about 18 per cent. This is low enough for many of the uses to which softwoods are put, and even in those yards where there are also kilns, one is unlikely to find softwood being kilned, for it is usually taken direct from the stacks. For this reason it is important that it should be so piled as to allow air to

* 'Unsorted' from Finland and Sweden consists of first, second, third and fourth qualities; from Russia consists of first, second and third qualities—a fourth quality is sold separately. The actual quality of unsorted varies widely according to the place of origin and the shipper. Some timber marks, therefore, have a much higher reputation than others. The term unsorted does not imply that the timber has not been sorted; it means that a number of grades are included in the same parcel.

† See Appendix II, page 200.

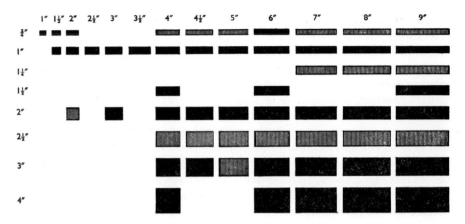

Fig. 8. Table of softwood sizes, showing generally available sawn sections in softwood. The shaded sections are less common. For finished sizes subtract $\frac{3}{16}$ in. from each dimension.*

circulate around each piece, and this is achieved by inserting small battens under each row, as can be seen in the illustrations. The timber is then said to be 'in stick'. Hardwood will also be found 'in stick', but this is usually only one stage in its process of seasoning and it will almost certainly be kilned before use in order to reduce its moisture content to the appropriate amount for the purpose to which it is likely to be put. Even if air drying could reduce the moisture content enough it would be unlikely to do so within a time that is short enough to meet the demand: softwoods take roughly two to three months for every 1 in. thickness for air drying to 18 per cent moisture content and hardwoods about one year.

The reduction of moisture content of timber is probably the most important factor determining its stability in use, and the subject will therefore be dealt with in greater detail in the next chapter.

HARDWOODS

By contrast with softwood there are hundreds of commercial varieties of hardwood imported from many parts of the world, and whereas the softwood industries have been highly developed in the producing countries, this is not generally so in those countries from which the hardwoods are produced; and the commercial handling of the two sides of the trade are very different. In 1957 over 200 different species of hardwood were imported. At a yard an architect will see that softwood is stacked in 'square sawn' sections, whereas the hardwoods may well still be in a pile of logs. He will learn that in their conversion and sale different systems are used.

The hardwood areas are mostly in tropical and semi-tropical countries, many of which are less industrialized than those parts of the world in which the softwoods are produced (see map, fig. 1).

* BS 1860 adds the following sections: 3 in. by $1\frac{1}{2}$ in.; 3 in. by $2\frac{1}{2}$ in.; 4 in. by 5 in.; 5 in. by $1\frac{1}{2}$ in.; 7 in. by $1\frac{1}{2}$ in.; 8 in. by $1\frac{1}{2}$ in.

The result is that the timber is exported in several different forms, depending on local circumstances, shipping arrangements and trade practices. For instance, teak trees are bought by auction three or four years before it is proposed to fell them, so that they may be killed by making a girdle through the bark in order that the logs shall become light enough to float down the rivers to the sawmills, where they are converted to planks for shipment. Muhuhu, on the other hand, comes from a small tree and, being suitable for flooring, is almost exclusively imported as short strip or blocks.

The chain of handling is a complicated one. The timber is usually bought in the producing country and shipped by the *importer*, who in turns sells it to the *merchant*. But it must be noted that *importers and merchants* may be combined, and occasionally *consumers*, i.e. large joinery works are also their own importers and merchants.

The importer or merchant dealing in hardwoods usually has saw mills, and carries out further conversion after receiving the timber. The yards and mills are mostly in London or Liverpool, close to the wharves, and the sight of large piles of logs and of sawn timber in stick will be familiar to most architects. Whereas softwood is mostly used up as soon as it is imported, hardwood is by tradition delivered by the importer to his customers in a 'seasoned' condition, and is therefore stored by him for a number of years before being sold.

When the timber leaves the country of origin, it is usually in one of three forms. It may be in the solid log (round or 'squared up'), or in square-edged stock, or in boules (logs cut through-and-through and tied with steel bands). Many importers and merchants prefer square-edged timber because of reduced handling and conversion costs, and savings in shipping space and waste. On the other hand, uncut logs have the great advantage that they can be converted to special requirements.

Grading is a more specialized process with hardwoods than with softwoods. This varies in different countries and some countries have grading rules which are most exacting. For instance, West African sawn timber is graded according to the rules of the National Hardwood Lumber Association of America, while Malaya has its own grading rules.

Hardwoods are graded according to quality in the country of origin, and for commercial purposes are sorted into: FAS ('first and seconds'); Selects; No. 1 Common; No. 2, etc. (see also page 168).

Qualities below No. 1 are, however, not very satisfactory for joinery, and architects' specifications should make it clear that lower grades are not acceptable. When the timber arrives at the importers' yards it is sorted again—especially if it is required for decorative purposes when matters of appearance are of importance.

The criteria by which the timber is then judged are: straight, even grain (or special figure); consistent colour; quantity and condition of sapwood; number and extent of heart shakes; freedom from decay, insect attack and fungi.

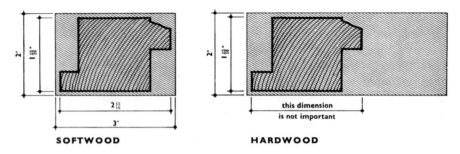

SOFTWOOD   **HARDWOOD**

Fig. 9. Diagrams showing the influence of timber yard practice on economy of dimensioning. On the left is a typical softwood section requiring a 3-in. by 2-in. sawn scantling. For softwood both dimensions are critical for economic design. On the right is a similar section applied to hardwood. Here, since hardwood is marketed in boards, the long dimension is less critical. It will be noticed that ⅜₂ in. is allowed on each face for finishing.

Heartshakes (i.e. cracks radiating from the heart: described and explained on page 33) may be very large and extend through the length of the log. Of less concern are end shakes, which open up in the ends of logs and are due to the extreme ends drying out and shrinking. The ends of some timber are painted in order to minimize this. Sapwood may be much softer and lighter in colour than the rest of the log, and may also be attacked by insects or fungi, to which it is particularly liable.

It is at this stage that the architect may wish to take a personal interest in the choice of the timber, and that it is useful to be able to recognize good from bad material, and to know how the wood which he inspects in the yard is likely to appear when wrought and finished.

Although all the different ways of converting timber are shown in text-books, the majority of logs are initially cut 'through and through' (see fig. 12, page 34), and the material is supplied to the user in planks of a number of recognized thicknesses.

These are 1 in., 1¼ in., 1½ in., 2 in., 2½ in., 3 in. and occasionally 4 in. unless the logs are specially converted. The planks are not, however, of standard *widths* as in softwood, and in purchasing a parcel of planks of a minimum width of, say, 9 in., some of them will exceed this figure by varying amounts.

From the architect's point of view the significance of this is that small sections are cut from relatively wide planks and it is only necessary in avoiding waste to consider the standard thicknesses. In softwoods, by contrast, both dimensions have to be taken account of.

Because of the great variety of hardwood trees, the available sizes vary enormously according to the species; whilst the average length of plank is 12 ft., widths vary from 9 in. to 18 in., and some woods can be had in much larger planks. Mahogany, for instance, can reach as much as 25 ft. by 4 ft. wide, and at the other extreme kingwood comes from trees whose diameters do not usually exceed 9 in. It is obviously worth while ascertaining in what sizes timber is available before making a choice from a small sample.

METHODS OF SELLING AND PRICES

The obtaining of softwood for a building is nearly always left entirely to the contractor, but it frequently happens with hardwoods that the architect wants to select the type and grade of hardwood, and that he will consult and obtain quotations from importers or merchants, receiving samples and possibly visiting their yards. It need hardly be said that the architect will be unlikely to be able to judge the comparative merits of different logs or planks without the help of a trustworthy merchant, but, as we have said before, such visits will increase his knowledge of the different species and their sizes, and his interest will encourage the merchant to supply appropriate material of good quality.

Softwoods are sold in bulk unwrought, by a measurement known as the 'Petrograd Standard'. This is 165 cu. ft., and typical prices in 1957 per standard were: seconds £140 a standard; unsorted (selected for joinery) £115 standard; unsorted (selected for carcassing) £100 a standard; and fifths £90 a standard. When sold in smaller quantities, it is bought by the foot run of a particular section and is often priced at so much per cu. ft. Unsorted for joinery would on this basis be about 14s. per cu. ft.

Hardwood is nearly always sold per cu. ft. and some representative prices for common sizes are: teak, Honduras mahogany, 50s. to 65s.; Japanese oak, 35s. to 60s.; iroko, 30s. to 45s.; West African mahogany, English oak, 25s. to 45s.; keruing, Jugoslav beech, 20s. to 25s.; English beech, 15s. to 20s.

These prices are variable and depend not only on the quality but also on the sizes of boards required.

It might be mentioned that hardwood for flooring is an exception to the rule, and blocks and strips are sold per yard super of material, which is commonly of 1 in. nominal thickness.

Reverting to softwood, much official encouragement has been given to the use of timber impregnated with preservative. Wolman salts and creosote are quite commonly used for impregnation which is carried out either by a limited number of firms who then distribute the timber to stockists, from whom the contractor may order what he requires, or by the timber merchants themselves. Treated softwoods cost about £10 extra per standard (1957).

SOURCES OF INFORMATION

The Forest Products Research Laboratory, which is part of the Department of Scientific and Industrial Research, issues information and undertakes to answer inquiries. The Timber Development Association undertake a similar service on behalf of the timber trade and are always willing to help. They also have available a set of fifty timber samples. (£2 10s. the set or 1s. 3d. each, 1957.)

2: Movement in Timber

All building materials expand and contract slightly with changes in humidity and temperature. In certain materials such as steel and concrete the amount of movement can be calculated accurately, and allowed for in design. But timber is subject to a greater degree of moisture movement than most other materials, and whilst it is common practice to make some allowance for this movement in specification and design, the ways in which it moves are complicated and not always fully understood. It is probably true to say that more trouble arises in joinery from this than from any other cause.

Unlike other building materials, wood is a natural organic substance and has a complex cellular structure. For its growth a tree requires water far in excess of the amount which is desirable in timber prepared for joinery. The extraction of the surplus moisture causes the timber to shrink, but the degree and manner in which it shrinks is influenced by the way it is cut out of the log during the process of 'conversion'; and to understand the different methods of conversion and why one piece shrinks more or less than another, it is necessary to know, in an elementary way, how the wood in the tree is formed.

THE GROWTH OF TIMBER

In a sapling *all* the wood carries the food and water necessary for the tree's growth, and this wood is known as *sapwood*. As the tree grows in height and girth, a new layer of sapwood is formed each season underneath the bark. The progressive layers of growth can often be seen as alternate dark and light concentric rings when the tree is cut across, and are sometimes referred to as 'annual rings', a misleading term since in some tropical countries there may be two seasons of growth each year. In trees grown in temperate climates, the light rings are the fast spring growth and the dark rings are the slower summer growth. When the tree grows older, the inner layers of growth cease to convey the sap, and the cells, of which the wood substance is composed, die. The sap is then carried only by the outer and relatively new growth layers, whose total width may be only $\frac{1}{2}$ in. and is unlikely to exceed a few inches.

At the centre of the tree is a substance known as pith and, although sometimes it can hardly be detected, it may be up to $\frac{1}{8}$ in. in diameter.

The major part of the trunk of an old tree will consist of the dead cells which comprise what is known as the *heartwood*. From the joiner's point of view this is the most useful wood, because the sapwood is often, and especially in hardwoods, of a lighter colour than the remaining wood—which may not be desirable in the finished piece of joinery. The sapwood is also more liable to attack by insects and fungus. It is not, however, otherwise inferior.

It must not be supposed, because the cells in the heartwood are dead, that the wood is weaker: it is, in fact, this wood which gives rigidity to the tree.

In large trees a series of splits, radiating from the heart, often develop after felling. This is due to uneven drying out, the consequent shrinkage

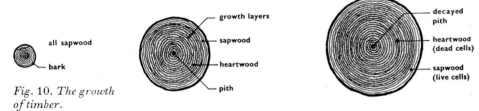

Fig. 10. *The growth of timber.*

causing the fibres to rupture. The splits are known as heartshakes, and whilst they have to be taken into consideration in avoiding waste during conversion, they do not adversely affect the surrounding wood.

CONVERSION

The important thing to know about conversion is, as has already been suggested, that the sections or planks into which trees are converted will behave differently and have a different appearance, depending on which way they are cut out of the trunk.

The simplest way of converting a log is to cut it through-and-through, but this results in about half the planks being cut tangentially to the growth layers. These planks, known as *flat-sawn* boards, are liable to warp when dried, and to shrink considerably across their width, as explained later.

Planks which are sawn radially (and known as *quarter-* or *rift-sawn*) are on the other hand less liable to warping during seasoning and have less shrinkage; conversion which produces as many planks as possible cut radially is therefore likely to produce the most stable timber but, because of the additional trouble and waste, is up to 25 per cent more expensive than through-and-through conversion.

If a decorative 'figure' or pattern of grain is wanted, this may determine the way in which the wood is converted, and may overrule considerations of stability, so that a flat-sawn board might then be preferable to a quarter-sawn board. For instance, in oak the figure depends on rays which are exposed only in quarter-sawn boards, whereas in Douglas fir, the characteristic figure, which depends on the exposure of the growth layers at an oblique angle, is displayed only in flat-sawn boards (see figs. 15–17, page 36).

The method of conversion may also influence the degree of movement and distortion that is likely to occur in the converted section from such other factors as sloping grain, the position of the heart, and of the knots. It will be appreciated for instance that since trunks of trees taper and the growth layers are in the form of cones parallel to the outside of the tree, planks

33

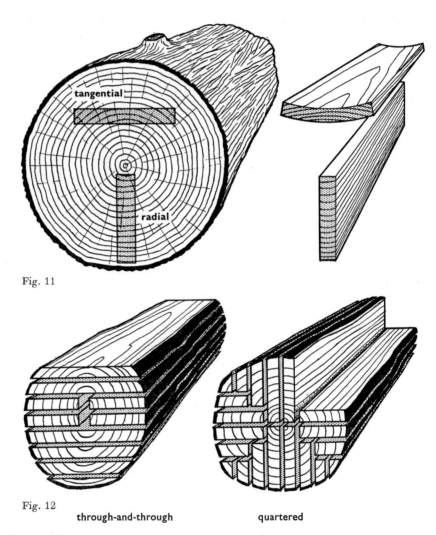

Fig. 11

Fig. 12

through-and-through   quartered

Fig. **11.** *A 'flat-sawn' board is one which is sawn from the log so that its plane is tangential to the growth layers. 'Quarter-sawn' boards are cut radially from the log. Since shrinkage in timber is greater tangentially than radially, a flat-sawn board will tend to 'warp', while the quarter-sawn board will remain flat. Fig.* 12. *Two methods of converting logs. 'Through-and-through' is most common, and the cheapest. It produces about two-thirds flat-sawn stock and one-third quarter-sawn. 'Quartering' is more expensive as the log has to be turned many times during sawing. It produces no flat-sawn stock, all the boards being quarter-sawn or approximately so.*

which are cut parallel to the axis, which is the common practice, will have sloping grain—a factor which, in excess, will encourage warping. When absolutely straight grain is required for such objects as wall-bars in gym equipment the timber should be cut parallel to the *outside* of the log. Also, it is better to arrange the conversion so that the pith comes in the centre of a section rather than on the edge; otherwise there will again be a likelihood

34

Fig. 13

Fig. 14

Fig. 13. *Cross section of a log of elm, showing the sapwood—the younger growth layers toward the outside of the tree—which is lighter in colour than the older timber, or heartwood. Small heartshakes are beginning to form at the centre of the log.*

Fig. 14. *The end of a typical hardwood log which has developed large heartshakes.*

35

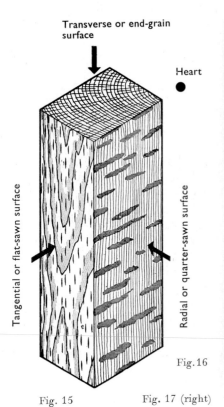

Transverse or end-grain surface

Heart

Tangential or flat-sawn surface

Radial or quarter-sawn surface

Fig. 16

Fig. 15

Fig. 17 (right)

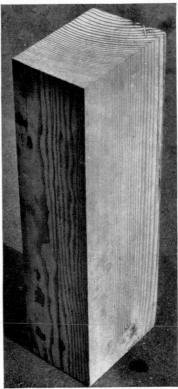

Figs. 15, 16, 17. THE STRUCTURE OF WOOD AND ITS EFFECT ON APPEARANCE. *The majority of the cells run longitudinally in the log, arranged in growth layers concentric about the heart. A flat-sawn face shows the contours of the growth layers as they undulate in and out of the surface; this is particularly noticeable in softwoods, where there is a strong difference in colour between the early and late growth in each layer. Smaller groups of cells known as rays run radially from the heart and these are exposed on a quarter-sawn face, showing as flecks or 'silver figure' in some hardwoods. Softwoods have a poorly developed ray structure and do not show this effect. Fig. 16 is a piece of Douglas fir, showing the characteristic figure on the flat-sawn face. Fig. 17, English oak, a hardwood which shows 'silver figure' on the quarter-sawn face.*

Fig. 18. CONVERTING ON THE BAND-RACK SAW. *The log is mounted on a carriage which runs on rails past the saw. After each cut the log is moved sideways by power ready for the next cut. The process is very rapid (and therefore economical) if the log is not turned on the carriage, i.e. if the log is converted by sawing 'through-and-through'.*

Fig. 18

of warping. This is called 'boxing the heart'. In large hardwood trees the pith and the wood immediately adjacent to it is often cut out and discarded even if there is not already a hollow formed by decay.

From what has already been said it will be apparent that when moisture is extracted from timber to make it usable as joinery it will shrink, either with or without distortion. Distortion, however, does not, for all practical purposes, occur except when the wood becomes either wetter or drier, and can be simply explained in terms of the general behaviour of wood when subjected to changes in moisture content.

MOISTURE MOVEMENT

Most people will have noticed that the wood from a newly felled tree is saturated with water. In fact, the amount of water may weigh considerably more than the weight of the actual wood substance. It is contained both in the cell cavities and also in the fibrous structure of the cell walls, and when the tree is dried the water held freely in the cavities is the first to be expelled. Up to the point where the water in the cell walls begins to be given up, there is no shrinkage, and the amount of moisture then in the timber is about 27 per cent to 30 per cent by weight of the amount of the wood substance.

Further drying causes the water in the cell walls to be given up, and the wood begins to shrink proportionately to the amount of water extracted.

If wood is dried in the open air it will continue to lose moisture as long as the air is dry enough to absorb moisture from it, that is until a state of equilibrium is reached. The amount of water in the wood at the time when equilibrium is reached will depend upon the relative humidity* of the air, and upon the species of timber; some species giving up their moisture more readily than others. In the open air equilibrium is reached when the timber has a moisture content somewhere in the region of 18 per cent. Inside most buildings, and particularly in those having central heating, the air has a lower relative humidity than the outside atmosphere, and consequently air dried timber used in them would lose considerably more moisture, with consequent shrinkage, until it reached equilibrium at a moisture content which might be as low as 8 per cent. In order to avoid such shrinkage, the timber has to be dried in kilns until it has a moisture content which is known to be appropriate to the anticipated humidity of the air in which it will ultimately be placed.

If timber remained stable once it had been sufficiently dried, the problem would be relatively simple, but in fact it continues indefinitely to absorb or dispel water according to the humidity of the surrounding air; and to shrink or expand accordingly.

Unfortunately, even the atmosphere in which the timber is to be used is

* The Relative Humidity of the air at any given temperature is the amount of water-vapour present, expressed as a percentage of the maximum amount possible in air at that temperature. The Moisture Content of wood is the amount of moisture it contains, expressed as a percentage of the weight of the wood substance itself when dry.

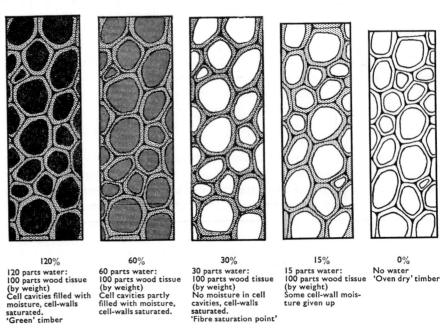

Loss of moisture from cell cavities.
No shrinkage.

Loss of moisture from cell-walls.
Shrinkage takes place.

120%	60%	30%	15%	0%
120 parts water: 100 parts wood tissue (by weight) Cell cavities filled with moisture, cell-walls saturated. 'Green' timber	60 parts water: 100 parts wood tissue (by weight) Cell cavities partly filled with moisture, cell-walls saturated.	30 parts water: 100 parts wood tissue (by weight) No moisture in cell cavities, cell-walls saturated. 'Fibre saturation point'	15 parts water: 100 parts wood tissue (by weight) Some cell-wall moisture given up	No water 'Oven dry' timber

Fig. 19. MOISTURE CONTENT: *cross-section of a piece of timber magnified* 800 *times.*

unlikely to have a *constant* relative humidity, and an average value has to be assumed in practice. Only in exceptional circumstances will conditions be such as to produce no movement.

So much for the variations in the atmosphere: there are also as serious variations in the timbers themselves.

In the first place, the amount of movement resulting from changes in moisture content differs for each species; it is not the same in the radial and tangential directions for any one species, the tangential always being greater than the radial; and there is no fixed relationship between the radial and tangential movements for every species. Fortunately, movement *along* the grain is so little in all timbers as to be of no practical importance.

In the second place, each species of timber reaches equilibrium with given humidities at different moisture contents: for example, teak in air at 80 per cent relative humidity and 77 deg. F. has an 'equilibrium moisture content' of 12·5 per cent whereas the corresponding moisture content for oak is 16 per cent and that of sycamore 18·5 per cent.

The equilibrium moisture content varies also with temperature, but the variation within the range encountered for joinery is not great, and for practical purposes we consider that it may be ignored.

When the time comes to decide what kind of timber to use in any particular design it is important to choose a species which will not move so much

Fig. 20

Fig. 22

Figs. 20, 21. METHODS OF SEA-
SONING: *Fig. 20. Air drying of softwood. The timber has been 'self-piled',
i.e. not spaced apart by sticks.
Although this method of piling does
not permit very free circulation of air,
it is often adequate for drying softwood.*

*Fig. 21. A control chamber at the
rear of timber kilns. The process can
be carefully controlled, and continuous records are automatically plotted.*

*Fig. 22. A joint between the stile and
rail of a glazed door, which has
opened up through moisture movement. The door was fixed some time
before the heating in the building was
turned on, and the shrinkage was
accentuated by the fact that the stile
was a very wide one.*

Fig. 21

Fig. 23. *Timber piled onto trolleys prior to entering the kiln. Note how the timber is stacked to allow the free passage of air around each piece.*

Fig. 24 *shows part of a typical battery of kilns – each one with its set of controls as already illustrated (Fig. 21, page 39).*

in the range of humidities in which it is likely to be placed as to give trouble or spoil appearance. For instance, if flat-sawn beech were chosen for a window board 9 in. wide, and subjected to a range of humidities between 55 per cent and 65 per cent relative humidity, it would move more than $\frac{1}{4}$ in.—which would obviously be undesirable. Figures showing the movement of different species have been ascertained by experiments by the Forest Products Research Laboratory, and those for some common joinery woods are set out in the accompanying table (Fig. 25, page 42).

Having chosen the timber, the appropriate moisture content must be decided upon, taking into account the levels at which the particular timber reaches equilibrium for various humidities. For simplicity we have grouped timbers into three classes: A those with low, B those with medium and C those with high levels of equilibrium, and have produced a graph, showing the levels of equilibrium of the three classes for all humidities. The graph also indicates the average range of humidities for heated interiors and also for external air. The table below has been compiled from the graph giving the moisture contents which we recommend for the three groups of timbers when used in joinery for specific purposes. Prior to the publication of these tables and graph the only information on the subject generally available has been the table issued by the FPRL and used widely by members of the Kiln Owners' Association, and the table in BS 1186, Part I: *Quality of Timber and Workmanship in Joinery*.* Neither of these tables takes into account the different moisture contents at which various species of timber reach equilibrum for given humidities—a factor which can be of some importance (see also fig. 26, page 43).

SUGGESTED MOISTURE CONTENT VALUES FOR SPECIFIC PURPOSES

	Hygroscopicity Group		
	A	B	C
	%	%	%
External joinery, except doors	13	17	19
External doors	12	15	16
Internal joinery in intermittently or moderately heated positions, except doors	11	14	15
Internal doors in intermittently or moderately heated positions	10	12	13
All internal joinery in continuously heated positions	9	10	11
Joinery in close proximity with sources of heat	8	9	10

DISTORTION

So far we have considered movement which occurs uniformly, but the same process of wetting and drying may also cause *distortion* in certain circumstances, some of which have already been mentioned when discussing conversion. This distortion is almost always caused by the difference between radial and tangential shrinkage and this explains why flat sawn boards are liable to cupping and why boards with sloping, twisted and interlocking

* See footnote, p. 170.

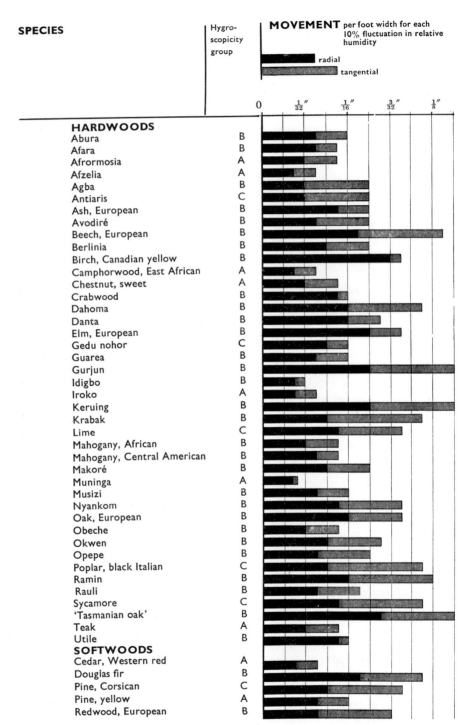

SPECIES	Hygro-scopicity group	MOVEMENT per foot width for each 10% fluctuation in relative humidity
HARDWOODS		
Abura	B	
Afara	B	
Afrormosia	A	
Afzelia	A	
Agba	B	
Antiaris	C	
Ash, European	B	
Avodiré	B	
Beech, European	B	
Berlinia	B	
Birch, Canadian yellow	B	
Camphorwood, East African	A	
Chestnut, sweet	A	
Crabwood	B	
Dahoma	B	
Danta	B	
Elm, European	B	
Gedu nohor	C	
Guarea	B	
Gurjun	B	
Idigbo	B	
Iroko	A	
Keruing	B	
Krabak	B	
Lime	C	
Mahogany, African	B	
Mahogany, Central American	B	
Makoré	B	
Muninga	A	
Musizi	B	
Nyankom	B	
Oak, European	B	
Obeche	B	
Okwen	B	
Opepe	B	
Poplar, black Italian	C	
Ramin	B	
Rauli	B	
Sycamore	C	
'Tasmanian oak'	B	
Teak	A	
Utile	B	
SOFTWOODS		
Cedar, Western red	A	
Douglas fir	B	
Pine, Corsican	C	
Pine, yellow	A	
Redwood, European	B	

Fig. 25. COMPARATIVE MOISTURE MOVEMENT VALUES FOR PRINCIPAL JOINERY TIMBERS. *The liability to distortion can also be gauged by the difference between the radial and tangential values, i.e. by the length of the shaded portion. This list does not exactly correspond with the list of selected joinery timbers given in Appendix I. Figures for African walnut, European walnut, meranti and sapele are not yet available. Central American cedar has the same figures as gedu nohor and mansonia has similar figures to lime.*

42

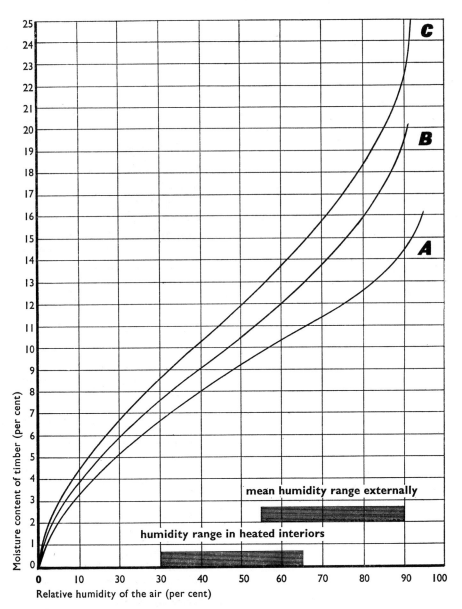

Fig. 26. EQUILIBRIUM MOISTURE CONTENTS FOR DIFFERENT RELATIVE HUMIDITIES: *The three curves represent the average values of hygroscopicity of three groups of timbers.*

USE OF FIGS. 25 AND 26: *The group to which a timber belongs is shown in Fig. 25. By referring to the appropriate curve in Fig. 26, the moisture content of the timber can be related directly to the humidity of the air. Given a range of humidity for the air surrounding any piece of timber, (1) the fluctuation in moisture content can be determined from Fig. 26 and (2) the amount of movement can be calculated from Fig. 25. For example, if a 9-in. wide flat-sawn board of ramin at 12% moisture content were to be used in a position where the average humidity of the air was as low as 30% (e.g. a radiator casing), its moisture content would drop to 7½% (Curve B). The drop in moisture content from 12% to 7½% corresponds to a humidity drop from 60% to 30%, i.e. a fluctuation of 30%. Referring to Fig. 25, the movement of flat-sawn (tangential) ramin is ⅛ in. per foot width for each 10% fluctuation in humidity. The shrinkage of the board would therefore be*

$$\frac{1}{8} \times \frac{30}{10} \times \frac{9}{12} = \frac{9}{32} \text{ins.}$$

43

grain are subject to distortion of one kind or another. Whereas one timber may shrink or expand more than another, it is quite possible that that with the lower movement may be the more liable to *distortion*, and whilst some indication may be provided by the straightness of grain, there are not at present any lists of those timbers which are specially liable to distortion. It has, however, been noted, as might be expected, that timbers in which the excess of tangential over radial movement is not great are least likely to distort, irrespective of the amount of total movement to which they are liable. Muninga, for example, has a low total movement whereas Canadian yellow birch has a high total movement, but both timbers are known to distort little, as in each the difference between the radial and tangential movements is small.

SEASONING

The process of drying timber for its various uses is known as *seasoning*, and until shortly after the first world war it was nearly always done in the open air without any artificial aid.

Timber was before then comparatively cheap, and it was still an economic proposition to keep it stored in yards for the long period of time that air seasoning requires.

The increase in cost of the raw material and the depletion of the stocks during both the wars of 1914–18 and 1939–45, however, have encouraged kilning as a method of drying because of the far quicker rate at which it achieves the required result.

One other major factor has furthered an interest in kilning and has, in fact, made it essential in modern joinery, and that is the increase of central heating in buildings.

Although by no means all of the total output of timber for joinery is kiln dried even now, it is none the less of the utmost importance that *all* joinery used in heated buildings, where the humidity is low, should be kilned; this is for the good reason that air seasoning will not reduce the moisture content to a figure below 18 per cent except in the most favourable weather, yet figures of 8 to 10 per cent are often needed.

Much softwood joinery is nowadays built into the work as it proceeds and is consequently exposed to the atmosphere for a considerable time, so that to kiln such timber would be a waste of time. Fig. 27 shows a record of the variations of moisture content which might occur during and after the erection of a new building. Ideally, all timber should be kilned to a specified moisture content and brought into the building only when it has dried out and normal heating is operating. This is obviously impracticable for all but the most expensive joinery—though nevertheless *essential* for floors laid over heating panels. It is so important, that such floor blocks are sometimes wrapped in waterproof paper to prevent the wood absorbing moisture on the way from the factory to the building.

The whole problem of preserving the correct moisture content until the final conditions are reached requires attention, and this will be dealt with

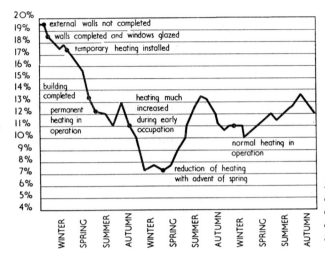

The graph labels:

20%
19% external walls not completed
18% walls completed and windows glazed
17% temporary heating installed
16%
15%
14% building
13% completed — heating much
12% — increased
11% permanent during early
10% heating in occupation
9% operation
8%
7% — normal heating in operation
6% — reduction of heating with advent of spring
5%
4%

WINTER SPRING SUMMER AUTUMN WINTER SPRING SUMMER AUTUMN WINTER SPRING SUMMER AUTUMN

Fig. 27. Graph showing an example of moisture content variations during and after erection of a new building.

in detail in chapter 8. In the meanwhile it is perhaps worth pointing out that it is very little use specifying a low moisture content if the timber is subsequently exposed to the wrong atmospheric conditions. Whilst a shower may not do much harm to normal joinery, exposure to a week of moisture-laden atmosphere would destroy the advantages of kilning, even though the timber might be painted with a traditional primer. It is sometimes thought that ordinary priming seals the wood but this is not so. Some notes on the efficiency of various primings and other finishes are given in the BRS digest *Questions and Answers*, 4th Series, No. 13, 1959, from which the following examples are quoted*:

	Percentage efficiency in preventing moisture absorption	
	At 7 days	At 28 days
Bituminous paint, two coats	90	69
First quality oil paint, three coats (red and white lead primer, undercoat, and finishing coat)	83	56
Lead paint, three coats (red and white lead primer, undercoat, and finishing coat)	76	45
Aluminium paint, two coats (aluminium paste in bronzing liquid)	70	35
Shellac, two coats	68	31
Copal varnish, two coats	58	20
Aluminium paint, two coats (paste in boiled oil)	47	12
Red and white lead primer, one thin coat	38	14
Beeswax and turpentine, two coats over cellulose sealer	10	3
Boiled oil and turpentine, two coats brushed	2	0
Raw linseed oil, one coat rubbed	0	0

* A preservative designed also to seal the timber temporarily against moisture has recently been put on the market.

45

In practice much standard softwood joinery is made from air-seasoned timber. Usually this is adequate because a great part of it will be used in windows and door frames which are either exposed externally where a low moisture content is not required or are of such construction that even fairly large movement can be tolerated. Such items as standard cupboards and doors, which because they are used inside require a lower moisture content, will often be made by specialist firms which have now become virtually separate branches of the joinery industry and in whose works kilned timber would normally be used. It is fortunate that the moisture content of air dried timber is usually at least as low as 20 per cent, which is low enough to stop active fungal growth.

Hardwoods are, by contrast, more frequently kilned: and the reasons are, first, that, on the whole, hardwoods are more frequently used in the kind of situations where low moisture contents are required; and, second, that softwood is imported in relatively small sections which by the time they are used have had an opportunity to dry out, whereas hardwood is often imported in log or in large sections: and, third, that in most cases a piece of hardwood of any particular size would take longer to dry out than a piece of softwood of equivalent size, and it is therefore important to use the limited space available in the kilns for hardwoods in order to meet the demand within a reasonable time.

The length of time needed for kilning will be governed by the amount of water in the green timber and the moisture content to which it has to be reduced. Also by the species of timber, and, of course, by the size of the section. As far as the latter is concerned, it has been found uneconomic to kiln hardwoods over 3 in. *thick*, but by the nature of the process the *width* of the boards makes little difference because the moisture is drawn mainly from the upper and lower surfaces of the piled timber.

In most kilns the drying is accomplished by introducing warm air into the kiln at controlled humidities, which passes over the upper and lower surfaces of the timber which is piled in stick. There are other forms of kilning using super-heated steam and radio frequency heating, and there are also methods in which chemicals are applied to the timber to assist the process. These are, however, the exception and are very rarely used commercially.

There is now a sufficient experience of kilning to ensure that, if it is done properly and in accordance with authoritative schedules, the timber will be thoroughly well seasoned, and be at least as good in service as the best air dried timber. There is a prejudice still against kilning, and there are those who consider that timber which has been first dried in the open and subsequently prepared and left standing in a warmed workshop for a long period will, as a result, be superior to kilned timber; but objective analysis of the results does not bear this out: on the contrary it shows that, owing to the control of heat and of humidity which kilning offers, the method has positive advantages in avoiding some of the distortion which may occur in air seasoning.

With this fact in mind it may be of interest to compare very approximately

46

the times which air drying and kilning are likely to take respectively, and a convenient rule of thumb guide for hardwoods is:

Air drying: One *year* per inch thickness (green to air dry, 18 per cent).

Kiln drying: One to three *weeks* per inch thickness (green to air dry 18 per cent).

It must be admitted that kilning in the early days was not always done well, and there was little control over certain defects which are associated with the process. These defects can still occur, but the means of avoiding them are known, and with the knowledgeable operators and the closely kept records which are common they are far less likely to occur than previously and, if they do, can be checked and the affected timber discarded. The most common of the defects are: *case hardening*, that is the drying out of the fibres on the outside of the piece of wood prior to those on the inside, causing uneven tensions which make the wood distort when, for instance, the section is machined or re-sawn. This can be overcome by introducing steam which prevents the outside drying out too quickly, but if overdone the remedy can be the cause of another defect called *honeycombing*.

When this happens the inside dries out too quickly and whilst the outside shows no failure, the inside of the piece of wood is full of small checks or splits longitudinally with the grain.

Case hardening can be detected by observing the behaviour of a typical cross-section taken from a piece of timber in the kiln and from which the inside is cut, forming a prong. If the timber is not evenly dried the prongs will distort: the appearance of a prong cut from a piece of timber at a late stage of case hardening can be seen in the diagram (Fig. 28). Honeycombing can be seen by cutting a representative sample in cross-section. The other faults which may occur, such as warping, twisting and bowing, can be minimized by careful stacking and even kilning. A special fault, known as *collapse*, to which some timbers are liable in seasoning, e.g. Tasmanian oak, western red cedar, cypress and hemlock, results in severe shrinkage and in the production of a corrugated surface on the quarter-sawn surfaces called 'washboarding'. It has been found that this defect can be remedied with complete success in kilns, by a process called *reconditioning*.

The schedules to which the kiln operator will work make it necessary for daily samples to be taken and weighed so that continuous records of the moisture contents can be kept. The only really accurate means of ascertaining the moisture content is to weigh the sample wet and then oven dry it and weigh it again. Electric moisture meters are available, and are described in chapter 8, but it should be stated that they give no more than an approximate guide to the condition of the timber throughout its full thickness. In addition, they have to be adjusted for different species and for temperature and should therefore only be used in the hands of an expert. Their chief merit is that they give a quick reading which is useful as a check.

If timber does not have to be dried below about 18 per cent, air seasoning is no doubt still the most economical method. The cost of kilning is approximately a tenth of the cost of the wood and must be reckoned as an additional item if low moisture contents are required.

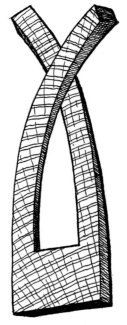

Fig. 28. Test for case hardened timber.

Before leaving the subject of seasoning, mention should be made of the expression 'water seasoning'. This is a misnomer. Certain timbers by tradition were and sometimes still are *stored* in the log in 'timber ponds'. This is done mainly to prevent the wood from checking badly and the ends of the log opening, which happens if they are exposed to the sun and drying winds. It also prevents the attack of certain insect pests and has been found to be a convenient form of storage facilitating handling especially for large and heavy logs. Amongst those species which were traditionally so stored were teak, rock elm, various species of mahogany, pitch pine and douglas fir.

We have explained that it is necessary to choose a species of timber suitable for the joinery that is being designed and to specify the appropriate moisture content. In spite of this, slight movement will almost certainly occur and this movement has to be allowed for in the design of sections and joints.

3: An Analysis of Construction

Nothing has been said as yet about the way in which wood, in the form of seasoned sawn planks, is made up into articles of joinery. Before anything can be made, there must be a design which will determine both what the article is to look like and exactly how it is to be put together from separate pieces of wood.

The design of some of the common articles of joinery, such as sash and casement windows and panelled and battened doors, has become so much a tradition that the details of their construction will not necessarily have to be described to the joiner or manufacturer, unless some departure is required from the usual pattern.* These articles are often produced with no more than a note from the architect of the sizes of the members; and in the ordering of mass-produced standard articles all that is required is a catalogue number. On the other hand, if the architect wishes to maintain a closer control or to depart from the accepted practice in construction, or to modify the appearance of such articles, he then must have enough knowledge of the methods at the disposal of the joiner or manufacturer to be able to give him proper instructions.

Equally, if he wants to have joinery made which is exceptional in size or for which there is no precedent, or whose particular character depends upon the way in which it is made, then again he must not only be able to give appropriate instructions, but he must also understand the technical means and visual consequences of the method of construction which he chooses.

The illustrations (Figs. 34–8 on page 53) exemplify these particular departures from standard construction, for which detailed instructions and drawings would be necessary:

(34) shows a dowelled joint for the junction between the stile and rail of a framed door, where the normal joint would be a mortice and tenon—a change in construction.

(35) shows a door in which the widths of the battens, the square rebates between them, and the curved light are all variations from the standard framed and battened door—a change in detailed design.

(36) illustrates a part of a large continuous area of glazing in wooden frames, and shows the problems involved when extra large sizes are needed.

(37) shows an acoustic reflector, and is typical of the kind of work for which there is unlikely to be any precedent, and about which there will not be any guidance in standard textbooks.

(38) shows continuous benching designed both for economy and also to

* Examples are shown in Appendix IV, page 207.

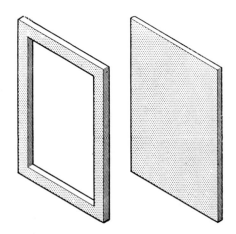

Fig. 29. *The two basic
elements of joinery:
skeleton frames and flat
areas of wood.*

obtain a particular character not associated with traditional methods of making such fitments.

These examples serve to show that it is not enough merely to learn to know parrotwise the details of what has come to be thought of as traditional practice. Instead one must understand the principles exemplified by such joinery and have a vocabulary from which to draw, not of complete components, such as windows and doors and so on, but of basic elements.

If one examines any article of joinery one may first be surprised by the subtlety with which the actual joints are made, and indeed since the function of the many joints used must be understood in order to design satisfactorily, the subject will be discussed later in full. It may also be apparent that all joinery is a process of putting together in some way or another a number of relatively small pieces of wood. These pieces, whose dimensions are governed by the size of the logs and the method of their conversion, are never large enough to comprise the whole article—unless one were to count a shelf as such—and some means has to be found of making them, as it were, larger, whether it be to form an open framework or a flat area of solid material.

An analysis of joinery suggests, in fact, that there are these two basic requirements:

1. To make *skeleton frames*, as, for instance, in door frames, casement windows, and the supporting framework to a counter.

2. To make *flat areas of wood*, as in doors, counter tops, linings and wall panelling.

Almost all joinery consists of these two elements, either separately or in combination, and it is therefore important to know how they are constructed and how they behave. Figs. 30 and 31 show two typical ways of forming frames, in which one important consideration is that the cross-section of the individual pieces shall be large enough and of the right shape to permit an adequate joint to be made at the corners. The choice of the appropriate

50

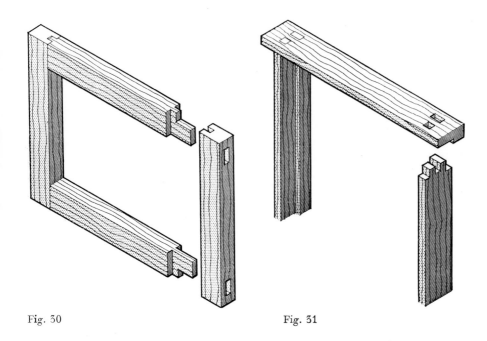

Fig. 30   Fig. 31

joints for frames for different purposes will be discussed separately, and for the moment one need be concerned only with the simple fact that frames of one sort or another are a common part of joinery, and that no better way of making them has been found than by joining four separate lengths of wood at their ends. It is obviously not practicable, for instance, to make such a shape by cutting out the centre portion of a large plank of wood, since two sides would have the direction of grain across the section and would have no strength. It would, of course, be possible to overcome this by using very thick plywood, but this would be uneconomical, apart from other objections, such as the difficulty of screwing or nailing into, or even of painting, the edges.

A frame made up in the traditional way is very stable, since the shrinkage along the length of the grain of each member is negligible, and the width of the members, where shrinkage would be likely to occur, is usually relatively small. For this reason, the frame is often used in conjunction with panels filling the centre, as one method of making the flat areas of wood which we are considering.

With the exception of shelves, or such components as consist solely of frames, there are indeed very few instances in joinery where it is not necessary to make sides or tops or bases which are wider than is normally obtainable in single boards. It is true that the top of a counter could be simply one very large plank and that, in modern construction, a panelled wall may consist of relatively few large sheets of ply. In the first instance, the appearance of the single plank may be particularly valued, though it is likely to be expensive, and in such a position allowance can fortunately be

51

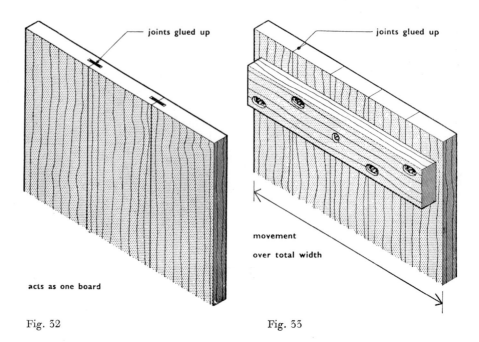

joints glued up

joints glued up

movement

over total width

acts as one board

Fig. 32   Fig. 33

made for the movement which will inevitably occur; in the second instance, advantage is taken of the special characteristics of plywood, one of which is that it has very little movement.

More usually any area larger than the individual plank has to be made up in one of the following ways:

(*a*) A number of boards with their edges accurately finished and glued together (Fig. 32). When the surfaces are sanded the joints can hardly be seen —and the separate boards can be distinguished only by following their grain. In 'carcass' work, which is the name given to the box-like casing of which the outside of a chest of drawers is typical, this method is commonly used. It has one great disadvantage, which prevents it being used, for instance for doors, where a constant width is important, and that is that the movement which takes place in each board is cumulative, and the total movement is equivalent to what might be expected from a single plank of the same width as the whole unit.

(*b*) In positions where the boards are used in conjunction with ledges, rails and other members in which the grain is in the opposite direction, the fixing between the two must be designed to make allowance for the movement of the boards. An example of such fixing is shown in Fig. 33. Since the boards will move as one, but the ledge will not move correspondingly because its grain goes in the opposite direction, the screws are made to run in slots and it will be seen that whilst such screws hold the boards close against the ledge, they do not prevent them moving laterally.

(*c*) Fig. 41 shows another elementary method of joining up small pieces of wood to make a larger unit, but both the principle and its applications are

52

Fig. 34

Fig. 35

Fig. 36

Fig. 37

Fig. 38

*Figs. 34 to 38 show examples of the
kind of joinery which cannot be
produced without detailed drawings
and specifications. These are discussed
on page 49.*

Fig. 39

Fig. 39. An illustration of the skeleton framing for benching. It compares with Fig. 57. The cross frames are prefabricated and the longitudinal rails are fixed on site.

Fig. 40. A detail of benching shown in Fig. 39, showing a joint in a longitudinal rail made over one of the cross frames. It also shows one of the plates for slot screwing the top to the frame.

Fig. 40

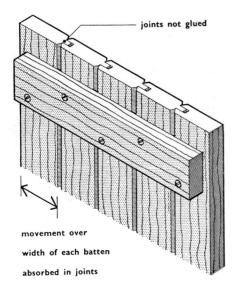

joints not glued

movement over

width of each batten

absorbed in joints

Fig. 41

different. Here the joints are not glued and each batten is free to move independently of the next. The joints will open and close with the movement of the battens, probably in an uneven manner. To avoid unsightly appearance, the joints are accentuated in a way which tends to conceal irregular movement. This is done sometimes by shaping the edges of each board in a 'V' as shown; half-rounds and square rebates are other possible variations. A ledge becomes an essential part of the system since the boards would otherwise fall apart, but it can be screwed or nailed to each board without slots because each board is free to move either side of the screw. By contrast, however, if each board were screwed twice in its width it would theoretically be necessary to provide slots; although, in practice, the movement across one board alone is not enough to make this necessary. Boards put together with unglued joints in the way that has been described are used where the movement across the total width must be kept low, and where it does not matter that the joints show.

(d) Fig. 42 illustrates what is perhaps the most commonly used method of achieving the flat areas of wood which we are considering. It consists of the stable skeleton frame with an infilling panel which can be allowed to move freely within the grooves that house it. Fig. 43 shows a variant in design embodying the same principle. Formerly, the panel consisted of solid wood and its size was limited by the amount of movement which could be accommodated in the grooves and also by the strength of solid timber in the thicknesses which are practicable for panels. With plywood it is obvious that this restriction in size does not apply and very large panels can be incorporated. Plywood, however, has not only the advantage that it can be produced in large areas, but also that the movement is negligible in both directions.

55

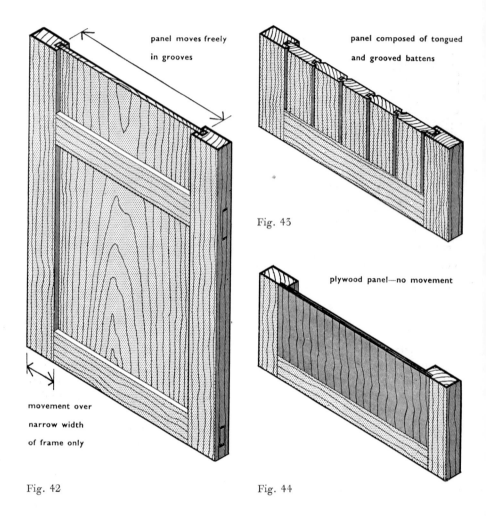

panel moves freely
in grooves

panel composed of tongued
and grooved battens

Fig. 43

plywood panel—no movement

movement over
narrow width
of frame only

Fig. 42

Fig. 44

Because of this characteristic it can be used in conjunction with a frame without allowance for movement.

(e) Fig. 44 illustrates how advantage can be made of the stability of ply-wood to provide a flush infilling to the frame. It would not be possible to achieve this with a solid wood panel since the joints at either side of the panel would open and close.

(f) Recognition of the considerable strength of plywood—yet another of its advantages—has enabled very light frames to be used in conjunction with it to produce large units which are thin compared with traditional framing, and which are very stable and very strong. The stresses in the unit are taken by both the plywood itself and also by the frame. When two sheets of ply are used, as in Fig. 45, the function of the frame is largely to keep the ply apart and to prevent twisting. In certain instances the frame is not jointed and the plywood is merely glued to the members of the frame which are laid out in a position to receive it.

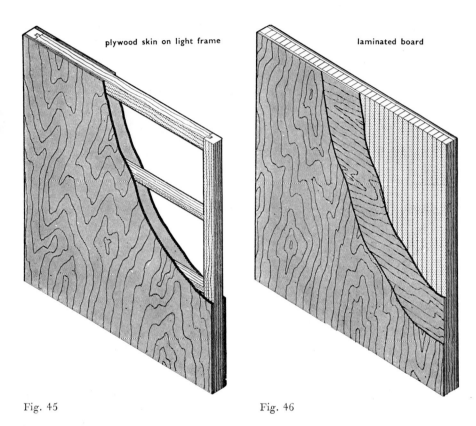

plywood skin on light frame

laminated board

Fig. 45   Fig. 46

(g) The methods so far described involve work in the joiners' shop, and the units are made to specific sizes. The unit shown in Fig. 46, however, is a manufactured composite board obtainable ready-made in large areas, and it is intended for cutting to the required size. It is used in much the same way as the glued-up boards described in (a) and since it has the low movement in both directions characteristic of plywood, it has largely replaced traditional 'solid' construction. Plywood of sufficient thickness to avoid twisting would probably be rather more expensive than the blockboard shown.

SKELETON FRAMES AND FLAT AREAS OF WOOD

As we have already explained on page 50 joinery components usually consist of the skeleton frames and the flat areas of wood which we have been discussing.

Thus: A window consists of a series of skeleton frames (Fig. 47).

A door consists of a flat area of wood. Doors, in fact, make a very convenient illustration since their various patterns exemplify nearly all the systems described above (Fig. 48).

A bookcase consists of flat areas of wood joined to form a box-like structure (Fig. 49). A table consists of a combination of a skeleton frame and a flat area of wood (Fig. 50).

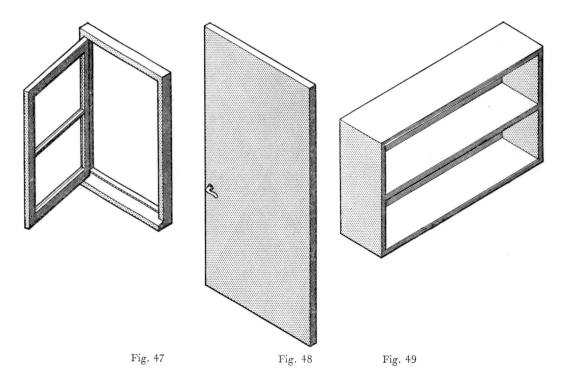

Fig. 47   Fig. 48   Fig. 49

A typical length of laboratory benching also probably consists of both, though the method of putting the units together may involve the use of separate connection pieces or rails which do not come strictly into either category (Fig. 51).

The choice of construction for different kinds of component and conditions of manufacture is discussed below, but before proceeding with this it should be made clear that in endeavouring to make a simple analysis of joinery there is a danger of excluding much that does not conveniently fit. We recognize that there are many miscellaneous items such as architraves, cornices and even such important components as staircases and their balustrades to which the analysis does not wholly apply.

Assuming, however, that for the most part this analysis of joinery is valid, it remains to discover what factors influence the designer in choosing any one of the systems which we have described. That is to say, why in one instance he would choose to use battens and ledges, and in another a framed panel; or glued-up boards rather than blockboard, and so on.

The variations are almost limitless, since there are so many different components, each of which can be made in many different ways. Every designer will have his personal preferences and will adopt methods to suit his particular requirements. These will no doubt be modified from time to time by experience and by the practical advice of the joiners or manufacturers who work from his drawings. Nevertheless, every design will be subject to certain constant factors, amongst which are:

58

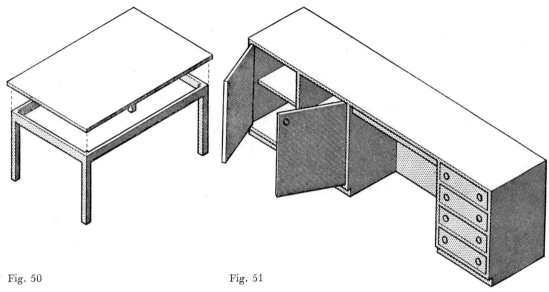

Fig. 50   Fig. 51

Character

The difference in aesthetic quality between traditional moulded wall-panelling and a flush veneered plywood wall lining must be obvious. The character of each is determined by the constructional details of the method used.

Again, if very high quality and finely finished work in hardwood were required, it would demand a different method of construction from a cheap counterpart in painted softwood.

Economy

When, for example, only a few cupboards are required in softwood, it would probably be cheaper for them to be made with solid sides; but similar cupboards made in numbers would be cheaper framed and panelled with plywood. On the other hand, if they were required to have a polished hardwood finish, it is likely that veneered blockboard would be more economical than solid hardwood boards jointed in their width. Although hardwood is itself generally cheaper than blockboard, the labour involved in jointing the boards accurately and 'cleaning up' the joints for a good finish adds considerably to the cost.

Movement

The elimination of undesirable movement, which we have already discussed, will often dictate the method of construction, as can be seen from the examples.

Characteristics of plywood and composite boards

The introduction of these boards, which have relatively little movement, has much altered the design of joinery; and a visit to any manufacturer's shop

59

will prove the extent to which traditional methods are being modified to take advantage of their stability. Nevertheless, it is also evident that, by contrast with some of the work of the furniture and cabinet-making industries, very little joinery is designed to take advantage of some of the other properties possessed by plywood. Whereas radio cabinets are frequently made from bent and moulded plywood, such items as drawers, which can be similarly made, are nearly always constructed in a traditional way, largely for reasons of economy.

Weather
Components which are exposed to the weather must be designed so that their construction will not suffer from the damp, and must incorporate only those materials which are weatherproof. For many years plywood was not satisfactory when used out-of-doors, and constructions which relied upon it failed. This has not, however, applied since the introduction of resin-bonded exterior grade plywood, though a prejudice against it still exists.

Finish
Even in two components which were exactly similar in shape, the construction might well be different according to whether the finish were to be polish or paint.

Size
The size of a component will clearly influence its construction, not only for reasons of strength, but also for convenience of handling and installation. For example, it would not be possible to transport a whole range of cupboards and drawer units if they were constructed as one in the shop; their construction would therefore have to be modified to enable them to be built in smaller units and joined in some way on the site.

Site work
Apart from the site fixing and fitting of separate factory-made components, so-called built-in cupboards and other components are often required in such small numbers that they can readily and cheaply be made by the joiner on the site. The choice of method here depends largely upon the type of firm employed; the specialist joinery manufacturers and the larger builders' shops have a preference for completing as much of the work as possible in the shop, and cutting site work to a minimum. This may involve apparently unnecessary duplication, such as having plywood backs to cupboards which will be fixed against a plastered wall, and yet still be more economical. On the other hand, many smaller builders may find it more economical to make use of the walls against which the components are to fit. This will require a modification in the design, probably entailing less work in the shop and more site work.

The accompanying illustrations of doors, cupboards and continuous benching serve to show how design is influenced by these considerations.

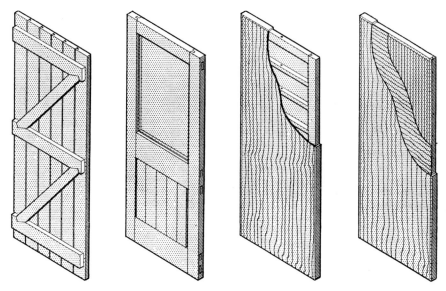

Fig. 52. Four kinds of door: ledged and braced; framed and panelled; flush plywood; solid laminated.

Four kinds of door are illustrated, each of which has characteristics which make it suitable for particular applications and for which one or other of the general methods of construction already described is especially appropriate (Fig. 52). *A Ledged and Braced* door is simple to make and cheap, and presents a neat, weatherproof face on the battened side; for these reasons it is often used for low cost exterior doors. It has no glued joints; the centre battens are free to move within the limits set by the two outside ones, which will always fit the width of the door frame. The diagonal braces are necessary to keep the door rigid and to prevent it from 'dropping' (i.e. sagging downwards from the hinge side). *Framed and Panelled* doors consist of a stable skeleton frame with glued joints, the openings of which are filled with thin panels of either solid timber or plywood. A door of this type can be divided into any number of panels, vertically or horizontally, separated by additional framing members. Openings can also be filled with glass. By contrast with ledged and braced doors they are associated with more expensive work and their construction allows considerable elaboration. The example shown has a glazed upper part, the lower panel being of tongued and grooved boards. *Flush Plywood* doors make use of the advantages of plywood to provide an unbroken surface. The type shown has two thin plywood faces glued to a 'core' of light softwood framing. The cavity is ventilated and a hardwood lipping conceals the core and the edges of the plywood. Because of their construction flush doors are very suitable for mass-production, and their manufacture has become specialized and economical. Owing to the fact that ordinary plywood does not withstand the weather, flush doors were for long not used outside, and the particular character which they have could not be

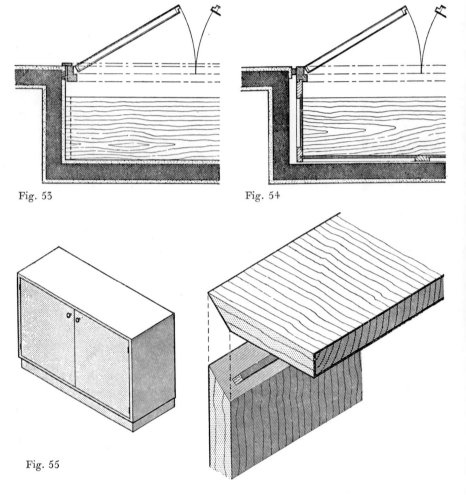

Fig. 53   Fig. 54

Fig. 55

made use of in this position. The introduction of synthetic resin glues in the
manufacture of the plywood itself and of the doors has, however, made this use
possible. *Solid Laminated* doors are made of thick blockboard, usually with
a facing veneer and a hardwood lipping. Being completely solid and of
uniform thickness, they are used in positions where extra strength, fire protection or sound insulation is required.

The examples of cupboards (Figs. 53 to 56) show the way in which
appearance, economy and other factors affect construction. Fig. 53 shows the
cheapest way of making a 'built-in' cupboard in a recess. The recess is first
plastered (or finished in a similar way to the walls of the room) and rough
timber grounds are incorporated for the fixing of a normal door frame.
Shelves are fixed to battens plugged to the wall. A better quality and more
expensive method is shown in Fig. 54. Here the cupboard is lined with
wood and the unit is made up as a complete 'carcass'; the door frame is of
hardwood, behind which is a softwood framing clad with plywood flush to

62

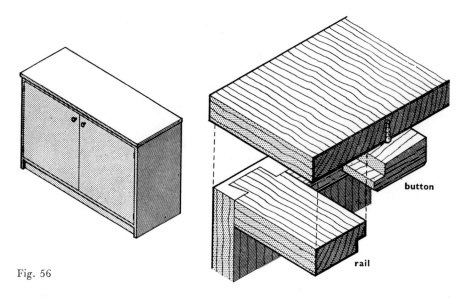

Fig. 56

the inside. Shelves are housed into the framing members. Some allowance in size must be made for building in, and the gap afterwards closed by a hardwood strip 'scribed' to the wall, or by other means. Some similar method of construction is essential if drawers are part of the design, since the carcass sides are required in order to support the drawer runners. The cupboard unit illustrated in Fig. 55 has been designed with its top returning flush with the sides, showing no end grain. To achieve this, it is necessary to use a mitred corner, which is expensive. The mitre shown in the example is, however, more economical than, for instance, a secret dovetailed joint which would be an alternative. A more economical method of constructing the cupboard, but which necessitates an alteration in appearance, is shown in Fig. 56. Here the top is allowed to oversail the front and sides, and is fixed with 'buttons' (i.e. small wooden cleats which are screwed into the top and engage in grooves in the carcass). The carcass sides are connected by rails. This arrangement allows for movement in the top, which is essential if the sides are framed.

Joinery components which are too large to be transported and installed as one unit have to be designed to be broken down into smaller pieces which can be fitted together on the site. Fig. 57 shows a simple way of doing this for continuous benching. The component is made as a series of complete carcasses, which are placed against each other or joined by rails, the top being fixed afterwards with buttons. Very little site work is involved, a consideration of some importance since more accuracy is possible if the major part of the work is done in the factory; this advantage offsets the otherwise uneconomical duplication of structure at the points where the units meet. Another method of achieving the same object is illustrated in Fig. 58. Here the benching is built up of separate cross-frames connected at the front and back by rails. Supports for shelves and runners for drawers

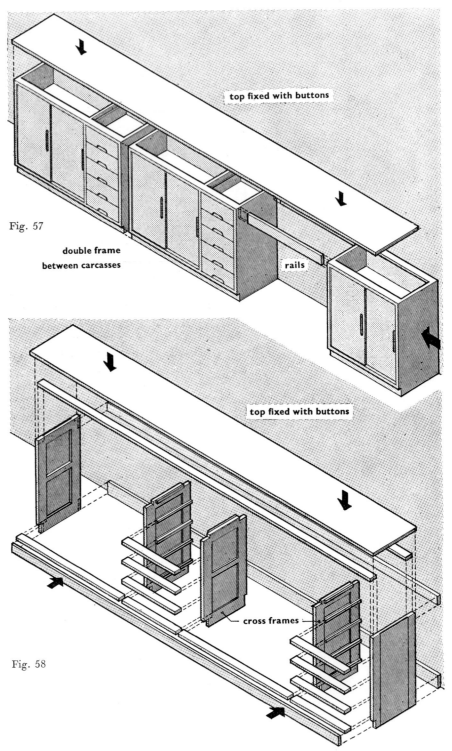

top fixed with buttons

Fig. 57

double frame
between carcasses

rails

top fixed with buttons

cross frames

Fig. 58

64

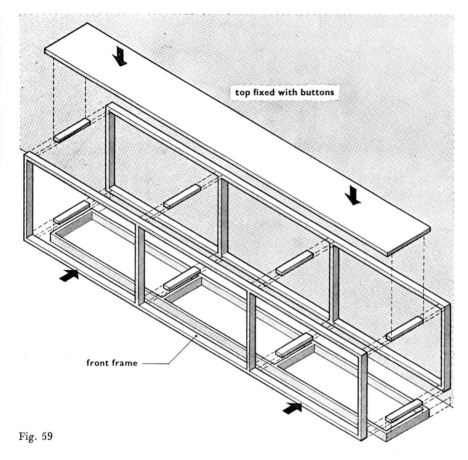

top fixed with buttons

front frame

Fig. 59

can be built into the frames. The whole unit is put together 'dry' in the shop, taken to pieces, and assembled on the site and the joints finally glued or screwed.

In some instances it may be more advantageous to construct the unit with front and back frames, as shown in Fig. 59. This might occur in a unit designed with a finely finished hardwood top and front, and sliding doors, the rest of the carcass being made of softwood. The hardwood front frame could be assembled and the doors fitted accurately in the workshop. This method would not, however, be suitable if drawers were included in the design, since the runners would then have to be made on the site.

NOTE: *Joints have been omitted from Figs. 57, 58 and 59, since they are intended to show only the general principles of construction.*

4: The Design and Machining of Sections

Having formulated some principles for the construction of joinery components one must next decide on the size and shape of the individual pieces of timber used.

In practice the designer will consider the shape of the sections and the way they are joined together at the same time, but for the sake of simplicity we are proposing to leave the design and choice of *joints* to the next chapter. This has the merit of following the sequence of actual operations in the production of finished joinery from the raw material; that is, the extraction of the logs; their conversion into sawn planks; their seasoning; their cutting to size and shape; the cutting of the joints by machine; and the putting together and finishing by hand.

It may be helpful if we stress at this point that because nearly all work is done by machine, requiring continuity in operation, the various stages in production are quite distinct: if a factory should happen to be making windows, one will find in one part of the shop a pile of rough sawn timber, unprepared but of the nearest nominal size to the full size dimensions shown on the drawings; and in another part a similar pile, but of timber shaped in section and cut to length; and in another a pile with the ends cut to form the joints; and finally a stack of the assembled windows.

Before the timber is cut to form the joints, it has undergone a process, or a series of processes, which gives it the particular shape in cross-section which is required; and although the means of achieving this shape are different from those used in producing extrusions in metal, it may be of help to think of the pieces of wood at this stage of production as being similar to lengths of metal extrusions.

The choice of size and shape of the sections will be largely based on the designer's wish for a particular appearance. Having this in mind, he may want to give the section a special profile; or he may wish to use sections that would exceed the size strictly required for strength, and so on. At one time there was little fear of his choosing sections that were inappropriate in size because there had grown up a sound tradition in design which, though we now view it as having limited scope, nevertheless met the economic and aesthetic requirements of the day. It required attention from the architect mainly in the refinement of the mouldings which were worked on the timber or applied to it.

Nowadays, whilst we look for new forms and new appearances, we must also be more economical; in addition there are plywoods and other built-up boards. These factors have encouraged architects and designers to review the old standards and to develop new shapes and new techniques.

Sometimes, however, a desire for novelty or for extreme economy may give rise on the one hand to sections which are disproportionately expensive, and on the other hand to designs incorporating sections which are too weak structurally.

If one adheres to traditional patterns as typified in Georgian work, the problem is relatively easy, for the sizes and shapes of the sections required will be similar to those which have been handed down and which can be learnt by study of actual examples or by reference to standard textbooks, such as *Modern Practical Joinery* by George Ellis. * If on the other hand one's design requires inventiveness and one is unable to rely on precedent for assurance that it will be satisfactory in practice, then it is as well to remind oneself of those factors which in addition to appearance govern the choice of size and shape.

THE SIZE OF SECTION

The size of section will depend upon:

1. *Mechanical and structural requirements*. When timber is used structurally, that is as an alternative to steel or reinforced concrete, the shape and size and position of the sections can be calculated. In joinery, however, the stresses are usually too varied to allow calculation and whilst each piece of wood will undoubtedly be of structural value its size will often be dictated by some of the other factors described below.

In the absence of calculation, and having taken these other factors into account, the designer must rely upon his judgment. This will be formed through his understanding of the properties of timber and his acquaintance with examples and study of the sizes which have proved successful in practice.† The old-fashioned habit of recording typical measurements in a notebook will help in making certain that one is aware of the results that are likely to be achieved by one's specifications. It is useful, too, in correcting the impression given by full-sized sections on a drawing which invariably appear misleadingly small.

The direction in which the longer dimension of any section is disposed in relation to the whole unit is, however, very largely dictated by structural considerations and two simple examples are shown in Figs. 60 and 61. In Fig. 60 the top and bottom members act as cantilevers and the section is most efficient with its longer dimensions disposed vertically. In Fig. 61 the converse is true because the greatest stresses are in the horizontal plane.

2. *Standard sizes of timber*. The size of the prepared section must be related to the sizes in which timber is marketed commercially, if one is to avoid waste. These sizes were given in the first chapter (pages 27–30), but it should be remembered that the standard practice is to draw sections in full size to the dimensions that they are to be after preparation, namely, reduced by $\frac{3}{32}$ in. for each prepared surface, and labelled to be taken out of the 'nominal'

* B. T. Batsford, London.

† Some examples are shown in Appendix IV, page 207.

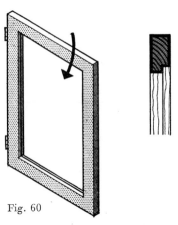

Fig. 60

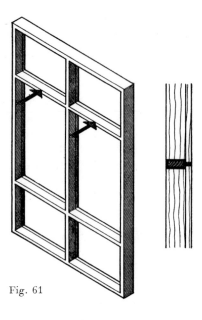

Fig. 61

Fig. 60. *The top and bottom rails of windows and doors act as cantilevers, resisting the tendency for the frame to 'drop' under its own weight. The section is therefore most efficiently disposed with its longer dimension vertical.*

Fig. 61. *The mullions and transoms of large windows are subjected to horizontal forces due to wind pressure. The longer dimension of the section would in this case be disposed most efficiently in the horizontal plane.*

or original size. Thus a window section in softwood drawn $2\frac{13}{16}$ in. by $1\frac{13}{16}$ in. would be labelled 'ex 3 in. by 2 in.'

This allowance can occasionally be reduced, although certain timbers require that it should be increased, but in general the rule applies, and any proposed departure from it would merit discussion with the manufacturers who were to carry out the work.

3. *Strength and quality of timber.* There is a relationship between the weight of timber and its strength which is helpful in making a comparison between one wood and another. The heavier the timber the stronger it is likely to be. We are most of us acquainted with balsa, a very light wood with little strength, and oak which by comparison is a heavy wood and is correspondingly strong: they both, incidentally, come in the classification of 'hardwoods' although balsa is, of course, extremely soft. For most purposes in joinery it is not necessary to discriminate between one wood and the next because the relative strength of most of the commonly used timbers does not differ greatly, but there may be occasions when a specially slender member is required, and the difference in strength between one timber and another may be of significance. The opinion is generally held that if hardwoods are used it is possible to employ smaller sections than if softwoods are used, but there can be no hard and fast rule. Apart from anything else, the quality of the wood in both hardwoods and softwoods may vary considerably, and the presence of twisted grain or large knots is likely to be more detrimental in a

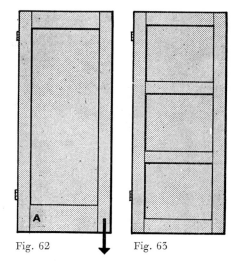

Fig. 62

Fig. 63

Fig. 62. The joint at A takes considerable strain due to the weight of the door, and is most effective if the moment arm is increased, giving a good length of joint.

Fig. 63. A door in which a number of joints take the load. Each joint, and hence the section of each rail, can then be smaller.

small section than any lack of strength in the timber itself. The beautifully moulded and delicate glazing bars of Georgian sash windows can be produced as well from softwood as hardwood, but they can be produced from neither if there are knots and other defects in the timbers. The quality of the actual timber used is therefore at least as important as the strength which the species may be thought to possess.

4. *The space required by joints.* However small a section may be it is always possible to join it rigidly to another section provided the stresses imposed on the joint are comparable to those which the section itself may be expected to withstand. In an assembled unit, however, the strength required of a joint may determine the size of a member. This is true of the bottom rail of a door where the tendency for the outer stile to drop (Fig. 62) must be withstood by the joint at A. The strength of this joint is increased proportionately by the depth of the rail, which in practice is often 10 in. or 11 in. although it is otherwise quite unnecessary for it to be so large. Fig. 63 shows that if there is a number of joints each assisting the other, then they can be smaller and the sections correspondingly reduced in size.

5. *Space required by fittings and hardware.* Once it is realized that it is most important to ensure that sections will accommodate the fittings which are associated with the particular piece of joinery being designed, the problem resolves itself into seeing that the cross-section is not cut away so much as to weaken it unduly; that there is adequate fixing for screws and that they will not split the section into which they are put; that even if the section itself is large enough the fittings are not such as will take away most of the joint between one member and the next.

Fig. 83, p. 80, shows a double glazed hopper window with rather complicated fittings. Many of the double glazed wood windows now on the market

Fig. 64

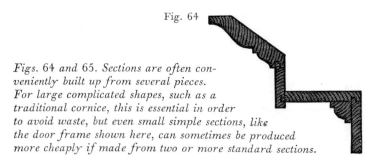

Figs. 64 and 65. Sections are often conveniently built up from several pieces. For large complicated shapes, such as a traditional cornice, this is essential in order to avoid waste, but even small simple sections, like the door frame shown here, can sometimes be produced more cheaply if made from two or more standard sections.

Fig. 65

are arranged to pivot and have inset espagnolette bolts. These require the section, which is made suitably large, to be deeply grooved throughout most of its length. One must avoid the temptation to adopt new kinds of fittings without first making sure that appropriate adjustments are made to the sizes with which, using other systems of opening and other fittings, one has become familiar. Similarly, one must avoid indulging in the invention of obscure profiles for the sections of such components as windows before ascertaining that it is possible to fix some kind of fitting to them. This is a question of the *shape* of the sections, which we discuss below.

THE SHAPE OF SECTION

1. *Economy*. Except perhaps for the influence of such practical matters as weathering, and rebating for glazing and others which are outlined below, the shape of the section will be governed principally by the desire for a particular appearance. Almost any shape *can* be produced, but some shapes cost more than others, and therefore attention to economy may affect the choice. Since the preparation is undertaken by machines, which take time to set up and for which cutters have to be ground, it is obviously expensive to demand non-standard* shapes for very short runs of material. On the other hand, for any reasonable quantity it is not disproportionately expensive to have cutters ground to special shapes, and the shape is then governed rather by its suitability for such joints as may be required, and by a common-sense attitude to cost. The cost of grinding an ordinary cutter is about 10s. If a large number of separate machine operations is needed, either because of an elaborate shape, or a particularly large section, or if very deep cut or undercut mouldings are asked for, involving special machining, the cost will increase. Even so, it must be remembered that the cost of machining is only a part of the total cost, which would normally be made up as follows: cost of timber—one-half; machining—one-quarter; assembly—one-quarter.

It would be absurd to try to cut an elaborate cornice (see Fig. 64) from one large piece of timber because most of the original piece of timber would be cut away and its cost wasted. Such large profiles have of necessity to be built

* 'Standard' sections in joinery are of two kinds: 1, trade sections (debased classical mouldings) developed by the trade through long usage, and 2, BS and EJMA sections.

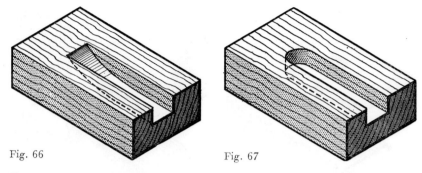

Fig. 66   Fig. 67

Figs. 66 and 67. Machined mouldings stopped in the length of a member will have curved ends; these illustrations show the effect produced by a spindle moulder (Fig. 66), and a router (Fig. 67).

up from a number of small sections, but economy will often be achieved, even in simple components such as a door lining, by using two plain rectangular sections (the lining and the 'planted' stop—see Fig. 65) instead of cutting the rebated stop out of the solid. It does not always follow, of course, that the cheaper method is the best.

If the quantity of material required is considerable, the number of operations will be of less significance because it will become economical to use a machine which has up to six separate cutters on it. This machine (Fig. 80, p. 79) is very expensive to set up, but once in operation produces the material at a rate which in large quantities more than compensates for the initial expenditure. Finally, when the quantity is of the order of that of standard mass-produced articles, the product must be regarded as having all its features unalterable, including the shape of the section, if it is to maintain its cheapness. Architects have assumed the right by tradition to modify at will the shape of sections used in joinery, but this no longer applies when, in order to achieve economy, large scale machinery is set up and a factory is organized to produce articles which are no less a standard product than say a motor car. We show in Fig. 79, p. 79, one of the special cutters used for this class of work, the cost of which is about £50. One change in dimension in a standard design might easily double the cost of manufacture.

As a general rule, the most economical joinery is composed of members having a constant section throughout their length, since this is in the nature of the machining processes. Sometimes, however, it is necessary to change the shape of the section at a point in the length of the member, and the machining will then need to be stopped off at that point. A 'gun stock' door* is a typical example of a design which could be produced by machine but which is more expensive than a door with straight stiles because more operations are involved. The illustrations above (Figs. 66 and 67) show the problem in another form. On the left is a stopped moulding produced by a spindle moulder, and on the right, that produced by a router. In both examples the

* i.e. a door in which the lower part of the stile is wider than the upper part.

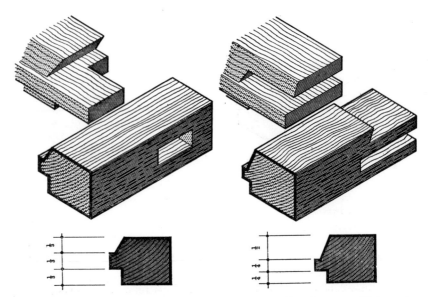

Fig. 68. *When designing sections it is important to consider the type of joint to be used at the points where they meet. This will often influence the proportions of the sections. The example illustrated here shows a typical casement section. Left, a mortice and tenon joint, in which the width of the tenon should preferably be one-third of the width of the members. If the section is designed, as shown, with its proportions coinciding with those of the joint, scribing cuts will be simplified. The same applies to the comb joint, right, which has four equal laminations.*

moulding finishes with the curvature of the cutter but if a square stopped end were to be required, it would have to be cut out by hand and this would add to the cost.

2. *Junctions with other members.* It is perhaps taxing the architect too greatly to ask that he should think of such details as follow when so much else is expected of him, but even if he does not consciously bring them to bear on his design of sections he will at least be aware of them, should they be raised by the manufacturer.

In the first place certain proportions have been adopted in practice for joints, and it simplifies their manufacture if, as shown in Fig. 68, the proportions of the faces of the sections on which they are cut correspond. The result of not doing so is shown in Fig. 69. It is quite possible that manufacturers will alter the profile from that shown on the architect's drawing to suit their machines rather than adjust the cutters of the machines which make the joints, and architects should make it clear in their specifications whether they agree to this being done or are prepared to accept the additional cost of strict conformity to their drawings. In the second place there are several methods used for 'returning' the profile at the junction of two members, as for instance the moulding on the rail and stile of a casement window. Some of these methods are cheaper than others, because they can be

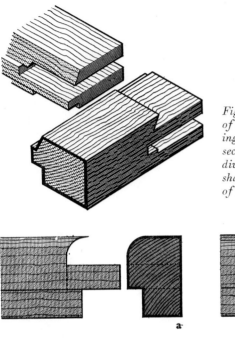

Fig. 69. This illustration shows the effect of designing a section without considering the type of joint to be used. The section illustrated has three equal subdivisions, while the joint has four. The shape of the scribing cuts, and therefore of the cutters required, becomes complex.

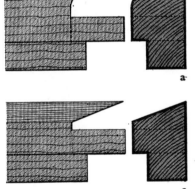

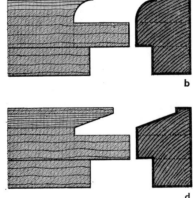

Fig. 70. Scribed joints and their influence on the design of sections. a and c show two sections (a 'pencil round' and a shallow splay) which cannot be satisfactorily scribed, as a feather-edge would result which would 'break out', or chip away, during machining. Some alternative method such as mitring the moulding would have to be used, and this may change the manufacturing process sufficiently to raise the cost out of proportion to the intended visual effect. By altering the section to provide a small square shoulder, as in b and d, this difficulty is completely overcome.

done wholly by machine. 'Scribing' is the cheapest of all, but if it is to be done successfully the profile of the section must avoid certain characteristics, such as 'pencil rounds' and shallow splays and undercuts (Fig. 70).

Illustrations of the various methods are given (Fig. 71) to show their several advantages and disadvantages and to suggest how they can be used instead of scribing if a profile unsuitable for the latter should be insisted upon. The methods are described below:

SCRIBE. In this method one member runs through uncut, while the other has its end 'scribed' or worked to the profile of the section. It is the most common method, and has many advantages: it allows great freedom in the

73

design of the joint, is easily and cheaply machined (one member only need-
ing special machining to form the junction) and can be used where two dis-
similar sections meet. However, it is not suitable for 'undercut' sections, and
the scribe is difficult to cut when the section has a pencil round or a shallow
splay, owing to the feather-edge which is formed at the intersection of the
scribe and the face of the member at that point.

MITRE. Although this method is in principle simple, in practice it has certain
disadvantages. It greatly restricts the choice of joint, and is difficult to produce by machine because very small inaccuracies in setting-out produce large
faults in alignment; for this reason it is mainly confined to hand work. The
two sections must be identical, although they can be of any profile. It has
the great advantage of neat appearance when made well, and this is generally
the reason for its being used for margins and picture frames.

MITRE (MOULDING ONLY). This method presents the same appearance
as the scribe when assembled. It combines some of the advantages of each
of the above methods; it allows freedom in the choice of joint, and while the
mitred portion will deal with undercut or shallow-splayed sections, the rectangular parts of the two members can be of different widths. It is, however,
almost impossible to produce well by machine, and so is confined to hand
work.

MASON'S MITRE. This method derives from masonry technique, and cannot
be said to be sympathetic to the nature of wood or woodworking. It allows
complete freedom in the choice of joint, the members generally being
assembled before the moulding is worked. Although this means that the
joint itself can be entirely machine-cut, the working of the moulding at the
joint can only be done by hand and is very expensive.

ROUTED MOULDING. This comparatively recent technique has been made
possible by the development of the routing machine (see fig. 81, page 80, for
section-cutting machinery). The moulding, whose shape is limited, is cut
after the members have been assembled, and turns the corner with the
circular arc typical of machine technique. While this may sometimes be considered aesthetically desirable, in certain positions it will be impracticable—
for instance, in glazing rebates. The example shown has a scribed rebate
combined with a routed moulding. One advantage which it has is the saving
in cutters, one moulding cutter only being required—in a scribed joint, a
'reverse' profile cutter is needed to work the scribe.

3. *Functional requirements*. All joinery components are required to 'do'
something: they are not abstract ornamental objects. Some of their functions
are 'mechanical' such as the work done by a shelf supporting a load, but
various other functions are often required; a sill must shed water, the meeting rails of sash windows must let in as much light as possible whilst also
admitting the least amount of draught and foiling the burglars' attempt to
slip a knife in to push back the catch, a glazing bar must be designed to
receive the glass and retain it, a door frame must be designed to provide a
check for the door, and so on. Profiles designed to receive paint will differ

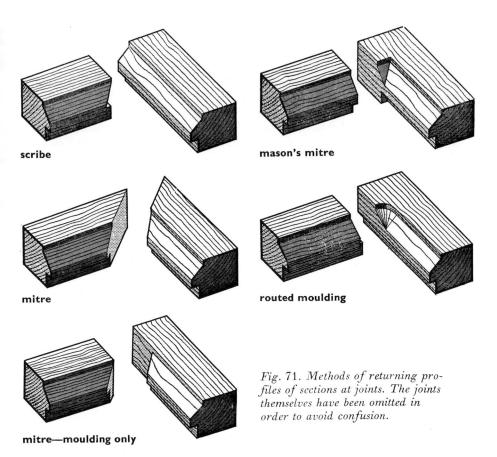

scribe

mason's mitre

mitre

routed moulding

mitre—moulding only

Fig. 71. Methods of returning profiles of sections at joints. The joints themselves have been omitted in order to avoid confusion.

from those for polish since successive coats of paint will clog narrow grooves and upset the intended visual effect.

No rule can be laid down for these factors but it is questionable whether all the elaborate grooves and sinkings shown on many window sections can be justified though it is recognized that they are intended to help keep out the weather.

It is also interesting to note that one requirement sometimes conflicts with another: in order to admit light the longer dimension of the section of an opening light in a casement window should be at right angles to the plane of the window, but to give it strength it has to be the other way round.

4. *Movement.* Very wide flat sections of solid timber such as are used in door linings and wide architraves are specially prone to warping. Proper seasoning and the selection of a quarter-sawn timber will do much to avoid it, but as an additional safeguard the back of the section can be cut out in a wide shallow groove. This does not add much to the cost of machining and has the advantage of ensuring that the section fits closely at both sides even if it tends to warp.

5. *Fittings.* Just as it is necessary to ensure that there is enough *room* to accommodate fittings, so is it necessary to see that the *shape* of the sections is appropriate and will allow the fittings to work properly. Every problem of this kind must be considered on its merits, and it will be enough to point out two examples: the awkwardness of fixing window fasteners to splayed sections, and the impossibility of fitting standard rebated mortice locks—which are produced with one set of dimensions—to the meeting-stiles of doors having rebates of different dimensions. It is easy to alter the dimensions of the rebates on the drawing board, but difficult when the doors have been made! Special locks can be made—but with unnecessary expense.

MACHINES

It is not necessary for an architect to have a detailed knowledge of the machines which produce in timber what he draws on his board, but if at the back of his mind he can picture what takes place in the factory it is likely to be of help to him, if only to avoid thoroughly impracticable designs: and at least it will add to his interest. The illustrations and the notes which follow endeavour to describe the purposes of the machines and such of their characteristics as influence design.

They are shown in order of the sequence of operations. Machines used expressly for *jointing* will be described in the next chapter, which is devoted to the design of joints.

Circular rip saw
The first operation in the preparation of a section, shown in Fig. 72, is to cut the timber out of larger stock to a size slightly greater than that of the finished section. This is usually done on a hand-feed circular rip saw of the type shown here. The width of the timber is kept constant by the *fence*, or guide, which is adjustable to widths up to 2 ft; other machines have a larger capacity. About $\frac{3}{32}$ in. is allowed on each face of the section in excess of the required finished size.

Cross-cut saw
The rough sawn section is cut approximately to length on a cross-cut saw, shown in Fig. 73. There are two common types of circular cross-cut saw; the first is similar in principle to the rip saw, the timber being fed into the saw which itself remains fixed. The second type, illustrated here, has a table on which the timber remains stationary while the saw-blade, mounted overhead, is pulled forward.

All woodworking machines are fitted with guards, which protect the operator from the saws or cutters, but in some of these illustrations the guards have been moved to show the action of the machines more clearly.

Surface planer
The timber, cut to length, and roughly sawn to size, must now be planed smooth on two adjacent faces, as shown in Fig. 74. This operation is carried

Fig. 73

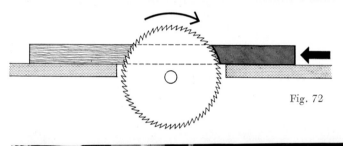

Fig. 72

Fig. 72. CIRCULAR RIPSAW.

Fig. 73. CROSS-CUT SAW.

Fig. 74. SURFACE PLANER.

*These machines are
described on p. 76.*

revolving cutter

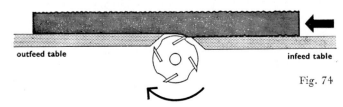

outfeed table   infeed table

Fig. 74

77

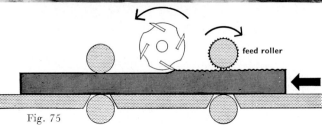

Fig. 75. THICKNESSER.
Fig. 76. SPINDLE MOULDER
WITH RING FENCE.
Fig. 77. SPINDLE MOULDER
AS USED FOR STRAIGHT WORK
WITH TWO STRAIGHT FENCES.

*These machines are
described on p. 81.*

Fig. 75

feed roller

Fig. 76

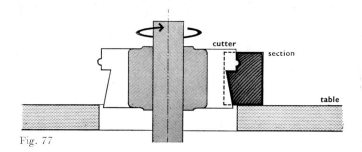

cutter
section
table

Fig. 77

Fig. 78   Fig. 79

Fig. 78. THE SQUARE BLOCK CUTTER: *this is the most versatile type.*

Fig. 79. THE SOLID PROFILE CUTTER: *expensive to make, this is used for mass-produced work, for which it is most economical since it can be quickly and easily sharpened without distortion of the profile.*

Fig. 80. FOUR-SIDED PLANER AND MOULDER, *often termed the four-cutter.*

These are described on pp. 81 *and* 82.

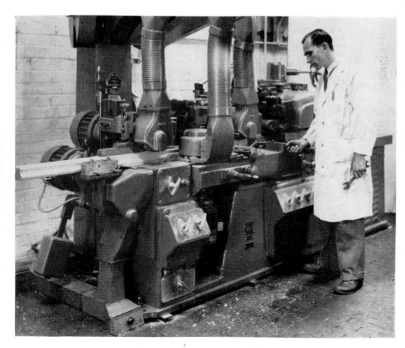

Fig. 80

79

Fig. 81

Fig. 81. ROUTER. *This is described on p. 82.*

Fig. 82. *Prepared sections of timber before jointing.*

Fig. 83. *In the design of sections, particularly in windows and doors, allowance must be made for fittings and hardware attached to them. This illustration shows a folding stay on a double glazed hopper window requiring a large recess to accommodate it.*

Fig. 82    Fig. 83

out on a planing machine, which has a revolving cutter with four, six or eight knives. The cutter is set slightly higher than the infeed table; this projection determines the thickness of the cut. The outfeed table is set level with the cutter. When one surface has been planed, the timber is fed into the machine again with the planed face in contact with the fence. Since the fence is fixed accurately at right angles to the cutter, the second face when planed will be square with the first.

A combined surface planer and thicknesser is made, sometimes referred to as the under-and-over planing machine.

One point to note in connection with all machines using revolving cutters is that, due to the rotary action of the knives, the apparently flat surface produced is actually composed of a number of very small concave cuts. If the knives are set out of alignment with each other, or the timber fed too quickly through the machine, this effect becomes noticeable and the surface appears 'rippled'.

Thicknesser

The timber, which has had two faces planed at right angles to each other on the surface planer, is then fed through a thicknessing machine (see fig. 75, page 78). The timber is fed under a power-driven feed roller with one of the previously planed faces downward on the infeed table. The cutter is mounted overhead, and the distance between it and the table—which determines the thickness of the finished section—can be accurately set to any dimension by raising or lowering the table. This is done simply and quickly by the turn of a handle (the large wheel on the left side of the machine). The timber is passed through once for thickness and again for width, after which the section will be accurately rectangular.

Spindle moulder

If any shape of section other than rectangular is required, the moulding (which is the term used for any irregular profile) must be cut either on the spindle moulder or the router.

The spindle moulder consists of a flat table, in the centre of which a vertical spindle rotates. The spindle is so designed that a number of different types of cutterblock, carrying shaped cutters, can be easily attached to it. The shape of a cutter is the 'reverse' of the required profile; the timber is fed past the cutter and the cut is kept even by means of fences.

The photograph, Fig. 77, page 78, shows the normal arrangement for straight work, with two straight fences. For curved work, a ring fence may be used (Fig. 76); this illustration also shows the action of the cutter (the machine has been stopped to illustrate this more clearly). The spindle moulder is a very versatile machine and may be used for double-curved work, as in handrail wreaths, and for making many types of joint as well as cutting sections.

There are three main types of cutter for moulding machines; the French spindle head, the square block and the solid profile cutter.

The French spindle head is the simplest, consisting of a narrow cylindrical extension to the spindle with a vertical slot, into which independent flat cutters are placed.

The square block (Fig. 78, page 79) is the most versatile; it has four sides to which flat cutters are bolted in any position. Its great advantage is that complex profiles can be split up into smaller sections, each being cut by a separate, simple cutter. Flat cutters can be ground to special profiles.

The solid profile cutter (Fig. 79) is a steel casting with outer edges ground to the required profile. This is a very expensive process, and the use of this type of cutter is restricted to those profiles which are mass-produced. Given these conditions, however, the solid profile cutter is most economical since it is quickly and easily sharpened (on the inner faces) without the possibility of distortion of the profile.

Four-sided planer and moulder

This machine, often termed the four-cutter (Fig. 80, page 79), is a mass-production machine in which the operations of planer, thicknesser and spindle moulder are combined. The timber is fed by a power-driven feed past cutters which plane or mould the four faces of the section in turn. For high quality work it is considered that the timber should be planed and thicknessed, in order to 'take out the warp', before being passed through this machine. For average work, however, the timber is often fed into the machine rough sawn. Due to the great amount of work involved in setting up the cutters and aligning gear, the machine must be run for a considerable time on any particular job (say about four hours) to justify the overhead expenses. Several thousand feet run of timber must therefore be required, as the feed rate of the machine is very high.

(The ducting above the machine is for the purpose of carrying away the wood chippings from the cutters.)

Router

This machine is specially suited to certain moulding and grooving operations which could not be carried out on the spindle moulder; for instance, where grooves are curved or turn corners (see photograph, Fig. 81, page 80). The cutter of the router revolves at very high speeds above a flat table, and the timber is fed sideways into the cutter from any direction. The high-speed router may also be used for cutting irregularly shaped holes and depressions.

5: The Design and Machining of Joints

If one collects together all the joints which have been used in joinery from time to time one finds that there is a bewildering number. We have noted some 100 which are quite common. It might have been supposed that in current practice only a small proportion of these would be used, but in fact it is surprising to find that very few of them are considered to be obsolete, despite the introduction of machine working and of new glues. Having examined all of them, and obtained the opinion of many manufacturers, we have selected eighty which are in common use and which we discuss here in detail.

Many traditional joints, especially those for use externally, were put together with white lead, without glue, and relied for their strength solely on their mechanical properties. For instance, they were pinned or wedged so that they could not be pulled apart. It might be thought that as modern waterproof glues would make the mechanical properties of the joints less important, since more reliance could be placed on the glues, there would be considerable changes in their design, but in practice the traditional methods of making them persist. The main exception is the 'comb' joint which has been designed specifically for machine production and relies for its strength on glue. It will be seen that the gluing surfaces or 'glue lines' as they are called are more extensive than in traditional joints used for the same purpose. When one is concerned with an industry that has become largely mechanized one is accustomed to look for the effect of machine production on design. Although in joinery the joints are now almost exclusively prepared by machine, it would appear that the nature of the raw material has had more influence on their design and shape than the tools which make them. Such differences as exist at the moment between hand-made and machine-made joints are only differences of detail, and these are mentioned in the notes about the individual joints given below. On the other hand some joints which were laborious and expensive to make by hand can be quickly and cheaply made by machine, and are therefore used more freely. The dovetail is a typical example of such a joint. It is now often used for joining the back of a drawer to the sides, for it is as easy to make by machine as the traditional method of grooving the sides and slotting in the back.

The principles of jointing
The objects of all joints are to fix one member to another in such a way that
   (a) as much of the strength of the individual pieces is maintained as possible;

(*b*) the actual joint takes place within the section of the wood. In carpentry, by contrast, many joints are formed by lapping the two pieces of wood over each other;

(*c*) the joint shall be as little visible as possible: the butting of two pieces of handrail is, for instance, very difficult to see if well done. The avoidance of 'end grain' on visible surfaces also governs the design of some joints, since end grain will often be obvious even after painting or polishing;

(*d*) the joint shall withstand dampness, especially when it is to be exposed to the weather;

(*e*) the joint shall be easy to make: particularly that the two pieces to be joined shall be easily located, and that it shall be possible to hold them together whilst the glue sets. In some joints such as dovetails they are automatically held together, in others pins and wedges are used, and in others, screws;

(*f*) it should not be possible to see through the joint if it should open as a result of shrinkage;

(*g*) when reliance is placed almost wholly on the glue, there should be as large as possible a gluing area;

(*h*) where necessary adequate allowance shall be made for movement. This applies in the joint between battens in a battened door. Arrangements such as the forming of a bead, and V-joints to avoid unsightly cracks in such positions, are a tradition;

(*i*) the joint shall be so designed as to avoid stressing any part of it in such a way as to cause splitting;

(*j*) the joint shall be reasonably economical to make, by minimizing the number of machine operations and by avoiding wastage of timber.

'Best traditions of the trade'

Specifications often call for joinery work to be put together in the 'best traditions of the trade' or to be 'properly framed up', and if this is to have any meaning for the architect he should at least know which joints are appropriate to use in various situations. It may be that there are several alternative joints which are equally good but which have certain special characteristics, and if the architect is very particular in his design he will wish to know what these characteristics are, and what effect they will produce, and to show in detail on his drawings which joint is to be used. It may be, for instance, that he would wish to have a dowelled joint between the head and stile of a door instead of a mortice and tenon joint, although both joints are considered to be sound practice. Often no joints are shown or specified by the architect, in which event their choice would naturally be made by the manufacturer, but the architect should then at least have sufficient knowledge when inspecting the work, either at the factory or on the site, to decide whether the joints accord with good practice.

Glues, screws and nails

It is necessary to discuss glues, screws and nails since all joints except those

84

designed for movement have to be glued, and there are legitimate uses for screws and nails which should be recognized. Formerly, when animal glues, which were not weatherproof, were used, it was common practice to joint up larger members in external work in white lead. This acted as a protective 'gap filler' but did little to stick the members together: it is little used today, because of the introduction of new glues.

For all practical purposes three main kinds of glue are used in this country and their characteristics are discussed below:

Animal Glues made from bones and hides—known as Scotch glue—or from fish, are still favoured by some, especially for interior work and for cabinet making, since all joiners are accustomed to them by tradition; they are strong and durable in *dry* conditions; they do not stain the wood, and they can be cleaned off or machined without blunting the blades. Although they have to be applied hot they have a long 'pot' life, and they are convenient and economical to use.

Casein Glues made from soured milk are used in assembly work and in plywood and veneering. They are supplied in powdered form, mixed with water and applied cold. Their main disadvantages are that they are irritating to the skin, they stain woods, particularly oak and mahogany, and the joints lose their strength if wetted, although they regain it on redrying. There are a number of varieties of these glues with differing characteristics; some are claimed to avoid staining and others to be waterproof. As a class they should therefore not be used indiscriminately.

Synthetic Resin Glues have two great advantages over the other two mentioned above; first that they are extremely resistant to moisture and second that they are immune from attacks by moulds and bacteria.

There are three main types, those based on Urea Formaldehydes, those based on Phenol Formaldehydes and those based on Resorcinol Formaldehydes. In each type there are several varieties, some in powder form and some in syrup form, and usually with a hardener supplied separately. The method of application also varies, sometimes requiring heat to obtain setting. They all require greater care in the gluing operation and their 'pot' life is relatively short. They also have a dulling action on tools. Nevertheless, the variety of their forms and their marked superiority in weather resistance has encouraged their use.

It will be seen that properly chosen and used, synthetic resin glues can be relied upon under all conditions. An architect could justifiably specify them for all joinery work, but it must be recognized that some smaller firms may not have had much experience of them, and it would be reasonable for him to permit one of the other kinds to be used in work that is not subjected to moisture.

The development of the synthetic glues has been associated with those parts of the industry dealing with specialized work such as plywood manufacture, aircraft or ship production, and has produced its own technology.

The choice of the right grade and its application requires more care to obtain good results than was necessary when only animal glues were used,

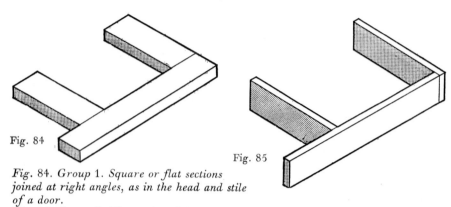

Fig. 84

Fig. 85

*Fig. 84. Group 1. Square or flat sections
joined at right angles, as in the head and stile
of a door.*
*Fig. 85. Group 2. Flat sections joined at right angles, as in the construction of
a bookcase.*

but now that most joinery is produced under factory conditions where modern techniques are more readily assimilated, they are in fact understood and widely used.

Screws of various sizes and materials are used in joinery for five main purposes. First to hold joints together until the glue sets; second, as the sole means of fixing flat surfaces together, such as battens screwed on a wall, or ledges on a drawing board (with slots to allow for movement); third, to fix components in such a way that they can be demounted; fourth, to fix fabricated components in position in a building; and fifth, to secure fittings of all kinds.

When screws are used to enable components to be taken to pieces or parts removed, such as glazing beads, they may have to be visible, and they are then usually used with brass cups which enable the screw to be removed and replaced without enlarging the hole. Otherwise, they are usually kept out of sight and if used, for instance, to secure a polished hardwood architrave they could be counterbored and covered by pellets of the same hardwood or used at the back in conjunction with slotted plates.

When concealed, steel screws are used for cheapness and for strength, but they are liable to rust and also to stain certain woods, notably oak. Brass screws, though less strong, do not have these disadvantages. Where screws are used in association with fittings they should preferably be of the same metal as the fitting or at least of a matching colour, e.g. chromium plated screws for aluminium fittings. Needless to say, steel screws even when painted are liable to rust and it is possible to obtain them galvanized or otherwise rustproofed.

Nails are used in inferior work for holding joints together whilst the glue sets; they are then a poor substitute for screws. Round wire or French nails are often used in these positions. Oval wire nails, panel pins and veneer pins and other special nails are however legitimately used for fixing such items as linings, skirtings and beads and plywood panelling. They are punched in and concealed with putty or other filling material which may then be painted or polished.

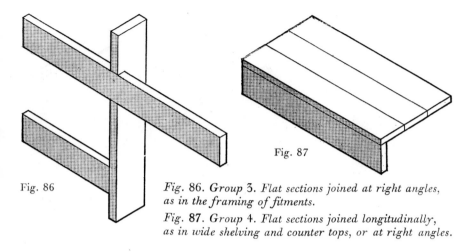

Fig. 86

Fig. 87

Fig. 86. Group 3. *Flat sections joined at right angles, as in the framing of fitments.*

Fig. 87. Group 4. *Flat sections joined longitudinally, as in wide shelving and counter tops, or at right angles.*

Analysis of joints

To revert to the joints themselves we have collected them into eight groups according to their functions. We have taken the principal joints from each group and described them in some detail, with notes about the remainder.

The eight groups are as follows:

GROUP 1. Square or flat sections joined at right angles, as in the head and stile of a door (Fig. 84).

GROUP 2. Flat sections joined at right angles, as in the construction of a bookcase (Fig. 85).

GROUP 3. Flat sections joined at right angles, as in the framing of fitments (Fig. 86).

GROUP 4. Flat sections joined longitudinally, as in wide shelving and counter tops, or at right angles (Fig. 87).

GROUP 5. Flat sections joined longitudinally allowing movement as in matchboarding.

GROUP 6. End-to-end joints as in a handrail or in an extra long sill.

GROUP 7. Joints between 'built up' boarding including lippings.

GROUP 8. Miscellaneous fastenings.

GROUP 1: SQUARE OR FLAT SECTIONS JOINED AT RIGHT ANGLES, AS IN THE HEAD AND STILE OF A DOOR

The joints in this group are those used in such situations as the junction of the rails and stiles of doors, and elsewhere where the pieces of timber have the relationship shown in the sketch. It may be asked why with modern glues one could not butt one member against the other and rely upon adhesion at the point of junction. In the first place glue is less reliable when applied to end grain, and is also stronger in shear than in tension; but these considerations apart, the diagram Fig. 89 on page 88 shows that, even if the glue were strong enough, the wood when so joined might easily fail.

87

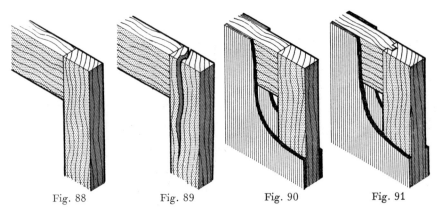

Fig. 88   Fig. 89   Fig. 90   Fig. 91

In a glued butt joint (Fig. 88), the glue might be at least as strong as the wood; but the joint will nevertheless fail by splitting (Fig. 89), owing to the grain structure of the wood. Failure is due to a bending moment producing tension across the grain. When this is taken by other means, e.g., plywood covering (Fig. 90), a butt joint is practicable. In practice, the butt joint is difficult to manufacture as it does not 'locate' itself. A tongue and groove is often introduced to overcome this difficulty (Fig. 91). The problem where bending moments are taken by the joint itself is to provide con-

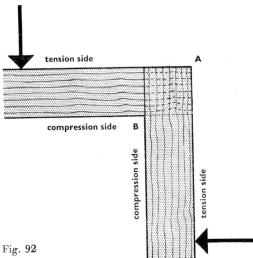

Fig. 92

tinuity between fibres taking tension in one member and corresponding fibres in the other. This necessitates the overlapping of part of both members (Fig. 92) so that tensile fibres of the two members meet at A, and compressive fibres meet at B.

Figs. 88 to 92 also illustrate the principles of design which are used in over-coming the likelihood of failure.

The most common joint used in practice is the mortice and tenon, of which there are various forms for different situations as described below. The dowelled joint is an alternative for the mortice and tenon, but whereas certain advantages can be claimed for it it is not nearly so often used. The comb joint is also employed as an alternative to the mortice and tenon but is mainly restricted to the construction of windows. All these three kinds of joint succeed particularly in fulfilling the functions listed above.

Mortice and tenon joint
Figs. 93 to 95 show one of the most commonly used of the mortice and tenon joints. As distinct from that in Fig. 103, p. 92, which is the simplest

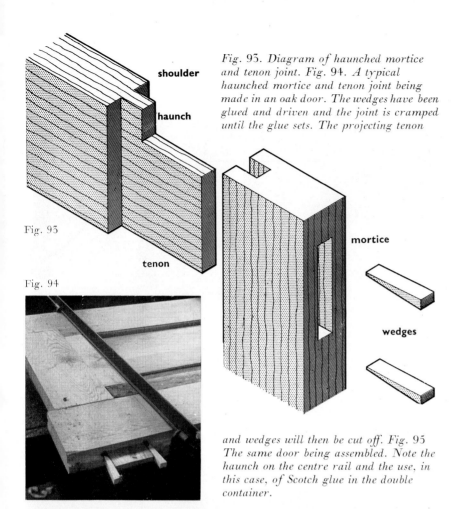

shoulder

haunch

Fig. 93

tenon

Fig. 94

Fig. 93. Diagram of haunched mortice and tenon joint. Fig. 94. A typical haunched mortice and tenon joint being made in an oak door. The wedges have been glued and driven and the joint is cramped until the glue sets. The projecting tenon

mortice

wedges

and wedges will then be cut off. Fig. 95 The same door being assembled. Note the haunch on the centre rail and the use, in this case, of Scotch glue in the double container.

Fig. 95

89

Fig. 96. *A dowelled joint prepared to receive a loose tongue. The joint is not satisfactory unless there are two rows of dowels as in these examples, and is improved by having the tongue or stub tenon. (See also Fig. 111, p. 94.)*

Fig. 98

Fig. 97. *The comb joint as would be used at the corner of a casement window. The slots have been arranged to coincide with the mouldings on the section. The splay to the section in this example has been made after the joint by the use of a router. (See also Fig. 112, p. 95.)*

Fig. 99

Fig. 98 *shows a machine-made lapped dovetail joint. (See also Fig. 113, p. 96.)*

Fig. 99. *A form of housed joint is used universally in the construction of traditional closed string staircases where the treads and risers are jointed to the stringers. In this position the grooves are made wider at one end than the other and wedges are inserted to increase rigidity and to secure the members while the glue sets. (See also Fig. 124, p. 98.)*

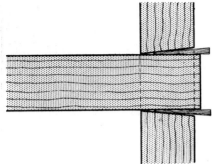

Fig. 100. Diagram showing section of mortice with wedges.

form of the joint, it is designed for use where the vertical member does not continue past the horizontal member and where it is necessary to retain sufficient material at the top of the vertical member to withstand the pressure of the wedges. It will be seen that the tenon is cut away for part of its length leaving what is known as the haunch. This helps to prevent warping and also prevents a gap showing if the joint should open. When mortice and tenon joints were made by hand the craftsman introduced a number of refinements to increase their efficiency. For instance the mortice was cut slightly wedge-shaped as shown in Fig. 100, so that when the wedges were inserted and glued to it, the tenon was virtually converted into a dovetail. This is still done in good joinery despite the fact that the mortices are cut by a machine which would normally cut a parallel sided slot. The tapers are made by tilting the wood, in which the mortice is cut, to each side in turn, and it should be stressed that, if the architect wishes to be sure of obtaining a really good joint, he should specify that the mortices should be so tapered. In addition the wedges were sometimes cut in such a way that they gripped mainly near the shoulders so that any shrinkage which occurred in the vertical member would not cause the joint to open.

In principle all mortice and tenon joints are the same. Each consists of one or more tongues known as tenons on one member and slots or mortices in the other. The tenons are inserted into the mortices and fixed with wedges and glue. The thickness of the tenon should preferably be one-third the width of the section, and the depth of the tenon restricted to five times its thickness. For most mortice and tenon joints the mortice is cut right through the member and, when inserted, the tenon shows on the outer edge. When the main purpose of the joint is to locate one member relative to another and when the joint will not be subjected to tension, a short tenon, known as a 'stub' tenon, can be inserted into a shallow mortice and be fixed by gluing and possibly also by pinning, but without wedges.

For cabinet work and for joinery of extra high quality where the best possible workmanship is demanded, a special kind of mortice and tenon can be used. In this joint, the mortice, which is wedge-shaped, is not carried through the member in which it is cut, and the tenon is correspondingly short. Before the tenon is inserted, however, wedges are driven partially into

91

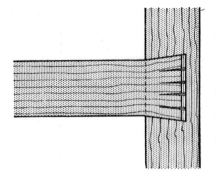

Fig. 101. Section through a stub tenon with foxtail wedging.

it so that when the joint is cramped up they secure the tenon in the mortice, as shown in the drawing, Fig. 101, secretly, without exposing either the wedges or the end grain of the tenon.

This process, which is known as foxtail wedging, is expensive, possibly doubling the cost of the joint. The wedges should be of hardwood, and the work has to be very accurate for, once made, the joint cannot be taken apart and reassembled should there have been any error in the making.

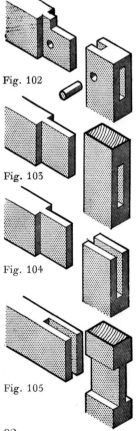

Fig. 102

Fig. 103

Fig. 104

Fig. 105

Fig. 102. PINNED MORTICE AND TENON.
In large sections the mortice is sometimes secured with a circular piece of wood known as a pin or dowel or peg in addition to the usual wedges. In very small sections, where wedges are impracticable, the pin alone may be used.

Fig. 103. THROUGH MORTICE AND TENON.
This is a simple version of the mortice and tenon joint used for the junction of intermediate rails. The tenon is sometimes cut down or 'reduced' to provide shoulders at the top and bottom so that if the tenon shrinks it does not expose an opening into the mortice.

Fig. 104. OPEN OR SLOT MORTICE.
A cheap easily made joint used in positions where good appearance is not essential: suitable for heavy external use. It should be glued and pinned or screwed. Since it cannot be wedged it may be held together by draw pinning. In this process the holes in the two parts of the joint are not exactly opposite each other so that as the dowel is driven home the two members are drawn together.

Fig. 105. TEE BRIDLE. *There is some dispute about the use of this joint and various joinery manufacturers have offered the following opinions:*
'Seldom used in joinery.'
'Of general use, particularly where members vary in thickness.'
'Constructional joint used extensively in the Middle Ages to carry loads.'
'Used principally for site assembled work.'

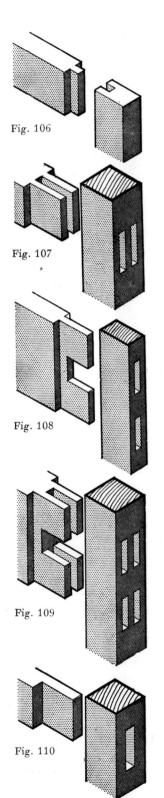

Fig. 106

Fig. 107

Fig. 108

Fig. 109

Fig. 110

Fig. 106. STUB TENON WITH CONTINUOUS GROOVE. *As shown here this 'stopped' tenon is used to locate one member in relation to the other and is valuable only in such situations as the construction of flush doors where the members are afterwards covered by sheet material. 'Stub tenon' also refers to a joint in which a short tenon is made on the end of one member with shoulders on all four faces. It is used mainly at the bottom of a vertical member to keep its foot in position; for example at the junction of a window mullion with a sill.*

Fig. 107. DOUBLE TENONS. *Used in thick sections (e.g. 2½ in. upwards) and particularly in lock rails where mortice locks are specified. Can be made with haunches for top rails or with reduced tenons (i.e. having a shoulder at top and bottom).*

Fig. 108. TWIN TENONS. *Used in deep rails, sometimes with reduced tenons, or with haunches. The two tenons shrink less in their mortices than would one deep tenon.*

Fig. 109. TWIN DOUBLE TENONS. *Used where the timbers are both wide and deep, as in the middle and bottom rails of heavy doors. Cutting away for the lock between the tenons weakens the joint but to nothing like the same extent as it would if the tenon itself were used.*

Fig. 110. BARE FACED TENON. *Used where the two members are of different thicknesses: notably in framed and ledged and battened doors, and in rails in tables.*

93

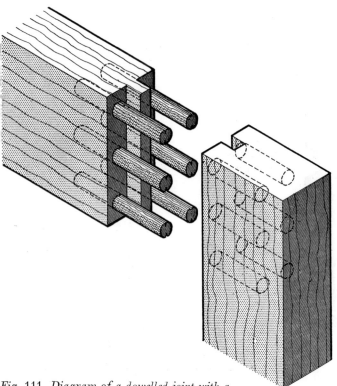

Fig. 111. Diagram of a dowelled joint with a stub tenon, or alternatively a cross-tongue. (See also Fig. 96 on p. 90.)

Dowelled joints

We have already mentioned that the dowelled joint is an alternative for the mortice and tenon, and is normally associated with the manufacture of mass-produced doors and of furniture, although some manufacturers use it almost to the complete exclusion of mortices and tenons in all their work and consider it to be superior if properly made. From the point of view of the efficiency of the joint it is claimed that there is less likelihood of any gap appearing between the rail and the stile if the stile should shrink away from the shoulders, as is possible in a mortice and tenon joint; and if made with a double row of dowels and with a cross tongue it is considered quite as strong as the latter. There is also a slight saving of timber as compared with mortice and tenon joints since there are no tenons to be cut on the end of the rail. As may be seen from the illustrations the joint consists of a number of hardwood dowels which are glued into accurately-prepared holes in either member to be jointed. The dowels should have small grooves formed in them to allow the surplus glue to squeeze out of the holes. The cross tongue is often omitted in cheap work and the dowels are sometimes reduced in number to provide only one row. In this form it is inferior to a mortice and tenon and is not an acceptable substitute.

The comb joint

This joint is the most obvious example of a new joint developed for manu-

94

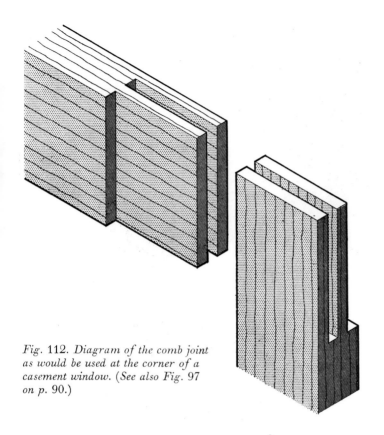

Fig. 112. *Diagram of the comb joint as would be used at the corner of a casement window. (See also Fig. 97 on p. 90.)*

facture by machine, and relying upon the additional strength and durability of modern weather-resisting glues, which should always be used with it. It has been used mainly in the construction of casement windows and particularly in connection with the EJMA standard pattern. There seems no reason why it should not be used in other places, since, if one accepts the reliability of synthetic-resin glues used in normal production, the joint is a very sound one, the effect of which is to form a lamination over the area of the joint.

The design of the joint gives a proportionately greater gluing area than would a mortice and tenon. There should be at least two tongues on each member, and the two members are held together whilst the glue sets by dowels, or by special white-metal pins of star-shaped section.

GROUP 2: FLAT SECTIONS JOINED AT RIGHT ANGLES, AS IN THE
CONSTRUCTION OF A BOOKCASE
The joints in this group can be sub-divided into two categories: those designed to join the *ends* of two boards to form a right angle, and those designed to join the end of one board to another board which continues past it.

The three most common examples of the first category are the dovetail, whether made by hand or machine; the corner locking joint sometimes called a 'box' joint; and the tongue and groove joint (Figs. 113, 115, 123). Mitred joints in one form or another are also regularly employed when the particular

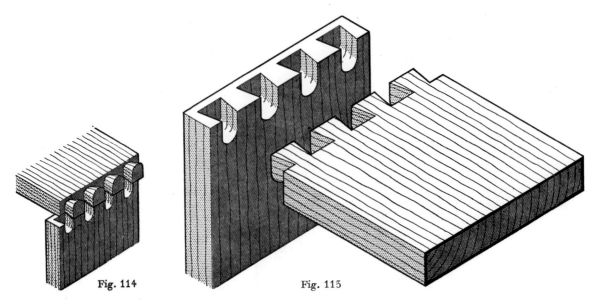

Fig. 114   **Fig. 113**

Fig. 113. LAPPED OR STOPPED MACHINE DOVETAIL. *A useful joint made by machine and commonly used for drawer fronts. Its characteristics are that it is strong in tension, and that it is neat in appearance. Fig.* 114 *shows how the two pieces of wood are held together for machining, the work being done on both pieces simultaneously. The two pieces are clamped at right angles into position in an attachment, then moved along the lines of a jig, producing the shape shown on the sketch. The rounded portion is one of the features of the joint which distinguish it from a handmade dovetail. When put together the appearance is similar to a hand-made joint except that the dovetails and the spaces between are equal in the machine-made joint whereas in the hand-made joint there are fewer dovetails and they are usually much thinner. (See also Fig.* 98, p. 90.)

Fig. 115. CORNER LOCKING JOINT. *This is essentially a machine-made joint, relying on glue for its strength. It is made on an attachment to a vertical spindle moulder. It has been associated with the manufacture of boxes and instrument cases, and also with shop-fitting. It does not usually feature in builders' joinery, but provided its appearance were acceptable there seems no reason why it should not be used as a cheaper alternative to a dovetail joint.*

Fig. 115

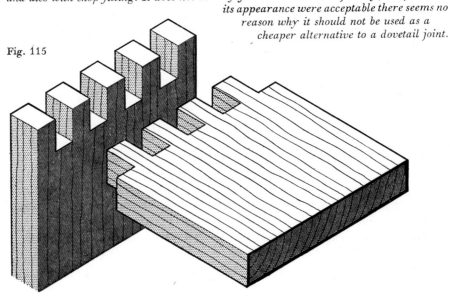

appearance which they give is required by the designer.

In the dovetail and tongue and groove joints, the two pieces of timber are held firmly together at least in one direction by the way the pieces of wood are cut to form the joints: and in the corner locking joint they are held by the restraint of the glue which is spread over the extensive 'lines' offered by the 'teeth'.

In the second category, the commonest joint is a simple housing described overleaf (Fig. 124), with variations which both improve its appearance and increase its strength, and which are described on page 101 (Figs. 135–9).

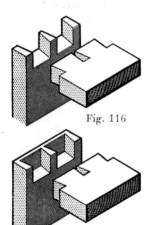

Fig. 116

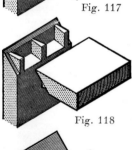

Fig. 117

Figs. 116 and 117. COMMON AND LAPPED DOVETAILS. *These are traditional hand-made joints requiring skill and time. They are expensive to make and can be justified only when their refined appearance is particularly desired. This would mainly apply to polished hardwoods. It is common practice to make the angle of splay of the dovetail 1 : 8 for hardwoods and 1 : 7 for softwoods.*

Fig. 118. MITRED SECRET DOVETAIL. *A joint which is rarely used owing to its cost, and which can be made only by hand. It is seldom seen except in cabinet work, and as an exercise for joinery apprentices. Its obvious merits are that it combines the strength of a dovetail with the appearance of a mitre.*

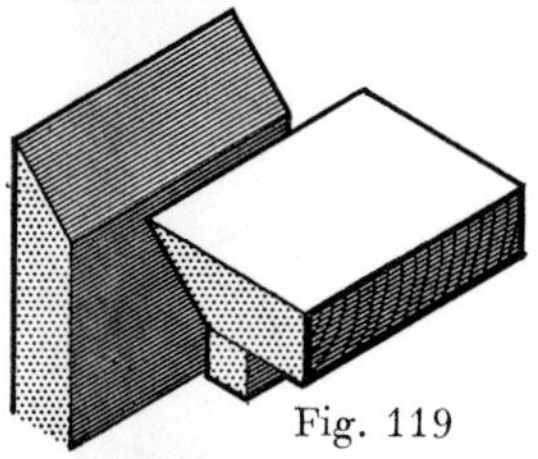

Fig. 118

Figs. 119 and 120. MITRES, WITH BLOCK AND WITH LOOSE TONGUE. *It will be seen from the various illustrations that the visual effect of a 'mitred' joint is quite different from that of dovetail and from other joints which do the same job: in the mitred joint the means of holding the joint together can easily be hidden and there is no visible end grain.*
In Fig. 119 the joint is merely glued and possibly pinned, and the block can give either permanent or temporary reinforcement, and need not come to the face of the joint. Its chief function is to 'position' the two pieces to be joined and to hold them during cramping. Both these joints are difficult to cramp, especially in wide boards, and some difference of opinion exists as to whether the mitred joint with loose tongue is really satisfactory in practice, since there are a number of ways of cutting a tongue on the solid.

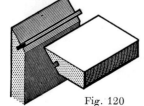

Fig. 119

In Fig. 120 the tongue, which likewise need not come to the face, also locates the two pieces as well as giving additional strength. To be of any value, the tongue must be of cross grained timber or of ply.

Fig. 120

97

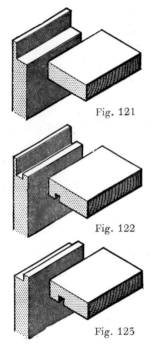

Fig. 121

Fig. 121. REBATED JOINT. *This is a joint which can be cheaply made. It has little strength and is often fixed with pins or screws as well as glue. It is used in small cupboards, boxes and backs of cupboards. The purpose of the rebate is to help locate the two pieces to be joined, and to prevent the end grain showing on one face.*

Fig. 122

Fig. 122. TONGUED AND LAPPED. *This joint has the characteristics of the lapped joint with added strength given by the tongue. It is sometimes used as a cheaper alternative for drawer fronts. It is, however, not a very sound joint since the short grained end which laps over the tongue is narrow and therefore weak.*

Fig. 123

Fig. 123. TONGUED JOINT. *This joint by comparison with Fig. 122 has a larger section of short grain lapping over the tongue and is correspondingly stronger, but the end grain is not hidden. It is frequently used for the junction of the head and jambs of door linings where the end grain would in any event not be visible.*

Fig. 124

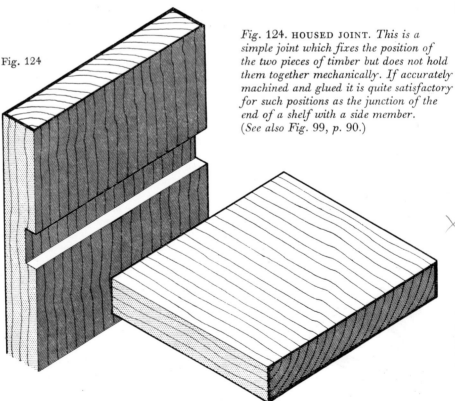

Fig. 124. HOUSED JOINT. *This is a simple joint which fixes the position of the two pieces of timber but does not hold them together mechanically. If accurately machined and glued it is quite satisfactory for such positions as the junction of the end of a shelf with a side member. (See also Fig. 99, p. 90.)*

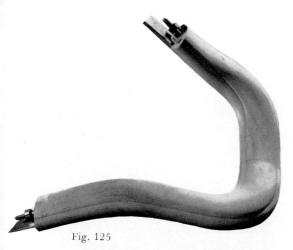

Fig. 125

Fig. 128

Fig. 126

Fig. 127

On this and the following page are illustrated the principal machines used for the preparation of joints.

Fig. 125. *A typical example of wreathing with joints formed with handrail bolts.* (See also Fig. 170, p. 109.)

Fig. 126. OVERHEAD RECESSING MACHINE. *The recessing machine illustrated is mounted with a jig for cutting housings in a staircase string. It is similar in action to Fig. 128.*

Fig. 127. TENONING MACHINE. *Although tenons may be cut on a spindle-moulder, much greater speeds can be obtained for repetitive work on a machine specially designed to carry out the whole operation, including scribing the shoulders and cutting to length, in one operation. These machines may be constructed to cut the joint on one or both ends of the section and are therefore known as single- or double-ended tenoners. The photograph shows a double-ended tenoner, and the caterpillar tracks which automatically feed the sections across the cutters. This machine is set up to cut slots in the ends of the sections, to make comb joints.*

Fig. 128. A HIGH-SPEED ROUTER, *a machine which has been developed fairly recently but which is proving to be very useful. The high speed of rotation gives a very clean cut.*

99

Fig. 129

SPINDLE-MOULDER WITH ATTACH-
MENT FOR CUTTING THE 'BOX' OR
'CORNER LOCKING' JOINT. *As can be
seen from Fig. 129 the attachment
provides a number of cutters arranged
in a spiral on the spindle. Four boards
are being cut simultaneously by being
moved on the carriage past the cutters.*

MORTICE-CUTTING MACHINES. *Fig. 131
shows the action of the chain morticer and
the hollow-chisel morticer (see also
Figs. 130 and 132). Sometimes both
tools are mounted on the same machine.
The links of the mortice chain have
sharp cutting edges and dredge out the
mortice, leaving a round hole at the
bottom: the hollow chisel, on the other
hand, has a sharp square cutting edge
with a drill revolving inside so that a
clean square hole is formed. Since
mortices are usually rectangular several
holes with the hollow chisel have to be
made, side by side, to make the joint.
The hollow chisel method is therefore
the more expensive.*

Fig. 130

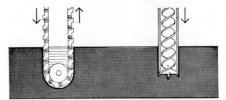

Fig. 131

Fig. 132

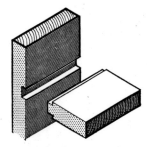

Fig. 133

Fig. 133. SHOULDERED HOUSING. *A joint which is useful if there should be grooves or mouldings on the member which is shown horizontally in Fig. 133. It is more expensive than the simple housing, and it is questionable whether it has any advantages over it, except where there are mouldings.*

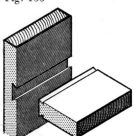

Fig. 134

Fig. 134. DOUBLE DOVETAIL HOUSING. *This is similar to the simple housed joint except that a dovetail is cut on the top side and bottom of one member to prevent the joint pulling out. Since the two boards have to be slid together the difficulty of making the joint increases with the width of the boards. It can, however, be made relatively easily up to 2 ft. 6 in., although it is of course more expensive than the simple housing. It is a useful joint for those positions where one member is liable to bow and requires restraint.*

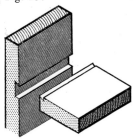

Fig. 135

Fig. 135. SINGLE DOVETAIL HOUSING. *A similar joint to the double dovetail, but one which is more commonly used, though it is still relatively expensive by comparison with a simple housing.*

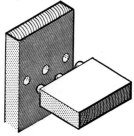

Fig. 136

Fig. 136. DOWELLED JOINT. *An alternative to the simple housed joint, at present more often used in furniture and cabinet making than in builders' joinery. One of its disadvantages is the danger of the joint opening and showing a crack. On the other hand, the holes for the dowels do not weaken the wood so much as a groove, thus avoiding any distortion which the groove might cause.*

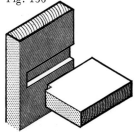

Fig. 137

Fig. 137. STOPPED HOUSING. *This joint is similar to the simple housing shown in Fig. 124 except that the groove is 'stopped' back from the front face so that the joint is concealed. It is frequently used in shelving.*

101

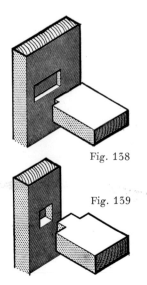

Figs. 138 and 139. STOPPED HOUSING FOR RAIL AND DOUBLE STOPPED HOUSING. *Two other forms of stopped housing. They are applicable to the junction of rails with uprights, as would be found in the construction of a chest of drawers or in skeleton framing.*

Fig. 138

Fig. 139

GROUP 3: FLAT SECTIONS JOINED AT RIGHT ANGLES, AS IN THE FRAMING OF FITMENTS

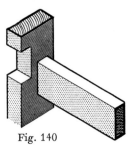

Fig. 140. FACE HOUSING. *A straightforward, cheap joint consisting of the housing of one member into the face of the other. It would have to be fixed by pins or screws. It is used commonly when the member shown horizontally in the sketch continues past the vertical member. It would normally be restricted to rough work or to concealed positions.*

Fig. 140

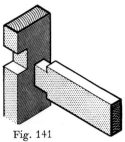

Fig. 141. SHOULDERED FACE HOUSING. *A slightly more elaborate joint than that shown in Fig. 140. If there are a number of housed joints required close together, it has the merit of taking less from the vertical member.*

Fig. 141

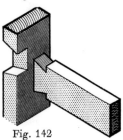

Fig. 142. SINGLE DOVETAIL HOUSING. *This is a stronger joint than those in Figs. 140 and 141, particularly in tension.*

Fig. 142

102

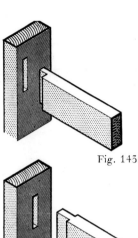

Fig. 143

Fig. 143. BARE-FACED TENON. *A joint used often in fitments, particularly where the rails and uprights are flush, and when it is desirable to conceal the actual joint.*

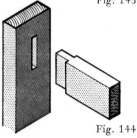

Fig. 144

Fig. 144. MORTICE AND TENON. *When the rail can be set back to give greater room for the tenon, an ordinary double shouldered tenon is commonly used.*

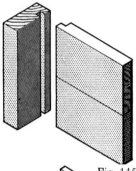

Fig. 145

Fig. 145. *A joint used where several boards forming a flat surface meet a member with the grain in the opposite direction.*

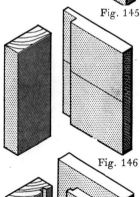

Fig. 146

Fig. 146. *This joint is considered to be inferior to 145. It must, of course, be remembered that timber shrinks more across the grain than in its length, and if the total width of the boards shown horizontally exceeds 10 in. to 12 in. it will be necessary to allow for differential movement as in fig. 147.*

Fig. 147

Fig. 147. *A joint allowing movement. The wooden buttons are nowadays often replaced by metal straps or angle cleats, which when used, for instance, in a table would be fixed by two screws to the rail and one screw through a slot into the top.*

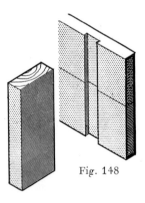

Fig. 148

Fig. 148. Another example of a typical joint used when several boards forming a flat surface meet a member having both its grain and its plane in the opposite direction.

GROUP 4: BOARDS JOINED LONGITUDINALLY, AS IN WIDE SHELVING AND COUNTER TOPS, OR AT RIGHT ANGLES

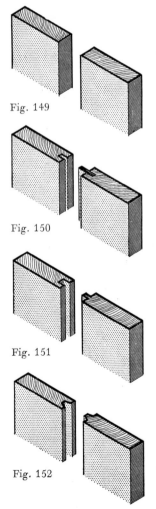

Fig. 149

Fig. 150

Fig. 151

Fig. 152

Fig. 149. SQUARE, EDGE-TO-EDGE OR RUBBED JOINT. *A traditional, cheap method of joining boards, which is quite satisfactory when accurately made and properly glued. It can be made by hand or by machine. Its limitations are the difficulty of aligning the boards in long lengths, and the danger of the single glue-line failing and leaving an open joint. In this respect, it would, for instance, be unsuitable for a draining board. for which the boards are usually tongued, as shown in Fig.* 150.

Some manufacturers consider the straight butt joint to be much improved by splaying and rebating; the profile on each board being complementary and made with the same cutter. The advantages of such a joint would not be worth the extra labour involved if it were made by hand, but, as with a number of the joints in this group, machines enable special profiles to be cut economically, and it will be found that different manufacturers show preferences for one or other method, depending upon the machine which they have installed. It would obviously be unreasonable for an architect to insist on any particular pattern of joint unless he had some special reason for doing so.

Fig. 150. CROSS (OR LOOSE) TONGUED JOINT. *A very common and economical joint which is stronger than the joint in Fig.* 149. *The tongue should be cross grained (when the individual pieces making up the length are known as feathers) or of plywood.*
When it is undesirable to see the tongue on the end of the boards it can be 'stopped'; this however is expensive.

Figs. 151, 152 *and* 153. TONGUED AND GROOVED JOINTS. *Versions of tongued and grooved joints whose purpose is to give alignment and greater gluing area. Fig.* 151 *is the traditional hand-made joint, largely replaced by the joints in Figs.* 152 *and* 153.

104

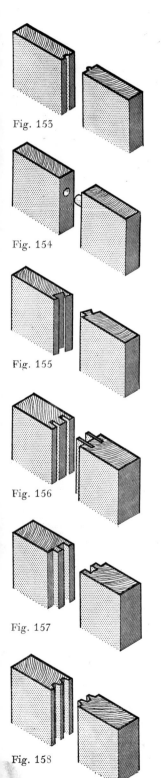

Fig. 153

Fig. 154

Fig. 155

Fig. 156

Fig. 157

Fig. 158

The latter are more appropriate to machine production, and whilst they provide for good alignment, they are easier to glue and assemble than the square cut tongue.

Fig. 154. DOWELLED EDGE-TO-EDGE JOINT. *A joint which is not very often used: it would have to be made largely by hand, and is more likely to be found in furniture and cabinet work than in joinery. The dowels help to align the boards.*

Fig. 155. THE LINDERMANN JOINT. *This is a special tapered dovetail joint which can be made only on an elaborate machine. The cost of installation of the machine cannot be justified unless a great volume of work is required of it, and there are not many of them in this country.*
The dovetail produces a mechanical locking of the joint, but it would obviously be difficult to assemble unless provision were made to overcome the friction in sliding long boards together. For this reason the dovetail is slightly tapered in its length, and assembly is done by machine. Although it is glued, no cramping is required, and the jointed boards can be handled straight off the machine. The maximum thickness of board normally worked is $1\frac{1}{2}$ in.

Figs. 156, 157 and 158. CROSSED TONGUED, AND TONGUED AND GROOVED JOINTS. *These are typical edge-to-edge boards similar to those shown in Figs. 151, 152 and 153 but used for boards having thicknesses over, say, $1\frac{1}{2}$ in. The version shown in Fig. 157 can be made with one cutter, which avoids the need for two specially matched cutters.*

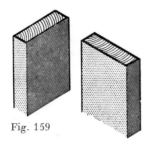

Fig. 159

It is often necessary to join boards along their length but at right angles to each other. The joints used are similar in principle to those we have just discussed, and may be compared with those in Group 2 where the ends of the boards rather than the sides are joined, and the grain is therefore in a different direction.

Fig. 159. BUTT JOINT. *Whilst the edge to edge joint can be used very satisfactorily to join boards when they are flat, since it is then fairly easy to cramp them and to keep them from bowing, the equivalent joint shown here for boards at right angles is not so satisfactory. Nails, screws or blocks are necessary to overcome the likelihood of bowing and to hold the two pieces together whilst gluing, and in practice it is used mainly in backings.*

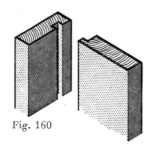

Fig. 160

Fig. 160. TONGUED AND GROOVED. *One of the most common joints used in joinery: it should be compared with the joint in Fig. 123 (Group 2) which, though of similar pattern, is less strong since the grain is in the opposite direction and the projection beyond the groove is more likely to break off.*

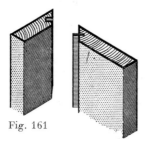

Fig. 161

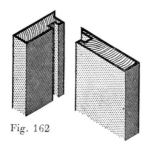

Fig. 162

Figs. 161, 162 *and* 163. CROSS TONGUED AND MITRED, TONGUED AND MITRED AND LAPPED AND MITRED. *These are all designed to make the actual joint between the boards appear on the corner. The joint in Fig. 161 is difficult to cramp but is a good joint if carefully made. The joint in Fig. 162 is a good sound joint and is used for corners of fittings and cupboards and elsewhere where both faces are seen. The joint in Fig. 163 is not so strong as that in Fig. 162 and requires blocks, nails or screws. The lap is inclined to lift if it is made too thin.*

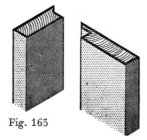

Fig. 163

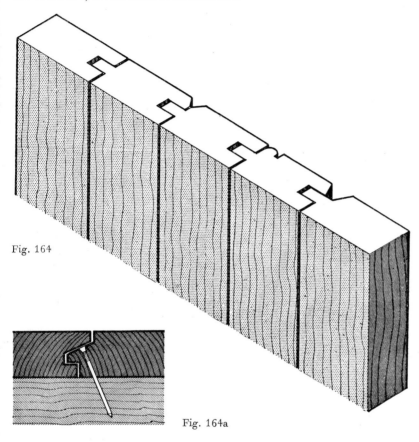

Fig. 164

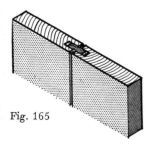

Fig. 164a

Fig. 164. TONGUED AND GROOVED MATCHING JOINTS. *The illustration shows four loose joints which are examples of a variety of joints which should be used when the boards are fixed individually to cross members such as joists or battens, and the moisture movement across the width of each board is to be taken up in the joints. The mouldings shown in three of the joints are intended to disguise the opening which occurs when the boards shrink. The mouldings could, of course, be made on both sides of the boards. It will be noticed that the tongue is not as deep as the groove which receives it, so as to ensure that the shoulders shall fit tightly. Fig* 164a *shows how the joint can be modified for secret nailing.*

Fig. 165. LOOSE CROSS TONGUE. *An alternative to the joints shown in Fig.* 164.

Fig. 165

107

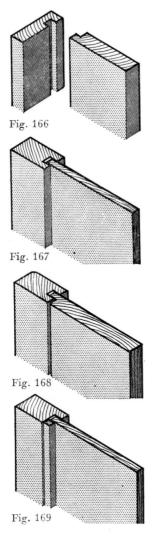

Fig. 166

Fig. 167

Fig. 168

Fig. 169

Fig. 166. UNGLUED TONGUED AND GROOVED JOINT. *A simple joint which would be applicable to vertical boarding on the corner of a building, for instance.*

Figs. 167, 168 *and* 169. PANEL JOINTS. *The illustration show three basic methods of inserting panels in frames. Each allows for moisture-movement of the panel, but has a different appearance. Elaborations of these methods, including a wide variety of mouldings, were commonly used in traditional work, particularly in the design of doors, and details can be found in many older books.*

GROUP 6: END-TO-END JOINTS, AS IN A HANDRAIL OR AN EXTRA LONG SILL

A satisfactory neat joint is difficult to make when the end grain of two pieces of wood butt. The two main methods of making the joint are to cramp the two pieces by some fixing device, and to cut the pieces or insert dowels into them so as to provide gluing lines along the length of the grain. It is not satisfactory in practice merely to glue the two surfaces of end-grain. The difficulty of making the joint is emphasized by the fact that the most successful and widely-used method requires a specially-designed metal bolt known as a 'handrail bolt'. As a matter of common sense, joints in the lengths of sections should therefore be avoided and components designed within the lengths of timber normally available.

108

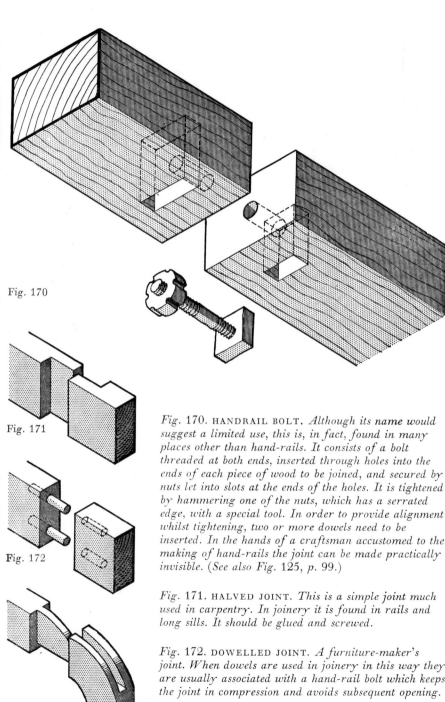

Fig. 170

Fig. 171

Fig. 172

Fig. 173

Fig. 170. HANDRAIL BOLT. *Although its* **name** *would suggest a limited use, this is, in fact, found in many places other than hand-rails. It consists of a bolt threaded at both ends, inserted through holes into the ends of each piece of wood to be joined, and secured by nuts let into slots at the ends of the holes. It is tightened by hammering one of the nuts, which has a serrated edge, with a special tool. In order to provide alignment whilst tightening, two or more dowels need to be inserted. In the hands of a craftsman accustomed to the making of hand-rails the joint can be made practically invisible.* (See also Fig. 125, p. 99.)

Fig. 171. HALVED JOINT. *This is a simple joint much used in carpentry. In joinery it is found in rails and long sills. It should be glued and screwed.*

Fig. 172. DOWELLED JOINT. *A furniture-maker's joint. When dowels are used in joinery in this way they are usually associated with a hand-rail bolt which keeps the joint in compression and avoids subsequent opening.*

Fig. 173. SLOT MORTICE AND TENON *A joint which could be used to join the ends of straight members, but in fact is more usually associated with the junction of curved members.*

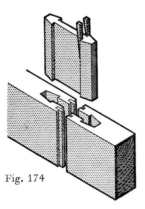

Fig. 174

Fig. 174. HAMMER-HEADED KEY. *A traditional joint which would now more often be made with a hand-rail bolt. It is still used for special work where, for some reason, the traditional practice is required, although it does not appear to have any particular advantages. The key and wedges should be made of hardwood.*

GROUP 7: JOINTS BETWEEN BUILT-UP BOARDS
Joints in this group are discussed in chapter 6: see pages 123–5, 130–3.

GROUP 8: MISCELLANEOUS FASTENINGS
In this last group we give some notes on metal fastenings. Already in the introduction to this chapter (page 86) the legitimate uses of nails and screws have been described. It is, however, useful to be able to identify the most common varieties, and to know their characteristics. As with many other components used in traditional construction, there is a bewildering range. In wood screws alone, a principal manufacturer's catalogue shows some fifty types, each of which are made in many sizes. Steel countersunk head screws, for instance, are made in lengths from $\frac{1}{8}$ in. to 8 in., each length in a number of diameters, indicated by a screw-gauge number. The smallest gauge is 4/0 and the largest 40. Thus 1-in. screws can be obtained in screw gauges 1 to 18. Besides steel and brass, screws are made in stainless steel, aluminium alloy, gun-metal and nickel-silver. Steel screws may be self-colour, or finished Japanned, sherardized, black-oxidized or plated BMA (bronze metal antique), copper, chromium, cadmium or zinc.

Heavy-cut steel nails of roughly-square cross-section, to be used mainly in rough work, known as clasp-nails, floor-brads and joiners' brads, are made from 1 in. to 8 in. in length, plain steel or galvanized. Sprigs and tacks range from $\frac{1}{4}$ in. to 1 in. Steel wire nails can be obtained from $\frac{1}{2}$ in. to 10 in. long in gauges 3 to 20 SWG (the smallest number in this case being the thickest), galvanized, sherardized, annealed, blued and in a number of different patterns. Wire nails and cut nails are covered by BS 1202.

Fig. 175

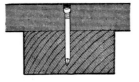

Fig. 175. OVAL LOST-HEAD WIRE NAILS (*sometimes called American wire nails*). *These have the advantage over the round wire nails with flat heads (French nails) that they can easily be punched below the surface and concealed by stopping. They are therefore very commonly used for fixing such items as architraves and picture rails on site. They are made from $\frac{1}{2}$ in. to 3 in. in length.*

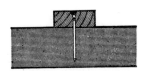

Fig. 176

Fig. 176. PANEL PINS. *These are thin wire nails with very small heads, as the name implies, useful for fixing mouldings, plywood panelling, insulating board linings and for other work where there is no great stress. Veneer pins are even smaller than panel pins, and 'needle points' are fine steel needles which can be snapped off flush to the surface.*

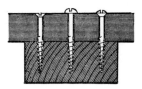

Fig. 177

Fig. 177. WOOD SCREWS. *Screws clearly provide a stronger fixing than nails, besides causing no jarring or damage to the timber when they are inserted. This illustration shows three patterns commonly made in steel and brass; counter-sunk, round and cup raised-head. These are covered by* BS 1210.

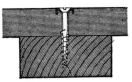

Fig. 178

Fig. 178. BRASS CUPS. *The object of brass screw cups is to enable screws to be taken out and replaced occasionally without disfiguring the wood. Glazing beads and removable panels to ducts should be fixed with cups and screws for this reason. They consist of small brass rings which are glued into a slightly larger counter-sinking than that required for the screw. Needless to say they alter the appearance, and, in the authors' opinion, give a more finished look to the screwhead.*

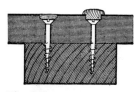

Fig. 179

Fig. 179. PELLETS AND PLUGS. *Where, for the sake of appearance, it is desired to conceal screw-heads, and where the joinery is to be polished so that putty cannot be used, the traditional practice is to counterbore the screws and to fill the holes with wood pellets or plugs. Pellets are usually circular, and cut from the same wood as the component in such a way that the top shows long grain to match the surrounding wood. They cannot, therefore, be cut from dowelling, as this would show end-grain on the exposed face. Plugs project above the surface and make no pretence at concealment and need not therefore be made of the same wood as the component itself.*

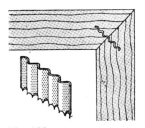

Fig. 180

Fig. 180. CORRUGATED FASTENER. *This is not a fastening usually found in books on joinery. Nevertheless, it is found in some joiners' shops, in out of the way positions such as the backs of fittings and plinths. Properly it is suitable for packing-cases, but provided it is only intended to hold the two sides of a joint together whilst the glue sets, there seems no reason for its being banned in better work. It is made of steel, sharpened at one end to cut through the timber when it is hammered in.*

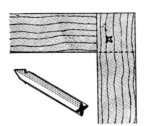

Fig. 181

Fig. 181. METAL STAR DOWEL. *This has been associated with casement windows of Scandinavian origin which employ the comb joint. The dowel is made of white metal and is so designed that it will not split the wood. Its primary function is to fix the joint whilst the glue sets.*

6: Plywoods, Boards and Veneers

Everybody knows what plywood looks like, and most people recognize block-board and hardboard, but it is difficult to acquire a knowledge of the multi-tude of types, grades and sizes even of these boards, let alone of all the other boards of various kinds available today. The stock list of one plywood im-porter, for instance, shows six thicknesses, three grades and twelve sheet sizes for Finnish birch plywood alone. Yet, plywoods, blockboards, laminboards, hardboards, chipboards, composite boards, veneered boards and plastic and metal surfaced boards are nowadays used in profusion in all kinds of fittings. They are usually fixed by joiners and whilst the trade has readily absorbed such changes in technique as have been occasioned by the use of plywoods and blockboards, not all joiners are yet accustomed to some of the more unusual boards, especially those which are plastic- and metal-faced. Those who deal in joinery will have to be increasingly versatile to manage all the varieties of board nowadays commonly used.

One must ask oneself how much an architect needs to know about their characteristics, and their qualities and prices and where they can be used to advantage. Since there are so many boards and so many factors to be taken into account he cannot know about them all, and we do not propose to attempt more than to sort out some of the information which he would find useful in his day-to-day practice. For the rest, reliance must be placed on the advice of suppliers and manufacturers and on the data contained in BSS and other literature. He will, however, want to know in general terms what kinds of board are available and to what uses they are most often put.

One can at once make certain distinctions: many of the boards may be used in relatively thin sheets as coverings to framing, or in thicker sheets either of the same material or in combination with other materials (e.g. plastic sheets glued to thick plywood) as structural materials, which are rigid in themselves and in which it is possible to make suitable joints to form carcasses: further, plywoods, blockboards and hardboards may be used in the state in which they are produced to receive some such finish as varnish or paint, or they may be used specifically as cores for veneers of one kind or another.

Apart from other considerations it is often a debatable matter as to whether it is more economical to construct a frame and to cover it with ply sheeting or whether to use a thicker ply or blockboard without the framing. To some extent this will depend on the preference of the joinery manufacturer chosen for the work: but it will also depend very largely on the amount of work being done. Firms who make mass-produced fitments find it cheaper to make the framework because they can set up their machines for long runs, and

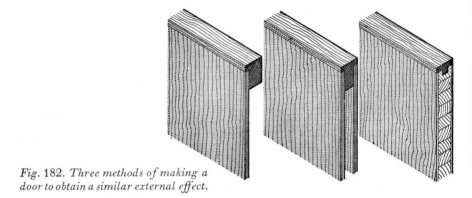

Fig. 182. Three methods of making a door to obtain a similar external effect.

reduce the cost of labour to an extent which enables them to take full advantage of the less expensive material. Other firms, however, given the choice of making the framing for, say, a wardrobe door and covering it both sides with ply or of producing the same door in lipped blockboard of equivalent thickness, would prefer the latter, and would produce the door at no greater cost.

We refer again later to veneering but it is interesting to note that because plywoods and blockboards are so often veneered, and because veneers are best applied when there are suitable presses available which not every manufacturer possesses, there has grown up a distinct branch of the trade whose firms are known as 'panel makers'. A joinery manufacturer making, for instance, veneered cupboards and drawers may well send a carefully documented list of all the component parts to such a firm who in turn will send back a series of panels, veneered, lipped and of the correct dimensions which will subsequently be jointed, moulded if required, assembled and polished by the manufacturer.

PLYWOODS

Plywood boards are built up from a number of veneers glued together, with the grain of each veneer at right angles to the next. They come from Scandinavia, Canada, Europe, Russia and Great Britain, but the sheet sizes follow a general pattern and the table below shows by way of example the standard sheet sizes provided by one British manufacturer.

Three-ply and multi-ply

Lengths: 120 in., 108 in., 96 in., 84 in., 72 in., 60 in.

Widths: 60 in., 54 in., 48 in., 42 in., 36 in.

(In any combination, long or cross grain.)

Thickness in mm.	4	5	6	8	9	12	15	18	22	25
Thickness in inches	$\frac{5}{32}$	$\frac{7}{32}$	$\frac{1}{4}$	$\frac{5}{16}$	$\frac{3}{8}$	$\frac{1}{2}$	$\frac{5}{8}$	$\frac{3}{4}$	$\frac{7}{8}$	1
Number of plies	3	3	3	3 or 5	3 or 5	5	5 or 7	7	7 or 9	9

When ordering plywood in the United Kingdom it is important to remember that the first dimension quoted is taken to denote the length of the board, that is, the measurement parallel with the grain of the face veneer.

114

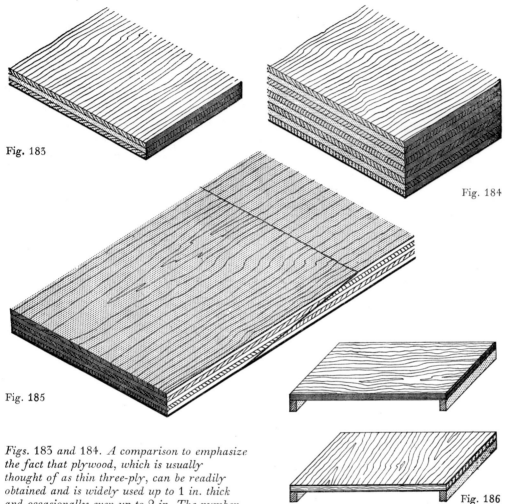

Fig. 183

Fig. 184

Fig. 185

Fig. 186

Figs. 183 and 184. A comparison to emphasize the fact that plywood, which is usually thought of as thin three-ply, can be readily obtained and is widely used up to 1 in. thick and occasionally even up to 2 in. The number of plies in the thicker sizes varies and the greater the number the stronger the board. In the thin ply the centre ply is sometimes twice as thick as the outer plies.

Fig. 185. The joint used in manufacture to produce exceptionally large plywood boards. When glued up under pressure the joint is hardly distinguishable and has great strength.

Fig. 186. These diagrams show plywood and blockboard used to take a load between bearers: the point to notice is that the direction of the grain of the outer veneers in the plywood should be in the direction of the span, whereas in single veneered blockboard it should be the opposite, so that the core blocks are in the direction of the span.

72 in. by 36 in. is a LONG GRAIN board with the face grain in the 72-in. direction. The reverse size 36 in. by 72 in. is a CROSS GRAIN board. In boards which are to be either bent or veneered, the distinction is essential: for bending, the direction of the outer veneers should be in the direction of the bend, and for veneering it should be at right angles to the grain of the veneer, as discussed later. It will be noticed that the number of plies for a

115

given thickness varies. Generally, the greater the number the stronger the ply and the more expensive.

The quality of plywood is governed by the quality of the face veneers used and by the type of glue. Grading varies as between one country and another, and, since it is not a simple matter to grasp, probably the most practical course is to specify a grade with which one is familiar and add 'or equivalent'. Reference could be made to BS 1455:1956 *British-made Plywood for General Purposes* which gives grades for the veneers (the front and back being assessed separately) and four kinds of bonding.

The grades for the veneers in this BS are as follows:

'*Grade* 1 veneer shall be of one or more pieces of firm, smoothly cut veneer. When of more than one piece, it shall be well jointed and reasonably matched for grain and colour at the joints. Veneers shall be approximately equal in width, but slight discolouration and an occasional closed split shall be permitted. It shall be free from knots,* worm and beetle holes, splits, dote, glue stains or other defects which would be objectionable when the plywood has to be used in its natural state. No end joints are permitted.

'*Grade* 2 veneer shall present a solid surface free from open defects. Veneers when joined need not necessarily be matched for colour or be of equal width. A few sound knots are permitted, with occasional minor discolouration and slight glue stains, isolated pin worm holes not along the plane of veneer and occasional closed splits of maximum one-tenth of the lenth of panel. This grade shall admit neatly made repairs of wood inlays which present solid, level, hard surfaces, and are bonded with an adhesive appropriate to the type of the plywood. No end joints are permitted.

'*Grade* 3 veneer may include wood defects excluded from Grades 1 and 2 in number and size which will not impair the serviceability of the plywood. It may also include manufacturing defects, such as rough cutting, overlaps, gaps or splits, provided these do not affect the use of the plywood. No end joints are permitted.

'*Grade S* veneer. Specially selected grade to be the subject of agreement between manufacturer and purchaser.

'*Note.* The following are the uses for which plywood made with the grades of veneer defined above are considered suitable:

Grade 1. For use in its natural state.

Grade 2. For use where subsequent painting and/or veneering is intended.

Grade 3. For use where it is not normally visible.'

Before the British Standard was revised in 1956, it divided plywood into 'interior' and 'exterior' types according to the adhesive used in manufacture. The present Standard does not do this but provides for the use of four kinds of bonding which correspond to the four kinds of adhesive given in BS 1203 *Synthetic resin adhesives for Plywood*, as on facing page.

---

* 'This shall not exclude the occasional "dormant bud" which resembles a sound knot, not more than $\frac{1}{8}$ in. diameter, of the same colour as the surrounding wood. Also permitted are occasional areas of disturbed grain, up to $\frac{1}{2}$ in. diameter, where dormant buds have been overgrown.'

BS 1455 Designation	Corresponding type in BS 1203 (where appropriate) and the definition of properties
Bonding WBP	Type WBP—*Weather- and boil-proof.* Adhesives which by systematic tests and by their record in service have proved highly resistant to weather, micro-organisms, cold and boiling water, steam and dry heat. Such glues are more durable than the wood itself.
Bonding BR	Type BR—*Boil-resistant.* These adhesives have good resistance to weather and to the boiling-water test, but they fail under prolonged conditions of full exposure to weather for which the WBP adhesives are satisfactory. They will withstand cold water for many years and are highly resistant to micro-organism attack.
Bonding MR	Type MR—*Moisture (water)-resistant and moderately weather-resistant.* To this group belong those glues that will survive full exposure to weather for only a few years. They will withstand cold water for a long period and hot water for a limited time, but fail under the boiling-water test. MR adhesives are highly resistant to micro-organism attack.
Bonding INT	Not defined by BS 1203. Adhesives comply with the requirements of Bonding INT if they make strong and durable bonds in dry plywood, and have a limited resistance to cold water; they need not be able to withstand attack by micro-organisms.

Boards manufactured to comply with BS 1455 are required to be marked with the following:

(*a*) Manufacturer's name.

(*b*) BS 1455.

(*c*) The grades of the front and back veneers (e.g. 2-3 or S-1).

(*d*) Bonding (i.e. WBP, BR, etc.).

(*e*) Nominal thickness.

The specification of the bonding is designed to ensure that the layers of ply do not come apart under various conditions. It has no bearing on the durability of the exposed face which will weather in the same way as the solid timber from which the veneer is cut. Unless, therefore, the face veneer is of teak or other very durable wood, it will require a protective finish when used outside. There are, however, specially manufactured plywoods in which each veneer is impregnated with wood preservatives which makes them resistant to fungal and insect attack and produces a board which will withstand extreme conditions of exposure.

Very often plywood is used in situations where a decorative wood finish is required, and in order to obtain it a special veneer may have to be applied as a separate process. This, of course, adds to the expense, and it should be borne in mind that there are plywoods on the market which are ready faced on one side with decorative woods. The choice is limited, but amongst them are hardwoods such as Japanese oak, Australian silky oak, sapele and maple. Plywoods are otherwise commonly made of the following:

ALDER. Ply made from alder is mainly imported from Poland and Russia.

Light reddish brown with darker brown flecks.

Grain varies from straight to very wild.

Texture even. Takes stain and paint very well.

BEECH. Beech plywood is imported from Central Europe.

Logs steamed for peeling give a brown wood known as red beech.

Unsteamed veneers are known as white beech—a light brown colour, straight grain, showing 'silver grain' flecks.

Takes stain and polish well.

More liable to moisture movement than most other woods used for plywood.

Should not be chosen, therefore, where stability is particularly required (e.g. large sheets in panelling with butt joints).

BIRCH. Very commonly used.

Manufactured in Finland, Poland and Russia.

White to pale brown in colour.

Fine but irregular grain.

An excellent base for veneered work.

Takes paint, varnish and polish well.

DOUGLAS FIR. Well-known durable Canadian softwood which makes a strong plywood.

Colour: yellow to red brown.

Rotary cutting shows strong grain with pronounced difference between summer and winter wood.

Grain apt to show through paintwork and even through veneers.

GABOON. Colour—pale red. The best plywood timber.

Straight grain, even texture, smooth finish.

Excellent for veneering, painting, polishing and all general purposes.

GUAREA. Varies from creamy-white to brown.

Fine grain, hard smooth surface, good for all finishes.

LIMBA also known as AFARA. Colour similar to light oak, useful for matching solid oak. Occasional black heart.

Smooth surface good for stain, wax or polish.

Interlocked grain of pleasing appearance, variable density.

MAKORÉ. Usually warm red colour. A very fine grain hardwood, giving exceptionally good sanded finish.

OBECHE. Pale yellow. Firm texture but grain softer and more open than other species.

SAPELE and other mahoganies. Red-brown of various densities, texture less uniform but harder than gaboon.

By the nature of its manufacture, plywood is uniformly strong and dimensionally much more stable than natural wood; also, when unrestrained, it is less inclined to warp than solid timber, though it is not wholly free from this trouble, especially if the outside veneers are not of equal strength and their grain is not in the same direction. This matter is referred to again later. It can be used in sheet form in sizes much greater than would be possible with solid timber, and it can be moulded during, or bent after, manufacture.

As has already been suggested, in its smaller thicknesses it forms a most useful material as a covering for framing, whilst in its greater thicknesses it

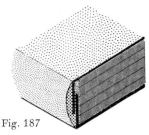

Fig. 187

SOME TYPICAL EDGE TREATMENTS TO
DOUBLE SIDED METAL FACED PLYWOOD, *as
recommended by one of the principal manufacturers:*

*Fig. 187. Common method where the metal covering is
galvanized steel. The edges are turned over and
soldered, and the whole joint covered with solder to
improve its appearance and to seal it against moisture.*

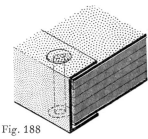

Fig. 188

*Fig. 188. A method used exclusively for heavy industrial
doors covered with steel sheet. The edge is protected by
a sheet metal channel riveted through the panel.*

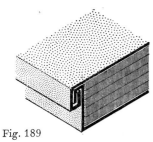

Fig. 189

*Fig. 189. Very extensively used in steel or aluminium
faced ply, particularly partitions for cubicles.
The fold is made mechanically.*

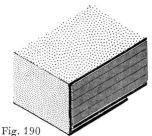

Fig. 190

*Fig. 190. A cheap and satisfactory joint for steel or
aluminium faced ply where only one face is seen,
e.g. for duct covers.*

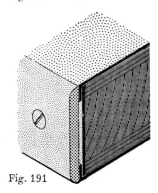

Fig. 191

*Fig. 191. The principal method for finishing doors
faced in steel, aluminium or zinc. The edging consists
of ⅛ in. flat zinc strip fixed with wood screws.
For double swing doors a rounded aluminium extrusion
can be used instead of the zinc strip.*

119

is often used structurally, as in work tops, stair risers, cupboard doors, and occasionally to form the carcass of cabinets without any additional framing. Its use in this way can, of course, only be justified when its strength and stability or the large sizes in which it is produced are made full use of, since it is, on the whole, more expensive than solid timber of equivalent thickness and type.

In furniture design advantage has been taken of the possibility of bending and even moulding it. Its properties are properly exploited to provide both form and structure, as can be seen, for example, in many chairs with moulded plywood seats, backs and arms.

Plywood can be faced on one or both sides with a veneer of steel or aluminium, and is sold in this form as a stock item (or if specially required in copper, bronze, stainless steel, zinc and other metals). Having greater strength and resistance to mechanical damage, metal-faced plywood is useful for partitions and doors, removable panels, counter fronts, column casings and so forth. There are also special plywoods with a sheet lead core which are used to give protection against X-rays. Plywoods with embossed or etched surfaces are available to give particular 'decorative' effects.

Technique for Plywood

Plywood is produced, as is evident from what we have already said about it, as a sheet material, and it is mainly as such that it is used in joinery, though, of course, the sheet may be bent. Obvious examples are panelling, carcassing, column casings (which may be circular) and bent chairbacks and seats. By contrast with solid timber it is rarely used in narrow widths to form legs or rails or such other parts of joinery as are associated with mortising and tenoning.

We must again refer to the distinction between covering a framework with thin sheets and using the inherent strength of thicker sheets to form the structure. In the former, no joints will be made in the plywood itself, whereas in the latter the joints must be made in the thickness of the ply.

When used as a covering the plywood may be glued and pinned or screwed to the framework. The junction of the corners of the ply will need consideration since mitring with very thin ply would be difficult, and the edges will show unless the whole is to be painted, and even then it is usually possible to discern them. This is not to suggest that the appearance of the edges is necessarily undesirable but to point out that they need thought. It is important, too, to have adequate framing at the back to prevent bellying, which may well cause the frames to show through, as can be witnessed in many flush doors. Honeycomb cores have become a part of the door manu-facturers' repertoire for this reason.

With panels of thicknesses over, say, $\frac{3}{8}$ in., it is possible to use the material structurally and to form joints at corners in the ply itself. This is often done in the manufacture of boxes and painted carcassing; typical joints are shown in Figs. 203–6, on pages 123-4. The remarks already made about the edges also apply. It should be noted that it is quite possible to make dovetails and even

Fig. 192

Fig. 193

Fig. 192. Face view of some of the boards now available: squared hardboard (at bottom of pile), perforated hardboard, leather faced hardboard and enamelled hardboard (at the top of the pile), textured plywood, reeded hardboard and plastic veneered chipboard.

Fig. 193. Edge view of the boards discussed in this chapter, from left to right: plywood, blockboard, laminboard, hardboard, chipboard, plastic veneer, plastic panel.

Fig. 194. An example of the use of thick plywood with the edges left candidly exposed. Note the routed-out handles.

Fig. 194

Fig. 195

Fig. 196

Figs. 195 and 196. *Another example of thick plywood used with edges exposed, showing how thin ply is used to form the covering to the framework of the fitment; note the fixing of the hinges into the edge of the ply.*

Fig. 197. *A drawer constructed with a bent plywood sheet forming the sides and bottom: a means of construction which takes advantage of radio frequency gluing of plywood veneers to increase the rate of production—a technique which has previously been applied mainly to radio cabinets.*

Fig. 198. *Examples of moulded plywood used in the construction of chairs, to give form and structural strength.*

Fig. 199. *Plywood manufactured to a curve. The two half circles are to be joined to form the rail to a circular table. The joiner is making a scarf joint.*

Fig. 197

Fig. 198

Fig. 199

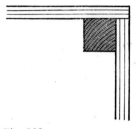

Fig. 200

Figs. 200 to 202. THIN PLYWOOD FIXED TO WROUGHT FRAMEWORK (*also suitable for hardboard or thin chipboard*).

Fig. 200. A simple and cheap solution whose disadvantage is that the edge grain of the ply is exposed. It would be suitable for backs of fitments. The ply would be pinned and glued.

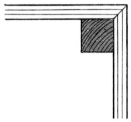

Fig. 201

Fig. 201. This is again a simple joint but requires more care in manufacture. The edges of the plywood are concealed.

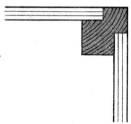

Fig. 202

Fig. 202. This requires more machining and cleaning off, but the actual corner will be less likely to get damaged, especially if the frame is in hardwood.

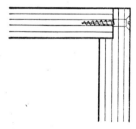

Fig. 203

Figs. 203 to 206. JOINTS FORMED WITHIN THE THICKNESS OF STOUT PLYWOOD. (*Joints 203 and 204 would also be suitable for blockboard and chipboard.*)

Fig. 203. A rough and cheap joint, which could be screwed, without gluing, for removable panels; the rebate helps to locate one board in relation to the other.

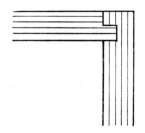

Fig. 204

Fig. 204. A common rebated joint relying mainly on glue. The edge grain of one board is, however, exposed.

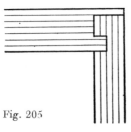

Fig. 205

Fig. 205. A modification of 204 designed to conceal the edge grain.

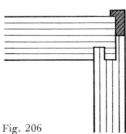

Fig. 206

Fig. 206. The same joint now between the side and front of a drawer and finished with a decorative hardwood cover slip. This is illustrated to show that where the additional expense is warranted quite intricate joints can be and are made.

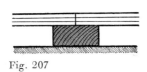

Fig. 207

Figs. 207 to 211. TYPICAL JOINTS FOR PANELLING

Fig. 207. A simple method of achieving a plain butt joint, especially with thin boards. Fixing would be by pins punched home and stopped.

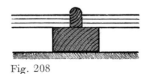

Fig. 208

Fig. 208. A joint which makes a feature of the division.

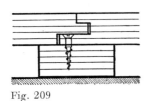

Fig. 209

Fig. 209. A secret fixing to grounds, with a butt joint: a more complicated method of achieving the same appearance as Fig. 207.

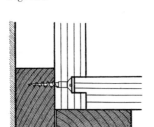

Fig. 210

Fig. 210. *An internal corner secretly fixed to grounds.*

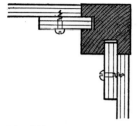

Fig. 211. *A method of fixing panels secretly to a post.*

Fig. 211

to screw into the edges of thick ply, provided the screws are thick enough to bite into two or three plies.

It will be realized that we have so far been thinking of boards without any lipping, and indeed in panelling, which is one of the most important ways of using ply, the boards are rarely lipped since here the edges will not show. Because of its relative stability plywood can be used in large areas in panelling with a straight butt joint. The panelling is fixed to grounds, and to this extent the ply might be said to be used as a covering rather than structurally, but, since it will quite probably have to withstand impacts, and in order for the grounds not to show through, the sheets must be thick. The grounds should be of well-seasoned timber securely fixed to the wall. They should occur wherever a joint in the panelling occurs and also at intervals between, their distance apart depending on the thickness and rigidity of the sheets applied to them. To give some indication of the spacing required, it is suggested that $\frac{3}{16}$ in. and $\frac{1}{4}$ in. panels should have supports at intervals of 18 in. to 20 in. *across* the grain of the face veneer and 30 in. to 36 in. in the opposite direction. Boards of $\frac{3}{8}$ in. would be adequately supported if the grounds *across* the grain were increased to 30 in. centres.

Plywood is often veneered and used in polished furniture and fitments where the appearance of the edge would be objectionable, and in such circumstances it is 'lipped' with an edging of solid timber, of the same kind as the veneer, unless a wood of contrasting tone or colour is specially required. The veneer may be taken over the lipping or stopped short of it, a matter to which we refer when discussing veneering. We also refer there to the necessity for putting a similar veneer on the back of the plywood in order to prevent the distortion which may otherwise take place.

The lipping now assumes two functions: it presents a suitable appearance and it provides a solid edging in which to make joints. It may even be extended in size to allow for moulding or shaping—which in turn may be left in the solid or subsequently veneered. Fig. 213, page 127, shows a fitment in course of construction, and the enlarged lipping can be seen at two stages, the first immediately after fixing a square section lipping and the second after it has been curved to receive a veneer. When it has been veneered it will leave the panel-maker, unless the works are themselves equipped as panel-makers, and go to the joiner for jointing, assembling and polishing. The diagrams, pages 123–4, show the methods of jointing used: the choice will depend upon the design of the fitment, and on the practice of the individual manufacturer, unless any one kind of joint is specifically ordered by the architect.

There are several ways of producing bends in plywoods. First the sections may be moulded during manufacture at the time of pressing by employing a special vacuum press. (See below.) These presses are usually able to produce bends in sheets of plywood up to 10 ft. long and 4 ft. measured over the curve. It is possible to produce a curve with as small a radius (internal) as $\frac{1}{4}$ in. with $\frac{1}{4}$ in. ply.

Secondly, flat panels may be steamed and then bent to shape. This should be done across the grain of the outer veneers and thicker plys (6 mm. and up) may need saw kerfs (i.e. a series of saw cuts cut in the concave side of a panel

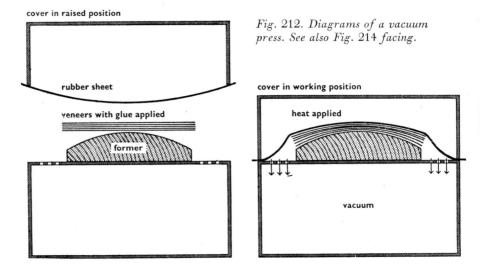

cover in raised position

rubber sheet

veneers with glue applied

former

cover in working position

heat applied

vacuum

Fig. 212. *Diagrams of a vacuum press. See also Fig. 214 facing.*

which is to be bent) in the back to relieve the resistance. By comparison with the first method a radius of about 1 ft. 6 in. with $\frac{1}{4}$-in. ply can be provided by this means.

Finally the curve may be built up by bending thin ply round and fixing to a solid wood framing.

HARDBOARDS

These boards come into the category of 'fibre building boards' and consist of ligno-cellulose fibres felted together and highly compressed. They vary in colour from light to dark brown and all of them provide large unbroken surfaces without grain, with at least one side always smooth. In joinery the 'standard' and 'super' grades of hardboard are often used as alternatives to plywood of equivalent thicknesses.

The table on page 129 shows the sizes and thicknesses in which they are commonly produced:

Fig. 213

Fig. 213. *A detail from part of a
fitment showing the lipped plywood
with the veneer which is to cover the
curved lipping applied to the board and
left ready for gluing to the lipping. This
part of the operation is done in the
vacuum press described and illustrated
below. The result after gluing and
sanding can also be seen in the photograph.*

Fig. 214. *A vacuum press extended to
allow insertion of the mould and the
veneers to be bent. The mould is placed
in position, the veneers with glue applied
laid over them, a rubber sheet is lowered
over the mould and the veneers, and air
is extracted through the 'floor' of the
machine. Heat is applied from above,
and after the appropriate period the
'moulded' panel is extracted.*

Fig. 215. *Parts of a veneered fitment in
which the lippings are designed to show
in contrast to the veneer and to be
rounded. The photograph shows them
being cramped on in square section and
at bottom left corner after veneering
and rounding of the lipping.*

Fig. 214

Fig. 215

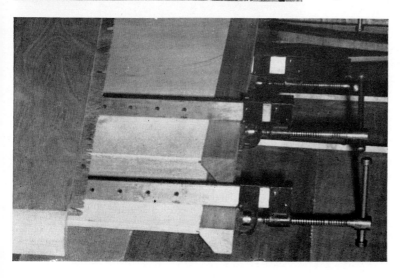

Fig. 216

Fig. 218

Fig. 217

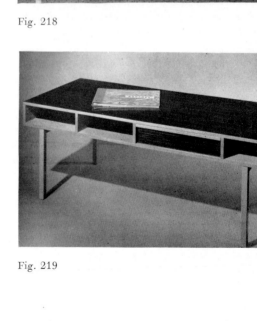

Fig. 216. Hardboard used in the entrance to an office. This example shows how the material can be curved.

Fig. 217. Hardboard used as a facing to doors in cupboards.

Fig. 219

Figs. 218 and 219 show pieces of furniture made with veneered chipboard. They illustrate how the material can be used to advantage if it is considered as a 'board', no attempt being made to imitate timber construction using narrow rails. The legs of the desk are of metal.

	lbs. cu. ft.	thickness	size of sheet
Standard	min. 50	$\frac{1}{8}$ in., $\frac{3}{16}$ in.	4 ft., 5 ft. and 5 ft. 3 in. by 4 ft. to 18 ft.
Super	min. 50	$\frac{1}{8}$ in., $\frac{3}{16}$ in.	4 ft., 5 ft. and 5 ft. 3 in. by 4 ft. to 18 ft. and as floor tiles

In addition there are softer boards known as medium hardboards:

Medium	30–50	4–12 mm. $\frac{3}{16}$ in., $\frac{1}{4}$ in., $\frac{3}{8}$ in., $\frac{1}{2}$ in. $\frac{5}{16}$ in.	3 ft., 4 ft., 5 ft. and 6 ft. by 4 ft. to 18 ft.

The medium hardboards are often used as pin-up boards, and also as ceiling and wall panels and as underlays for floor coverings. The 'standard' boards are widely used as sheet coverings in all forms of joinery and in the manufacture of flush doors: they are a most useful material for this purpose and their smooth surface provides an excellent ground for paints, provided they receive a suitable priming, but, like most materials, they move with changes in the moisture in the atmosphere and it is important to see that their edges are continuously supported and that as much support as possible is given over the whole surface of the boards in order to prevent bulging. This applies particularly to the thinner boards.

For positions liable to heavy wear and abrasion, the super hardboards are preferable to the standard grade. Being tougher, they are useful for tops, boat building and even for flooring, and in this connection it may be noted that some varieties on the market are sold specially for floors and have colouring incorporated during manufacture.

Some of the boards are what is known as 'oil tempered', a treatment which enables them to be used as shuttering for concrete and, if properly painted, in exposed positions.

'Standard' and super hardboards have been used for many years and their advantages and limitations are well recognized, but recently their range has been extended by the application or incorporation at the time of manufacture of a whole variety of special surfaces. These developments are likely to continue, and the only means of ascertaining what is available is to consult a stockist of wallboards. A recent visit to such a stockist produced the following: plastic faced, stove-enamelled, metal faced, wood veneered, embossed, perforated and 'leather faced' hardboards. Not all these boards are strictly connected with building joinery, but they will certainly be used in shop fittings, and it will probably be the joiner's job to fix them.

Technique for Hardboard

The material is essentially a sheet material suitable for covering frames or for framed panels: it is not practicable to form joints in the material itself except possibly edge-to-edge tongued and grooved joints.

It can be cut to size with woodworking tools and it can be drilled, but it is not wise to smooth or plane the surface, though it is possible to plane the edges.

It can be readily bent cold, but requires fixing to a framework.

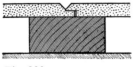

Fig. 220

Fig. 221

TYPICAL JOINTS FOR PANELLING IN HARDBOARD

Fig. 220. A lapped and V joint which makes a feature of the joint and allows movement particularly necessary with hardboard. The panels are pinned to the batten.

Fig. 221. A typical extruded aluminium fixing strip shown as an example of the great variety of metal fixing and cover strips used in connection with sheet materials, particularly with hardboards and plastics.

CHIPBOARD

There have for some time now been on the market a number of boards made from wood chips. They are produced by bonding the chips under pressure with synthetic resins, and they can be used in certain circumstances as an alternative to natural timber, plywood and blockboard.

The range of uses to which the boards are put follows a familiar pattern—furniture and fitments, panelling, flooring, partitioning, doors and so on. They are also sometimes produced with decorative finishes, and are offered as a base for veneering. It is claimed for them that they can be worked with normal woodworking tools and that they can be nailed and screwed. In certain respects, such as the saving of labour, stability and resistance to flame spread, combustibility and fungal and insect attack, they are claimed to be superior to natural timber.

Some of the Continental boards come with a layer of finer chips on the two outside surfaces and coarser chips on the inside, the object being to produce a board lighter in weight but of equal strength and with a smoother surface and greater stability.

One board of British manufacture is made 4 ft. wide in a continuous process which permits any particular length to be supplied without cutting to waste: otherwise the standard size is 8 ft. by 4 ft., $\frac{1}{2}$ in. and $\frac{3}{4}$ in. thick.

Generally speaking, all chipboards are considerably cheaper than plywood or blockboard, but in using them the following considerations should be borne in mind:

(*a*) The material is not as strong in bending as blockboard or plywood. In practice this means that whilst it is satisfactory for vertical surfaces such as the sides of cupboards, it requires greater support than blockboard and plywood when used horizontally: under load, as in a shelf, deflection increases with time, especially if the material is not veneered. Even when it is veneered, it requires more support than solid wood shelving of equivalent thickness if it is subjected to any substantial load.

(*b*) Like natural wood the material moves with changes in the moisture in the air: there is no grain and the movement is equal in each direction: for a 30° change in relative humidity a typical piece moves approximately $\frac{1}{32}$ in. for every 12 in. width and length. African mahogany, which has average values for moisture movement, would, by comparison, move $\frac{1}{10}$ in. radially and $\frac{3}{16}$ in. tangentially but would not, of course, have any significant movement in length. In practice there can be significant changes in the thickness

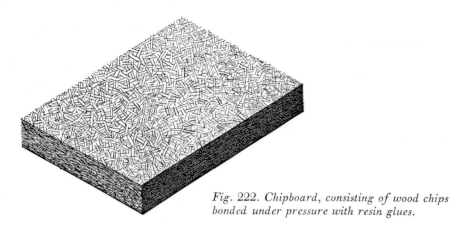

Fig. 222. Chipboard, consisting of wood chips bonded under pressure with resin glues.

of chipboard: a panel let into a groove in a solid member might swell enough to split the member, and it might be necessary to resort to making a saw cut in the thickness of the board to overcome the difficulty.

(*c*) Chipboard is variable in density and strength.

(*d*) Whilst it is possible to make dovetailed joints and mortices and tenons, they are not really appropriate to the material and simple sturdy joints such as tongues and grooves, loose tongues, laps and dowels are more satisfactory.

(*e*) Hinges and fittings can be adequately screwed to the material, and nails may be used in construction, but the holding power of screws is rather less than with some timbers; for instance, the holding powers of one No. 8 screw in the face are: birch, 356 lb.; obeche, 183 lb.; chipboard, 180 lb. (and if screwed into edge, 155 lb.).

Technique for Chipboard
Basically chipboard is worked and used in the same way as ordinary solid timber, but there are some slight differences in technique. High speed machine tools are an advantage; longer and thinner screws are advisable, though pre-drilling is not considered necessary; edges not covered in the construction should be covered by lippings; all woodworking joints are possible, but it is best to choose simple rebates, mitres and tongues. The material may be glued, veneered, painted, stained or polished in much the same way as plywood. It is essential, however, to follow the manufacturers' instructions carefully, more particularly since there is as yet no great experience of its use amongst joiners.

BLOCKBOARDS AND LAMINBOARDS
Blockboards and laminboards consist of a core of strips of wood, preferably quarter sawn, glued together and covered on both sides by one or by two fairly thick veneers. The difference between the two kinds of board is that in blockboards the strips are about an inch wide, whereas in laminboards they are about $\frac{3}{16}$ in. The idea for making such boards derived from the practice in early cabinet making of veneering over panels made up of quarter-sawn boards, 2 in. to 3 in. wide, and glued edge to edge.

131

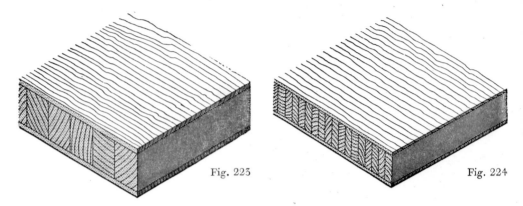

Fig. 223. *Single veneered blockboard. Frequently the veneers are of hardwood and the cores are of quarter sawn softwood about 1 in. wide glued together.*
Fig. 224. *Laminboard, usually of hardwood throughout, with cores of about ¼ in. width glued together.*

The thicknesses in which blockboards are available are ⅝ in., ¾ in., ⅞ in. and 1 in., and the standard sizes of boards are:

Widths: 120 in., 96 in., 84 in., 72 in.

Lengths: 72 in., 60 in., 48 in.

In blockboard with a single veneer each side, the width is in the direction of the grain of the cores, and as it is sometimes important that they should run in a particular direction, e.g. for shelving or partitions, it is a safeguard when ordering blockboard to state exactly how it is to be used.

Laminboards are obtainable in similar thicknesses, but they are also obtainable ⅜ in. thick and up to 2 in. They are less common and more expensive than blockboards, and in general are of a higher quality of manufacture.

Blockboards and laminboards are not as strong as plywoods of equivalent thicknesses, but have for long been used to replace the traditional edge-to-edge glued boards which formed tops and sides of cabinets and other fitments. Some makes can be procured in large sizes (up to 67 in. by 185 in.) without joints, and they form an excellent base for veneers, especially when large unbroken areas are required.

The veneers used for the faces of the boards are mainly of limba, birch or gaboon. Unlike plywood, there is at present no recognized grading, and it should be noted that neither kind of board is necessarily put together with weather-resistant glue. Blockboards usually have a softwood core, whereas laminboards are usually of hardwood throughout.

Technique for Blockboard
In almost all respects blockboard is similar to plywood in the way in which it is used.

Apart from not using it externally unless one can be sure that it is bonded with a synthetic resin glue, it is nearly always interchangeable with plywood. The joints used with it are the same, and so are the methods of lipping.

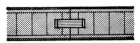

Fig. 225

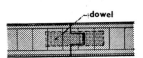

Fig. 226

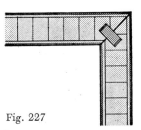

Fig. 227

Fig. 228

Fig. 229

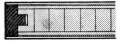

Fig. 230

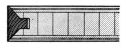

Fig. 231

Figs. 225 to 228. JOINTS FORMED IN THE THICKNESS OF BLOCKBOARD, PLYWOOD AND CHIPBOARD.

Fig. 225. Edge-to-edge joint with cross grained or plywood tongue. In so far as it is possible to obtain large boards one would naturally avoid this joint, but in very long runs or extra large panels it may be necessary. The scarfed joint (see Fig. 185, page 115) would be used if the joint were to be made in manufacture.

Fig. 226. An alternative to Fig. 225, with tongue and groove and dowels.

Fig. 227. A common corner joint with a cross grained or plywood tongue glued in. Especially appropriate where veneered panels are used.

Fig. 228. A simple housed joint.

Figs. 229 to 231. LIPPINGS FOR BLOCKBOARD, PLYWOOD AND CHIPBOARD.

Fig. 229. A standard lipping in which the lip forms a visible margin. If it is to be returned along two sides the corners would be mitred. This is the usual method of lipping if the panel is to be painted, but the margin usually shows. Even in veneered work the lipping is sometimes left exposed, and it is either matched to the veneer or purposely contrasted with it.

Fig. 230. This is an alternative for veneered panels, where the panel is veneered after lipping. Although the veneer stops right on the edge, this is found to be quite satisfactory under most conditions, and has a much cleaner appearance.

Fig. 231. A method of lipping which is frequently shown in textbooks, but which has certain disadvantages, principally that the size of the panel cannot be adjusted after manufacture, and it is therefore not suitable for doors which have to be 'shot' in fitting.

133

BATTENBOARDS, STRIPBOARDS

Battenboards are similar to blockboards except that their cores are not glued edge to edge, and are not generally used in high-class work.

Stripboards are not manufactured in or imported to this country, but are similar in construction to blockboard, except that their cores are up to 3 in. wide.

COMPARATIVE COSTS

Many factors influence the cost of materials, and it is rash to quote figures, but since everybody will want to know whether it costs more or less to use any one of the boards so far mentioned, we give below *approximate* figures (1957) for the supply of the materials. They make an interesting comparison.

	100 sq. ft. (without lipping, veneering or other finish)
$\frac{3}{16}$ in. Hardboard	60s.
$\frac{3}{16}$ in. Finnish ply	70s.
$\frac{3}{4}$ in. Douglas fir plywood (good two sides)	240s.
$\frac{3}{4}$ in. Finnish birch blockboard	230s.
$\frac{3}{4}$ in. Gaboon blockboard	251s.
$\frac{3}{4}$ in. Gaboon laminated board	301s.
$\frac{3}{4}$ in. Chipboard	110s. to 133s.
ex $\frac{3}{4}$ in. wrought softwood boards (joinery quality) glued edge to edge	approx. 200s.
ex $\frac{3}{4}$ in. wrought W. A. mahogany boards, glued edge to edge	approx. 450s.

As can be expected, manufactured boards are dearer to buy than equivalent amounts of softwood, and in order to equate the costs with those for hardwood one would have to add the cost of veneering and lipping, but nevertheless there are many situations where, if manufactured boards are used, the thickness of material may be reduced, and the amount of labour involved in preparing and jointing solid timber may be avoided, thus making the final cost at least comparable and probably less.

To give a more practical indication the prices of a single board 8 ft. by 4 ft. with various treatments would be approximately as follows:

	£	s.	d.
$\frac{3}{4}$ in. blockboard not lipped, unpolished	4	0	0
$\frac{3}{4}$ in. blockboard lipped	5	16	0
$\frac{3}{4}$ in. blockboard lipped and veneered (veneer supplied at 1s. per sq. ft. and compensating veneer at 2d. per sq. ft.)	8	5	4
$\frac{3}{4}$ in. blockboard with decorative plastic veneer	17	16	0

VENEERING

Veneering, which has been mentioned several times already, is nowadays closely related to the production of plywood and other laminated boards. Plywood, in fact, consists of a number of veneers and, together with blockboards, laminboards and hardboards, is made in presses which are similar to those used for decorative veneering. All of these boards provide better grounds on which to apply veneers than solid timber especially when large panels are required.

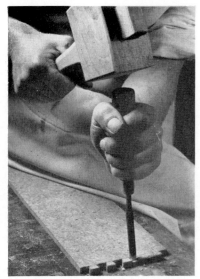

Fig. 232

Fig. 234

Fig. 233

Fig. 235

Fig. 232. Hand tools are not much used today when machines can do the work cheaper, nor is the dovetail a particularly suitable joint for chipboard, but this shows how it is possible to make such a joint, and demonstrates that chipboard can be worked to a large extent as natural wood.

Fig. 233. Planing the edge of a chip-board sheet (note that the sheet has already been grooved).

Fig. 234. Part of a system of partitioning. It is included to show how chipboard can be used for this purpose, and to illustrate the treatment of the joint: a hardboard slip locates the boards whilst the edge of the chipboard is chamfered to form a V.

Fig. 235. A typical joint between the side and back of a fitment. There is no effort made to conceal the joint, and reliance is placed largely on the screws. The illustration shows how plywood (the back) and blockboard are often used together, and also how the blockboard can be worked along the ends of the core (in this instance a simple rebate).

135

Fig. 236

Fig. 237

Fig. 236. *A veneer splicing machine. The veneers are glued edge to edge during the course of their travel through the machine. This method is used in making plywood. Thin veneers used for decoration are joined before application by a taping machine. The veneers are fed into the machine which draws them together and applies a strip of gummed paper along the joint. The paper is removed by sanding after the veneer is glued to its core.*

Fig. 237. *A view of a typical store of veneers. It is here that the architect should select and inspect the veneers he is proposing to use so that he will know the effect of the figure over the whole area of the veneer. It is not enough to choose from a small sample, which may be most misleading.*

Fig. 238

Fig. 238. *An example of rotary cut or 'peeled' birch. This should be compared with the illustration of the paldao veneer, Fig. 259, which is sliced.*

Fig. 259

In contrast with laminated boards, which are of comparatively recent invention, veneers have been used since ancient times: the Egyptians used, not only rare woods, but also gold, pearl and ivory veneers. The present practice of veneering in decorative woods, however, stems mainly from the eighteenth century. Used at first mostly for furniture, then for panelling in ships and railway carriages, and for pianos, it has been done more and more and is today employed in nearly all furniture manufacture and to an increasing extent in joinery. Wood is still the principal material of veneers, although it is not the only one: plastic sheets, as described later in this chapter, are also common.

There are, of course, very sound reasons for veneering; it is not just a matter of making an inferior wood look like a better one. For instance:

1. Some of the most beautiful woods come from rare trees and the best figured pieces from burrs which are rarer still. Quite apart from the cost, if these woods were used in the solid the supply would soon be exhausted.

2. The woods which are the most beautiful to look at in figure and colour are not always reliable for use in the ordinary way. Burrs, which are the diseased growths at the foot of the trunk, are an example. Some trees, such as kingwood and tulipwood, are also too small to give useful sized boards.

3. A veneered panel on a core of ply or laminated board is more stable than a solid wood panel made in the traditional way.

It will be seen that whilst there is emphasis on the use of woods which have exceptionally decorative figure or exceptional colouring—these provide what are known as 'exotic', 'rare' or 'fancy' veneers—there are sound arguments for veneering even with ordinary joinery hardwoods, and such veneers are those mostly used today. It is, in any event, no longer fashionable to make elaborate patterns out of contrasting exotic veneers.

There is a large number of veneers from ordinary timbers to choose from, but there are many others which come from woods which are not readily obtainable except as veneers. One must therefore be careful if one wishes to match, say, the solid framing of a cupboard with veneered doors or drawer fronts.

GRADES, COST AND SELECTION

Although the main centre of the trade is Paris, veneers are produced in this country and many other parts of the world. Unfortunately there is no universally accepted system of grading. An architect, however, should expect veneers free from knots, shakes, patches or other defects and can indicate this by specifying 'prime quality'.

The selection of a veneer requires much care. The cost of the material itself varies from as little as 2d. to as much as 1s. 9d. a square foot and some rare veneers may command up to 8s. a square foot. Even the difference between 2d. and 1s. 9d. might mean as much as £1 on the cost of a veneered door so that the choice must partly depend on cost as well as on appearance. Incidentally, the cost of the application of the veneer will be approximately 6d. to 1s. a square foot or slightly more if much selection and 'matching' have to be done. Also, veneered panels will usually require lipping, and this costs about 1s. 6d. to 2s. a foot-run depending on the size of the lipping and on the kind of wood used for it.

The intended use must be considered, particularly if the veneer is to be used externally: a stable oily wood such as teak would, for instance, be more satisfactory on an external door than say elm.

Size may also be important: veneers vary considerably in this respect, there being no standard dimensions. Lengths range from about 9 ft. to 17 ft., each piece being about 9 in. wide. The thickness to which decorative veneers are cut may be from $\frac{1}{250}$ in. to $\frac{1}{4}$ in. but long experience of those in the trade suggests that the best thickness is from $\frac{1}{28}$ in. to $\frac{1}{30}$ in.

When considering appearance it is dangerous to rely on a sample. Whilst mahogany or beech would perhaps be fairly represented by a small sample it would be impossible to judge the total effect of walnut or other woods having a strong figure. It is therefore advisable wherever possible to inspect the stock and select the actual material to be used, remembering that when polished the veneer will have a different appearance from the material seen in its natural state. Ideally samples should be polished, but an indication of the final colour can be obtained by wetting the surface. It is not our intention to write at length about the processes by which veneers are produced, but it is of help to have some elementary knowledge of what happens. This is explained in Figs. 240–3. The veneer may be produced either by 'slicing' with a knife or by 'peeling' (rotary cutting) and occasionally by sawing. Contrary to common belief most veneers are sliced and not peeled. Peeling is in fact restricted to cutting for plywood, and for veneers from bird's eye maple and burrs, and generally for woods which would either yield un-economical widths if sliced, or which display characteristic figure or marking on the tangential face. In order to carry out the slicing operation the log is cut up into 'flitches'. The illustrations show three common methods of flitching: squared up, half quartered and quartered. The half quartered gives narrower width, but allows the veneers to be cut in opposite directions which produces better results in some woods. The quartered flitches produce straight grain and the figure associated with radial cutting.

Figs. 240 *to* 242. THREE TYPICAL METHODS OF 'FLITCHING' *or preparing logs for cutting into veneers by slicing. The logs are cleaned, sometimes de-barked, and then flitched.*

Fig. 241. *Squared up: with the veneer cut in one direction through the whole log. Half quartered: producing the same kind of veneer as the squared up flitch but half as wide. Cutting can take place in opposite directions, which is an advantage in some kinds of wood. Both the squared up and half quartered flitches show 'heart' grain.*
Fig. 242. *Quartered: the pattern of the grain differs in veneers cut in this manner from those of the veneers from half quartered and squared up logs by the absence of 'heart' grain; the grain in quartered logs is straight and the figure which some woods show on the radial face is exposed.*

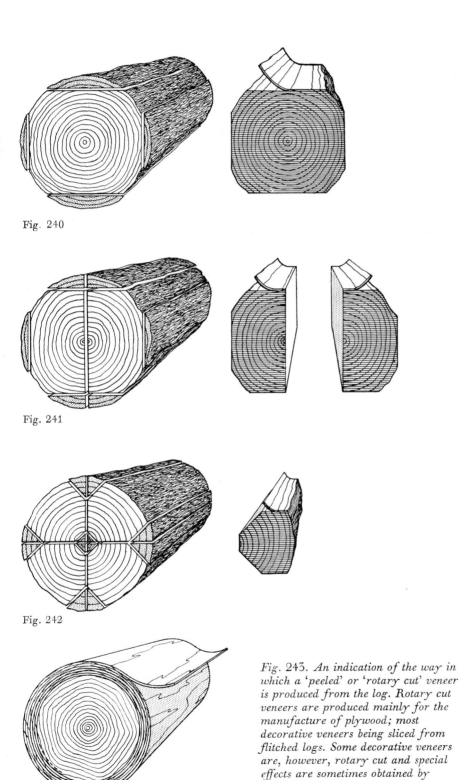

Fig. 240

Fig. 241

Fig. 242

Fig. 243. *An indication of the way in which a 'peeled' or 'rotary cut' veneer is produced from the log. Rotary cut veneers are produced mainly for the manufacture of plywood; most decorative veneers being sliced from flitched logs. Some decorative veneers are, however, rotary cut and special effects are sometimes obtained by rotating the log eccentrically.*

Fig. 243

139

Technique for veneering

Whether or not conscious patterning with veneers is required, the architect must be aware of the very different effects obtained by the way the relatively narrow widths of veneer are laid on the core: particularly when highly figured veneers are chosen. The whole subject of the arrangement of veneers is somewhat complicated and is best dealt with in practice by consultation, but even if the architect is not acquainted with the definitions employed in the trade he would do well to submit a sketch with his detail to show what he expects to get.

Briefly, the most important arrangements are: (*a*) 'side-matched': the 'leaves' as they are cut are placed side by side; (*b*) 'book-matched': every other leaf is mirrored by turning it over. If there is a diagonal stripe in the grain this will produce a herring bone effect; (*c*) 'quartered': four panels are arranged symmetrically to produce a diamond shaped pattern.

For all forms of veneering the first essential is a stable flat panel. If the core has a wood surface, the direction of the grain of the veneers should be at right angles to the grain of the core. This frequently involves cross veneering, which may also be necessary with coarse grained plywoods and some chipboards whose surface texture can show through a fine veneer.

Even if the moisture content of the veneer is the same as that of the core, as it should be, there is a tendency for the latter to warp when the veneer has been laid, and even on thick boards it is advisable to apply a compensating veneer on the reverse side. Ideally this should be of the same wood as the face veneer, but expense often dictates that it should be of a cheaper wood.

Until the introduction of plywood and the methods of manufacture associated with it, veneering was done by hand. The veneer was warmed by an iron and then stuck to the core with Scotch glue and pressed with a veneer hammer. In intricate work handwork is still resorted to today, but the cost may be as much as four times that of using panels ready veneered in a press before fabrication. It is important, however, to note that the synthetic resin glues nowadays associated with factory production of laminated boards are known to stain light coloured decorative veneers, and for them at least it is preferable to use other glues.

There are two matters of practical interest associated with veneering which deserve mention. The first relates to ready veneered panels which are machined and assembled afterwards. In order to avoid any unveneered wood showing on the outside corners of panels jointed at right angles, mitred joints are necessary as distinct from rebated joints or dovetails. The second is concerned with lippings. There is some difference of opinion about whether a veneer should be stopped before the lipping or taken over it. There seems no reason why the veneer should not be taken over unless the corner is likely to receive exceptional wear.

Finally, veneers can be applied to curved surfaces of even small radii, and by 'tailoring' can be fitted to shapes curved in two planes.

Fig. 244. An example of the application of veneering to wall panelling and to fitments. The whole of these veneers are here applied to chipboards which have been used both for the panelling and in the construction of the fitments.

Fig. 245

Fig. 247

Fig. 246

Fig. 248

Fig. 245. Plastic veneers used in a metallurgical laboratory, where easily maintained non-staining surfaces are required.

Fig. 246. Part of a bar in which plastic veneers have been used in a characteristic manner for bar and table tops where their resistance to alcohol and fruit juices and their cleanliness are of great value. Note also the bent plywood chairs.

Fig. 247. Murals and table tops in plastic veneer. The murals, part of the general panelling scheme and used in conjunction with natural timber, are made by an interlaminate printing process; the panels have the same hard clean surface as the ordinary decorative plastic veneers.

Fig. 248. A kitchen table with plastic veneered top and edges. Note the dark edge of the chamfer on the veneer—recommended to prevent chipping.

PLASTIC VENEERS, BOARDS AND PANELS

One of the few disadvantages of natural timber is the failure of most finishes applied to it to withstand the many and varied hazards to which they are put when exposed on counter tops and other positions where water, acids and alkalis may be spilt, cigarettes stubbed out, or where they may be chipped or scratched.

Decorative plastic veneers which withstand most of these hazards and which require only washing with soap and water for maintenance are now almost universally used in the construction of such fitments as are formed in kitchens and bars and so on. There are grades other than the 'decorative', which are cheaper and are used for balancing veneers, linings and industrial uses and which are usually brown or black; and some of them are less resistant to wear.

The most usual way in which the material, 'decorative' or otherwise, is used is as a veneer about $\frac{1}{16}$ in. thick, which is sold either in sheets or ready glued to plywood or other cores of any required thickness.

Sheets of plastic called 'panels' $\frac{1}{8}$ in. and $\frac{5}{32}$ in. thick are also available which are thick enough to be mounted on framing without any continuous backing. Both the thin veneers and the ready-veneered boards and the 'panels' are produced in sheets of 8 ft. or 9 ft. by 4 ft. in size, the exact dimensions depending on the manufacturer.

The 'decorative' plastics are expensive: a $\frac{1}{16}$ in. veneer unmounted and unfixed costing about 4s. a square foot (1957), the $\frac{1}{8}$ in. panel about 6s. 2d. a square foot and a $\frac{3}{4}$ in. ready-veneered blockboard about 10s. a square foot. Obviously it is important to avoid wastage and to design accordingly.

Although the $\frac{1}{16}$ in. sheets are called 'veneers', they and all decorative plastic sheets are built up of a series of veneers or laminations, the top one designed to produce a variety of gay colours and patterns with a finish which may be glossy, satin or matt. The sheets are made from layers of paper impregnated with phenolic resins and overlaid with a sheet of decorative paper, fabric or thin veneer of wood, on top of which is laid a transparent resin melamine sheet to give a very hard wearing surface. The laminates are subjected to pressures up to 5,000 tons and are cured at temperatures of about 160°C. The method of manufacture gives an opportunity for individual designs to be prepared on the paper incorporated in the sheet. They can be hand painted in special inks, silk screened or photographically reproduced.

It is a characteristic of many of the sheets that they are heat resistant up to a temperature of approximately 265 deg. F. A special grade which incorporates a sheet of aluminium foil as a conductor is produced to overcome the common complaint of cigarette burns on counter and bar tops, but even this grade will not withstand temperatures of over 265 deg. F if these are applied in large areas.

There are two other properties which ought to be mentioned. First, the materials only resist water above freezing point, and therefore they should not be used outside since the surface and colour may deteriorate. Second, although like all other joinery materials they move with changes in moisture

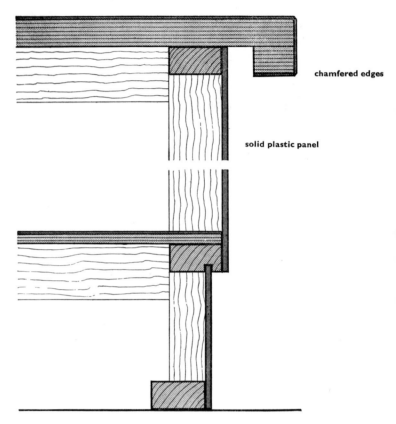

plastic veneer on plywood

chamfered edges

solid plastic panel

Fig. 249. A typical counter construction showing two ways of using plastic sheets: the top veneered to a core and the front of thicker panel of plastic fixed to stout framing of well seasoned wood. The top has no compensating veneer since it is adequately restrained by the framing and is not likely to be of large dimensions.

content they are, nevertheless, by comparison with normal timber, relatively stable.

Besides the now standard forms in which the veneers and panels are marketed, there are plain coloured ribbed core panels 1 in. and $1\frac{5}{8}$ in. thick, 8 ft. by 4 ft., which can be used structurally: also hardboards and chipboards faced with a variety of thin plastic surfaces incorporated in manufacture. The latter are not so hardwearing as decorative plastics, but would be suitable for counter and cupboard fronts and doors, if not for work tops.

Technique for plastics

The first thing to decide is whether to use the plastic in its veneer form on a solid core, or whether to design for the thicker panel which is structurally self-supporting. The illustration in Fig. 249 above shows two ways of using plastics on a counter. The best practice, however, is to use the veneer

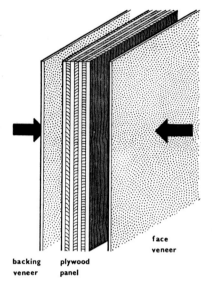

backing
veneer

plywood
panel

face
veneer

Fig. 250. Method of using thin plastic veneer by gluing to stout core at least ⅝ in. thick, with compensating veneer on back to prevent warping and keep out moisture.

on a core, especially since this eliminates the fixing screws and cover strips associated with the thick panels.

The problem then arises as to who is to bond the veneer to the board. Some manufacturers market ready-veneered boards, whereas others sell the veneers only, which then have to be bonded, either by agents who in turn sell the composite boards, or by the joinery manufacturer himself.

A joinery firm might obtain the veneer and stick it to the core in the shop, but there is some danger in this since they may not be expert in choosing the correct glues and may not have the appropriate presses which are desirable. It is true that the material is widely sold for amateur application, but usually for simple table tops and often with an 'impact' glue which, whilst it does not require pressure, is nevertheless a less efficient bond. It is preferable therefore to see that ready-veneered boards are obtained from specialists, even if cutting and fitting is subsequently done by the joiner. Just as with other forms of veneering compensating veneers are necessary, unless the panel is to be firmly restrained, and it is likely that the specialist firms would see that this is done.

Although ordinary woodworking tools can be used, this material is very much harder than wood and better results are obtained if high-speed woodworking machinery and powered tools are used. Because the technique is different from ordinary woodworking the manufacturers issue detailed instructions.

The material can be bent: there is no general rule, but certain makes of the $\frac{1}{16}$ in. veneer can be curved to small radii of 1 in. and even less. Curves of these small radii generally require that the material should be heated, and the ready-veneered panels will need to be treated or made up by the methods described when discussing plywood.

145

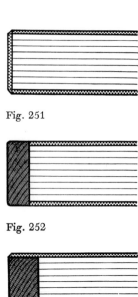

Fig. 251

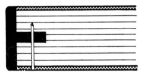

Fig. 252

Fig. 253

Fig. 254

FOUR TYPICAL METHODS OF EDGING
PLASTIC VENEERED BOARDS

*Fig. 251. With plastic veneer glued to edge. Note that
the edge is bevelled to save chipping and that this should
preferably be the vertical edge. The bevel shows as
a dark line.*

Fig. 252. With hardwood mastering the veneers.

Fig. 253. With a hardwood insert between the veneers.

Fig. 254. With a metal extrusion.

We show, Figs. 251–4, various methods of finishing the edge of plastic
covered cores, from which it can be seen that veneering the edge grain of
ply with some plastic veneer is common practice, though it should be
observed that the edges of the veneer itself should be chamfered to prevent
chipping of the decorative face. In addition, of course, there is a whole range
of aluminium and other extruded sections which are used as trim.

7: Transparent Finishes

'Timber does not deteriorate or "lose its nature" through age alone.'* There are in fact many examples of wooden objects several thousand years old which, for one reason or another, have been protected and in which the timber is still in a sound condition. It is common knowledge, however, that most timbers when left out of doors do in time become 'rotten'. This is not brought about by natural ageing but by fungal decay or insect attack: if exposed to extremes of temperature and constant wetting and drying most timbers will also suffer from warping and splitting and will deteriorate on this account too. In addition all timber exposed to the weather will eventually turn grey.

The fungal decay to which they are liable need not be due to Dry Rot (Merulius Lacrymans) or Cellar Rot (Coniorphora Cerebella), which are well known to those acquainted with building, but to any of a great variety of other fungi which, under certain conditions, attack timber: the results of their attack are often referred to as 'Wet Rot' since the fungi usually flourish when the timber is damp.

The most important reason for applying a finish to timber is therefore to prevent decay from fungi and insects: other reasons are (*a*) to prevent its absorbing moisture, which causes distortion; (*b*) to protect the timber against special forms of damage such as are occasioned by acids and alcohols, etc.; and (*c*) to improve the appearance, to enable it to be kept clean, and—in so far as transparent finishes are used externally—to preserve the colour of the wood.

FUNGI AND INSECT ATTACK

It is true that the heartwood of a few timbers (it does not apply to the sapwood) may be used both externally and internally without any protection even against fungi or insects, since these timbers happen to contain substances which resist decay. Of the commonly used joinery timbers there are in this category—besides teak whose durability is well known—afrormosia, afzelia, iroko, makoré, opepe, Western red cedar.

All but the last of these timbers is a 'hardwood' and Western red cedar is, in fact, the only common softwood having these special qualities. Although it is literally a 'soft' wood and is not therefore suitable for some joinery it is often used untreated for roof shingles, exposed siding and embedded plugs

---

* *Decay of Timber and its Prevention.* K. St G. Cartwright, M.A. (Oxon), and W. P. K. Findlay, D.SC. (Lond.). HMSO, 1947.

and other positions where advantage can be taken of its resistant qualities.

It will be noticed that oak does not appear in this list although most people will have seen untreated oak sills. Long years of experience have shown that oak is, in fact, reasonably resistant to fungal decay, and by tradition it is often used without protection.

Other woods used outside need protection and the best way to give this protection is to use one of the recognized chemical preservatives, as well as applying a waterproof finish such as paint. The function of the preservative is to reduce the risk of fungal and insect decay and of the paint to protect the timber against moisture movement, warping and splitting. In practice a chemical preservative is seldom specified and reliance is placed on the paint or other finish, yet where the danger from decay is greatest, such as at the back of door frames, a totally inadequate protection is given by only one coat of priming.

In theory it seems that the only satisfactory solution would be to apply to concealed faces a preservative followed by at least two coats of paint. In the opinion of the authors, the single coat of primer usually given, even if applied over a preservative, would do very little to prevent the absorption of moisture which can distort the timber and raise the paint film on the face.

Inside a building there should be no danger from fungal attack on wood, even if used (as it often is) with no preservative or other protection on the parts which are out of sight. Unfortunately there is a real danger, which is more often than not ignored, of destruction at some time or other by wood-boring beetles.

For this reason the authors' opinion is that it is advisable to treat all timbers internally, as well as externally, with a chemical preservative. This is, in fact, quite practicable since pressure-impregnated timber can readily be obtained throughout the country, but architects should make sure that the treatment will not affect whatever finish is applied. Anybody who has had experience of renovations or conversions, where all the timber including joinery work has been destroyed by furniture beetle, will appreciate that the initial capital cost is saved in the long run. Many hardwoods as well as softwoods can be pressure-treated. Treated timber should be used for joinery fitments such as cupboards as well as for structural work. The practical implications of this will be discussed in the following chapter on 'timber specification'.

It is true that, provided the beetle is not already in the wood, paints and polishes act as a deterrent to their entry by sealing the surfaces. They are, however, very rarely applied on all faces, and most people will have seen how the attack on, for instance, a polished chair is concentrated on the underside where there is no polish.

ABSORPTION OF MOISTURE

The question of the absorption of moisture was mentioned in Chapter 2. We return in Chapter 8 to the practical problem of how to prevent timber from absorbing too much moisture (pages 170–2).

SPECIAL FORMS OF DAMAGE

The resistance to damage and the hardness of the surface are important considerations. In situations where alcohols or chemicals may be spilt on to a
polished surface, some polishes would be entirely unsuitable. On the other
hand it is curious that french polish and wax, which are very susceptible to
damage by heat and water, are used for table tops where there is obviously
a risk of their being subjected to both. Ring marks from wet cups or glasses
are in fact often to be seen disfiguring french polished and waxed tables, but
it so happens that a professional polisher can fairly easily remove them and
match the surface or patch-polish it, whereas he would be unable to do so as
easily with oil seals, varnishes, celluloses or plastic polishes, all of which are
more resistant than either french polished or waxed surfaces to this form of
damage, as indeed to most other forms.

The authors carried out some simple tests which confirmed the opinions
which were generally voiced about the behaviour of a number of polishes
when subjected to some of the likely forms of damage. Each of six sample
panels were tested: photographs of some of them are shown overleaf to
illustrate what happened. Besides the other tests each sample was scratched,
but there was hardly sufficient difference in the degree of marking to make
any fair comparison. The results of the other tests, which we recognize as
being unscientific but nevertheless giving a general indication, are shown in
the table on page 150.

FINISHES FOR IMPROVING THE APPEARANCE

A decorative finish is usually required to enhance the wood and enable it to
be kept clean.

The most common finish applied to all sorts of joinery is paint, but besides
this there is a second group of finishes, all of which are more or less transparent: they are most often applied to hardwoods and the group includes
oils, varnishes, polishes and lacquers, and synthetic finishes. They can all be
used on external joinery, but some are more durable than others, and in the
main the discussion of them in this chapter is confined to their uses in connection with internal work.

Much has been written about paints, and knowledge of their characteristics and the means of applying them is readily available. This is not so true
of the transparent finishes, which we shall speak of broadly as 'polishes', and
it is therefore about these that we propose to write. The painting of joinery
is done—with the exception of priming—outside joinery works by an entirely separate trade. Although polishers are also a separate trade they have
by tradition been much more closely allied to joiners, and one usually finds a
polishing shop forming part of the works.

It so happens that refinements in the techniques of polishing, and particularly french polishing, have been jealously guarded, and for this reason
too there is less common knowledge about polishes than about paints. At the
present time the kinds of transparent finish which are in use are:

1. Oils. 2. Oil seals. 3. Wax polishes. 4. Liquid wax (stains). 5. French

	Cold water under cup left overnight	Ink spot	Hot cup	Cigarette burn	Gin
Oil seal	Nil	Nil	Nil	Through polish	Nil
Wax polish	Whitened	Stained	Dark ring	Through polish dark stain	White stain
French polish	Nil	Nil	White stain: polish melted	Through polish	White stain
Synthetic varnish	Slight mark	Nil	Very slight mark	Through polish	Nil
Cellulose lacquer	Nil	Nil	Slight destruction of film	Through polish	Nil
Synthetic resin finish	Nil	Nil	Nil	Nil	Nil

polishes. 6. Varnishes. 7. Varnish stains. 8. Cellulose lacquers. 9. Synthetic resin finishes (known loosely as plastic polishes).

For those who are not familiar with the various kinds of polish it is perhaps worth remarking that however different they may be in composition or properties, there are a number of basic operations which are usually undertaken in the application of all of them, especially if the architect has decided that the wood is to be fully polished.

These operations are sanding and scraping, stopping, filling, staining and colour matching, polishing and finishing.

When all these operations are undertaken with either french polish, varnish, cellulose or plastic polishes the difference between the various finishes is less easily discernible than is usually supposed. Indeed we doubt whether most people could for instance distinguish by a superficial inspection between a good cellulose lacquer and a french polish of comparable gloss. Oil polishes and waxes, and to some extent varnishes, are perhaps more easily distinguishable from the others and it must also be admitted that there is a subtle difference between oils, waxes and french polish which are rubbed in and varnishes, celluloses and other finishes which are applied on the surface. The quality of the final appearance of any polish is, however, always

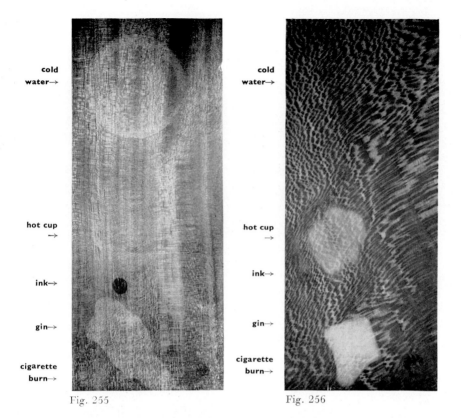

cold
water→

hot cup
→

ink→

gin→

cigarette
burn→

cold
water→

hot cup
→

ink→

gin→

cigarette
burn→

Fig. 255

Fig. 256

cigarette
burn→

Fig. 257

Fig. 258

FOUR NEWLY POLISHED
HARDWOOD PANELS
*tested for resistance to
damage (see table on
p. 150.)*
Fig. 255. Wax polish.
Fig. 256. French polish.
Fig. 257. Synthetic varnish.
*Fig. 258. Synthetic resin
finish.*

Fig. 259

Fig. 260

Fig. 261

Fig. 262

Fig. 259. STAINING *a mahogany table to match a sample.*

Fig. 260. FILLING *previously-stained mahogany. The filler is coloured to match the stained wood.*

Fig. 261. BODYING IN *on natural pine.*

Fig. 262. DULLING DOWN *with pumice powder to produce a semi-matt finish.*

Fig. 263. CELLULOSE SPRAYING.

Fig. 263

governed more by the degree of skill and care with which it is put on than by its intrinsic qualities. All the polishes can either be rubbed down or obtained in special form to produce matt and semi-matt as well as gloss finishes.

COST

In making a choice, the factors to be considered, apart from appearance, are cost, durability and resistance to damage, and the ease with which the polish can be renovated: it is a comparatively simple matter, for instance, for a polisher to strip a french polish as is sometimes required in order to alter the colour of the wood.

A comparison of the durability of various kinds of polish must take into account first whether the polish is to be used inside or outside. Broadly speaking varnishes are the most durable outside, and french polish is claimed as the most durable inside.

The cost of polishing varies considerably, and any one polish loosely specified could cost as much or as little as any other depending on the amount of preparation and care in finishing expended on it. It is impossible to give any accurate comparative or absolute figures, but since it is always useful to have some idea of the range of cost and to have in one's mind an approximate comparison we include the table on page 154.

PREPARATION OF THE SURFACE

Before any of these finishes are applied the wood has to be prepared: the object is to obtain a clean dry surface as smooth as possible, eliminating any roughness of the grain, scratches and tool marks, including those which are not easily recognized in the white but which would show up quite obviously on the surface after polishing; and possibly, either to alter or to make uniform the colour of the wood.

SCRAPING, SANDING AND FILLING

The surface has to be made even smoother than it is when left from the plane, and in good workmanship the timber would first be scraped along the grain with a small piece of sheet steel having one edge sharpened, and then rubbed with glass paper. Even then there will remain, with some timbers, an unevenness between the summer and winter growth rings, and a coarseness of the grain which will prevent the glass-like surface which is aimed at from being produced. To overcome this, and incidentally to provide even suction, a filler is used. If, however, a glass-like surface is not required, a surface dressing of gold size and turps or oil varnish can be used to equalize the suction.

Specifications should be very clear as to whether the filling process is required. It is not to be confused with 'stopping'*—the filling of holes—

* 'Stopping' may be either 'hard'—a conglomerate of beeswax resin and orange lac which has to be used hot—or 'soft'—a putty made of Plaster of Paris, whitening and oil. Both kinds of stopping can be coloured to match the wood.

1. The price of any type of finish depends more on the quality of workmanship entailed than on cost of materials.

2. The cost of labour is usually several times that of material. It may well be, for instance, 5:1.

3. The prices given below should be taken as being for good quality work on plain surfaces, including filling, staining and rubbing down, etc.

4. Rates for hand polishing should be measured per *foot* super but have been adjusted to read per *yard* super in this table for purposes of comparison.

5. Floor finishes which may superficially appear to be similar in specification are not of the same quality and are much cheaper, e.g. 'Body-in and twice wax' (for floors) 'Prepare and apply two coats of oil seal'. Both about 3s. yard super. The term 'body-in' is here used loosely and refers to the customary application of a coat of shellac without a great deal of rubbing.

(a) Proprietary preservative (two coats), 2s. per yard. Linseed oil (boiled) (two coats), 1s. 6d. per yard.		
(b) Wax (bodying-in and two coats) Oil seal (two coats) Varnish (four coats)	From 7s. to 10s. per yard.	1. The cheapest possible finish is one coat of wax. 2. For comparison knot prime, stop and paint three coats finishing gloss=about 7s. per yard. 3. Two coats of varnish might cost about 4s.
(c) French polish (full specification) Cellulose lacquers (full specification) Synthetic finishes (full specification)	From 20s. to 30s. per yard.	1. These prices relate to comparable finishes. 2. The higher price is largely applicable to the synthetic resin finishes. 3. All these can be applied to produce less highly finished surfaces and may then cost not more than half the figures quoted.

which one could expect to be done automatically by any reasonable firm: it is, on the contrary, a process which could add considerably to the cost, and a point should be made of ascertaining whether or not it is included in prices received for work.

FILLERS

It is beyond the scope of this article to describe all the various kinds of filler, many of which are patent. It is possible, however, to make a broad classification which may be helpful, and in the first place a distinction can be made between fillers used in paintwork and those used before polishing.

Reliable fillers used in paintwork are of two kinds: *lead paste* fillers for external work, and *leadless paste* fillers for internal work where the rubbing down of materials containing lead is prohibited under the Factory Act. They are applied fairly thickly with a broad knife and rubbed down across the grain. They should always be applied over a primer.

Fillers for transparent finishes are of three main kinds:

1. Direct filling, a combination of french polish and pumice powder. The polish is applied with a muslin bag containing pumice powder which gradually fills up the pores.

This kind of filling is used only in preparation for 'french polishing'. It is laborious, but is said to give the best results.

2. Paste fillers consisting of whitening or china clay in a medium such as methylated spirits or turpentine. These are applied with a rag and wiped off across the grain.

Different woods require fillers of different tints and the polisher may either add his own stain to the filler or obtain a tinted filler ready made.

3. Special fillers for plastic polishes and celluloses whose solvents would remove the medium of an ordinary filler.

STAINING AND MATCHING

The staining of wood is also a preparatory process which may be required for one of three reasons: either to conceal any uneven natural colouring, or to darken the wood or to make a cheap wood look like an expensive one. Fortunately more regard is now had for the natural characteristic appearance of many varieties of wood, and there is less desire to produce imitations.

We have already said that colour can be incorporated in paste fillers, but it is also possible to apply the stain separately.

There are a number of colouring materials which are useful in staining woods and, partly because they are not all soluble in any one medium, several kinds of stain are marketed. These are water, spirit, oil, varnish, wax, and chemical stains (for oak). Each of these has its own characteristics which determine the choice: broadly speaking, spirit (and especially naphtha) stains are preferable to water stains which tend to raise the grain, although there are craftsmen who prefer to use the latter. Oil stains are said to be the most lasting and can be used in conjunction with any kind of finish.

Varnish stains are strictly a 'finish' in themselves and are discussed later in this article.

Whilst dealing with the preparation of wood before finishing, mention should be made of the possibility of *bleaching*. This is done with proprietary preparations applied with a brush: many of them have a basis of oxalic acid. *Fuming* is another preparatory process in which the timber is subjected to ammonia fumes. It darkens the timber and is by custom more often applied to oak than to other timbers: fuming is usually followed by the application of a wax polish.

Yet another treatment for oak is *liming*: this consists of leaving slaked lime in contact with the timber until it has become a light grey and then brushing it off and wax polishing.

OILS

The use of linseed oil on hardwoods exposed to the weather is well known. It is usually put on in two coats, and either raw or boiled linseed oils are used. The boiled oil is the thicker of the two and dries more quickly. The oil improves the appearance of the timber but contrary to popular belief does very little to protect it against the effects of the weather. It collects the dirt and the dust and needs to be cleaned off and re-oiled at intervals as short as three to six months.

Another less well known use for linseed oil is as a polish. By a continuous series of applications and rubbing it is possible to obtain a fine lustrous finish which has the great merit of withstanding heat and water. The process is now rarely used commercially because it is laborious and thus an expensive one. It is said that continuous rubbing of linseed oil will produce instantaneous combustion—so would-be polishers should beware!

OIL SEALS

Various oils by themselves or in combination are used for the treatment of floors to produce hard, smooth, non-slip surfaces: there is much confusion in the names they are given by the trade, for some of the oils designed primarily as a basis for wax polishing are known as 'seals', whilst others with the same name are intended to be in themselves a 'finish' to the floor.

Most of these oils when used as 'primers' for waxing have a basis of tung oil, though linseed and other drying oils are sometimes used alone.

When designed to produce a 'finish', tung oil is used and is submitted to a heat process which alters its characteristics, especially in so far as it dries harder and is therefore longer lasting in use. A finish of this kind generally needs renewing every one to three years depending upon the amount of wear to which it is subjected. It renders the floor proof against dirt, grease, ink, water, and can be cleaned by damp mopping: on the other hand it does not produce a slippery finish and is often used in gymnasia. It can also be used as a polish to ordinary joinery components and, especially when rubbed down to produce a semi-matt finish, is very satisfactory.

WAX POLISHES

The simplest finish, with or without the preliminary treatment just described, which is practical and effective and reasonably cheap, is a wax polish. This kind of polish fills the grain adequately unless it is very open, and it is therefore not usually necessary to apply a separate filler: on the other hand the process of obtaining a high polish with wax may be speeded up by applying first a coat of one of the varieties of french polish discussed below, and this is termed 'bodying in'.

Wax polish itself consists of beeswax and turpentine and is applied as a

156

paste merely by rubbing with a soft cloth. Proprietary wax cleaning polishes which are obtainable in paste or liquid form are similar but have a spirit base: they can be used for treating raw wood but the paste type having more body is preferable to the liquid. In both these forms they are used for maintaining all the other polishes.

Properties of wax polish. Wax polish slightly darkens the wood and brings out its natural colour, imparting a sheen but not a gloss-like finish. The extent of the gloss depends upon the amount the wax is rubbed. Much of it is absorbed into the wood, and what remains on the surface stays relatively soft. For this reason it is more inclined to collect dust than other harder finishes.

It does not withstand the weather, heat, water or other liquids. For this reason it cannot be used successfully out of doors nor is it really satisfactory for table tops or other positions where it may be subject to heat or to water. It is nevertheless a most useful polish for doors, fitments, panelling and also for floors. It is easily applied on site. Scratches do not show on it to the same extent as on finishes with a high gloss, and it does not suffer from defects such as blooming, crazing, orange peeling, etc., to which other finishes are sometimes liable. A hint worth knowing is that the very obvious white marks which are formed by water can usually be removed by rubbing gently with a mixture of linseed oil and methylated spirits.

There are on the market liquid wax polishes which are applied by a brush instead of by rubbing in. After drying, most of them have to be burnished to produce a sheen though amongst them there are special water-wax emulsions which do not need burnishing afterwards.

Recently, silicones have been incorporated in the manufacture of both liquid and paste wax polishes to ease the spreading of 'hard' waxes, which are said to give the best polishes but which would otherwise be difficult to apply.

LIQUID WAX STAINS

There is a well-known proprietary combined liquid-wax finish obtainable in clear form or in combination with stains. It is claimed that it enables a stained and wax finish to be obtained in one coat; that it builds up a sufficient body in this one coat to provide a sheen after burnishing; and further that in its clear form it darkens the timber less than other wax polishes. It is widely used both in the furniture and building industries since it produces an acceptable finish at an economical price.

FRENCH POLISHES

Until the introduction of cellulose and other synthetic polishes, french polishing was recognized as the most important of the internal finishes, demanding considerable skill in its production. It is by no means superseded by other forms of polish, and despite its limitations many people consider that it gives a more beautiful finish than any other. Each craftsman built up his personal techniques and was reluctant to disclose the means which he learned from experiment and experience for obtaining particular results.

French polishing is not merely the application of a single polishing medium but a system permitting many variations by the choice of the basic polish and the incorporation of stains. In fact one of the main attributes of french polishing is the ease with which particular shades of colours can be introduced, and variations in colour in the natural wood eliminated, if required, to provide a uniform colour to match a sample. The 'colour' refers to shades of yellow and brown and grey, and it is not suggested that the wood can be stained bright blue!

Types of polish. The polish itself consists of a 'lac', which is a resinous encrustation from an insect found on trees growing in South-Eastern Asia, and afterwards dissolved in methylated spirits. The raw lac from the tree is processed by being melted and either flowed on to pieces of wood where it sets in thin layers and is then known as *'shell-lac'* (*shellac*) or dropped into water when it forms button-like discs and is then known as *'button'* lac. Button lac is a little lighter in colour than shellac.

These particular lacs, when mixed with methylated spirit, produce brown polishes which have a darkening effect in use. There is one other well-known variety—in all there are about twenty-eight—known as *'garnet'* polish which is darker but, having less body, is more transparent than most of the others.

'White polish' and *'transparent polish'* are made from bleached lac and do not have a darkening effect though they are considered to be less durable.

Application. 'Bodying in' is the first part of the process of french polishing after filling and staining—though the latter may be incorporated in the polish—and consists of a series of preliminary and liberal applications of polish. As already mentioned, wax polishing may also be preceded by 'bodying in' in exactly the same way with a lac. For economy—both in wax and french polishing—a polish known as 'brush' polish can be used. It has more body and consists of a lac to which gums have been added.

The next part of the process is known as 'bodying up' and consists in further thin applications of polish applied with a rubber (a pad of cotton wool wrapped in linen) with linseed oil as a lubricant. The number of applications and the amount of papering and of drying between them are matters of judgment and depend on the kind of wood and the finish required.

Finally the last coat of polish is softened by rubbing with another pad dipped in methylated spirits, the effect of which is to eliminate all rubbing marks and to produce a highly glazed surface. This is known as 'spiriting out'. French polished surfaces may be maintained by wax polishing.

Properties of french polish. French polishes are not ordinarily proof against heat or water or spirits: they are used outside on shop-fronts but need frequent renewal, even if special grades of polish are used. French polishes are associated by tradition with all kinds of furniture, doors, handrails and high-class joinery, but much of the work which formerly would have been french polished is now cellulosed, especially such things as tables, radio cabinets and factory made components which can be accommodated in the spray booths used in the process of cellulosing.

158

VARNISHES

A broad distinction can be made between the polishes which we have already discussed, and varnishes, celluloses and plastic finishes. The polishes are rubbed in and the others brushed or sprayed on and when well applied produce a more brilliant surface than rubbed finishes. Varnishes have a characteristic appearance and can usually be detected by the dust particles which almost invariably collect on the surface; in fact one of the difficulties in using varnish is to ensure that it is applied under suitable conditions: dust and draughts have to be avoided, and the air should remain at a constant temperature whilst the varnish dries.

There are two types of varnish, oil and spirit. The names derive from the media in which the resinous substances, which are their main constituent, are dissolved. Oil varnishes are the main type—and the notes that follow are concerned with them—spirit varnishes being used only for special purposes.

OIL VARNISHES

These are prepared from hard natural or synthetic resins, together with one or more oils. They dry and harden by a relatively slow process of oxidization, the time taken to oxidize depending on the nature of the ingredients and, of course, the conditions under which the process takes place.

There are many kinds of varnish and very often the individual varnishes retain the descriptive names of the uses for which they were originally compounded: for instance, church oak, crystal paper, elastic copal carriage, engine copal, pale copal yacht, front door, etc. They all fall within four main groups known in the trade as white, pale, medium and dark.

It will be noticed from this list that varnishes are made for both outside and inside use. In general, those for external use contain a larger proportion of oil (in relation to the amount of resin) to increase their flexibility and durability, and these are known as 'long oil varnishes'. Those with less oil are correspondingly known as 'short oil' varnishes and thus dry harder, without tackiness and with a more brilliant finish. Their use should be confined to interior work.

The nature of the oil, as well as its quantity and treatment, affects the performance of the varnish; those containing a proportion of 'tung' oil are more durable than those with only linseed oil and withstand extremes of exposure better. The use of synthetic resins instead of natural resins also makes the varnish more durable, and incidentally rather paler.

There are special varnishes, which can be used inside only, which are formulated to produce semi-gloss or matt finishes. These contain wax or other substances to dull the finish (those containing no wax have the advantage that, if necessary, they can be painted or varnished over without first removing the varnish). Sometimes it may be thought particularly desirable to retain the natural colour of the wood and for this yet another kind of waxless flat varnish can be obtained which is almost invisible when applied. It can be used as a finish or as a base for a gloss varnish, the point of the latter being that the resultant finish will not be as dark as it would otherwise have been.

159

Preparation for varnishing. The preparation of the wood for varnishing is not as elaborate as it is for other kinds of finish. It may, however, be necessary to stain the wood and in new work to equalize the suction over the surface to be treated: for this some craftsmen advocate sizing and others a coat of french polish. Alternatively the unequal suction can be overcome by applying extra coats of varnish, although this is likely to be more expensive. Unlike the polishes described previously, varnishes can be rubbed down with water as a lubricant using a special abrasive paper known as 'wet and dry'. This should be done between each coat.

Occasionally a pale varnish is used to add permanence to french polished work when it has to be exposed to the weather. There was a time, less than fifty years ago, when varnish was universally used over flat paints to give them life and gloss: ready-mixed gloss paints and enamels were not then known.

Properties of varnishes. It will be seen from what has been said about varnishes that whilst they do not produce so mellow a finish as french polish they can last much longer out of doors and they are none of them so liable to marking from water, spirits or moderate heat as french polish. The materials for varnish are expensive but the labour in producing a finish is less than that needed for french polishing: the whole process is cheaper, and is comparable to the cost of painting. The life of varnish is rather less than that of paint when used externally—on the other hand, varnish finishes deteriorate by cracking, whereas paint often deteriorates by 'chalking'. The former entails complete removal before retreatment but the latter forms an excellent base for further coats of paint.

VARNISH STAINS

Combined stains and spirit varnishes are sold under proprietary brands for floor margins and other amateur work where their cheapness and quick drying are welcome.

CELLULOSE LACQUERS

Whilst french polishes are applied by rubbing, and varnishes by brushing, celluloses are almost invariably sprayed on. The result of spraying is to produce a surface film in much the same way as the brushing on of a varnish, but in other respects cellulosing is more nearly akin to french polishing. It is in fact used as a substitute for it, and was developed in order that the characteristic appearance of french polish could be produced with less labour and skill and at less cost.

It is true that cheap cellulosing may consist of nothing more than the application of very few coats of cellulose on an unprepared ground: this would not constitute a satisfactory finish, and would admittedly bear no relation to french polish. On the other hand it is possible with cellulose to carry out many processes similar to those associated with french polish, and to produce more quickly, and at less cost, a finish which, in appearance, is hardly distinguishable from it. It would be natural to expect that the two kinds of finish would have different properties, and in fact cellulose is known not only to have a shorter life than french polish, but also to be harder and more brittle—but as a consequence to deteriorate eventually by cracking, which involves removal of the whole film if it is to be put right. Neither of the finishes is ordinarily suitable for exterior use. Experience has proved, however, that french polish, when used inside, has great durability although it is more susceptible than cellulose to damage by heat and water and spirits. These deficiencies in french polishing are irritating, especially to the owner of the polished object, but to the polisher they are less worrying since it is always possible to put right a small area and to match it with the remainder.

One must also take into account that sprayed cellulosing (brush-applied celluloses can be discounted for all large-scale work) requires mechanical equipment and special conditions for application. In general this means that the work must be done in a spray booth, and site work has to be restricted to a minimum. Portable spraying plant is available, but it is not of course convenient to use in, for instance, an occupied house.

The formulation of cellulose lacquers. At this stage the reader may be concerned to know exactly what cellulose is. Used with reference to polishes, the word is a loose term for nitro-cellulose. This is made from cotton treated with nitric and sulphuric acids and dissolved in solvents such as acetone or butyl acetate. To these are added natural and synthetic resins to increase gloss, and plasticizers such as butyl phthalate to lessen normal brittleness of the cellulose and give more flexibility. Nitro-cellulose when dry is almost 'flat', and it is consequently not difficult to produce semi-gloss and eggshell finishes without having to rub the work down.

Preparation for cellulosing. In order to obtain a good finish the preparation of the wood surface should be similar to that for french polishing. The wood must be 'dry' to avoid peeling of the cellulose coats, and all surface marks and scratches must be eliminated by papering. The grain should be filled and, if required, the wood stained and sealed.

The filling is done with either oil-thinned fillers (with a basis of barium sulphate, whitening, etc.) or waterfillers (with casein or gelatine) which are water soluble as a basis.

Stains and sealers are specially formulated for use with cellulose but serve the same purpose as in french polishing.

Finishing and burnishing. In cheap work glossy celluloses can be left without further treatment, but if the full process of polishing can be afforded, the cellulose can be bodied up and finished off in a variety of ways including hand rubbing. One of the finishing processes is known as a 'pull-over'. It is similar to the process of 'spiriting out' and is done by hand, using a solution of solvents and just strong enough diluents to dissolve the surface of the lacquer. Other methods of finishing are by cutting down with pumice powder and water and finishing off with wax or burnishing with a special cream.

It will be realized that it is important when specifying cellulosing to make clear what quality of polish is required and, as is advisable with all finishes, to work to a sample.

Cellulose polishing was developed in an attempt to overcome the deficiencies of french polish, and the introduction of synthetic resins has given rise to the development of so-called 'plastic' polishes which in turn are in some ways superior to both french polish and cellulose. Amongst other things, it is claimed that they are at least as durable as french polish and it is known that they withstand heat, water, grease, acids and alkalis and if specially formulated they can be used for outside work. The polishes are relatively new and there is not much experience of their use outside. They can be brushed or sprayed on. It is claimed that the surface, which is extremely hard, does not crack or flake and that it does not chip easily. Nevertheless, the one great disadvantage is that if they are accidentally scratched or damaged they are difficult to patch, and whilst it is possible to maintain them normally by sanding and applying additional coats, it is extremely difficult to get them off altogether should this be required. Some of them also have a marked darkening effect.

In general the material itself is expensive and since the preparation of the surfaces to receive the polish is much the same as that for french polishing and cellulosing but with stainers, fillers, and burnishing creams designed for use with the plastic polish, the whole process is relatively costly.

The polishes are made from synthetic resins such as phenolics, ureas and epoxies with thinners, and catalysts or hardeners.

There can be little doubt that for such positions as bar tops, fume cupboards, laboratory benches, shop counters and all joinery which comes into contact with substances which are likely to destroy either french polish or cellulose, plastic polishes ought to be most useful and a valuable addition to the range of available finishes. They can be applied by brush or spray, but owing to their quick rate of drying it is preferable that they should be sprayed: for this reason it is obviously more convenient to apply them in a workshop than on site, although the latter is not impossible. With cold-setting resins some hours have to elapse between coats, and it is important that on completion the surface be kept within a particular range of temperatures for several days, depending on the particular grade of polish.

There is, however, a technique used mainly in polishing furniture, in which the polish is 'stoved' in humidity-controlled ovens. The process takes in all about one hour. If this technique were extended we might perhaps look forward to a time when joinery components such as windows and doors leave the factory with a stoved waterproof finish.

It should be mentioned that the manufacturers of plastic polishes produce many grades each designed for a particular use and their advice as to selection and application should be sought, especially since most craftsmen are unfamiliar with the material and it is essential that instructions be closely followed.

8: Specification and Practice

A written *description* of the work to be done is necessary as an accompaniment to drawings, whether it appears in conventional form as a 'specification', or whether it is written into a Bill, or is contained in the drawings. Only under certain conditions, which we discuss later, may drawings with only general notes be enough by themselves.

On the other hand if the description is to be of value it must be accurate and intelligible and possible to interpret. This statement should hardly need making, but there are, in fact, very few specifications written, particularly those written for joinery, which bear criticial examination. It is usually assumed that they must be couched in a peculiar phraseology and that clauses which have appeared in previous specifications—which are followed as models—must be included whether they are pertinent or understood or not.

Many managers of joinery works have little esteem for the description which they receive, for no other reason than that much of what is demanded is almost impossible to provide, and would not be asked for if the implications of doing so were better understood. Timber which is 'entirely free from knots and all other defects' is frequently specified even for those positions where such a high quality would be quite unnecessary, because old specifications contain such a clause; when the original specifications were written such timber may have been readily available, but in present conditions it is not.

It is therefore most important to specify only what can be reasonably obtained and what one is prepared to insist upon having. Two or three pertinent clauses are more useful than several pages of jargon. It would be to the good if anyone writing specifications were to make no reference whilst doing so to any 'model' clauses or previous specifications, but instead were to write in straightforward language a simple description of what was to be done and the materials to be used, including nothing which he did not himself fully understand, but nevertheless including everything required to complete the work in every detail. It is, of course, difficult to be certain that all the necessary information is given, and that is why reference is so often made to former specifications, but we suggest it would be better to have a check list of the items which are likely to need description, rather than attempt to adapt existing clauses.

DIFFERENCES IN QUALITY

It follows from what we have said above that specifications ought not only to avoid asking the impossible but should quite distinctly differentiate between the qualities required for various classes of work. It is, in this respect, unfortunate that architects' specifications by custom require everything to be the 'best', whereas it must be obvious that where money is limited it would be reasonable to accept a lower standard of materials and workmanship. What in fact happens is that the manufacturer makes his own decision about the quality he will produce and hopes that the architect will be prepared to accept it. His decision will, of course, be based very largely on the practical necessity of keeping his price competitive with that of other manufacturers producing similar work. One manufacturer, to our knowledge, finds it necessary to have what he calls a 'housing' standard which is of a lower grade than that which he otherwise works to. Architects must be realistic about this. There is in general no recognized system of grading for workmanship in building and apart from the influence of economic restriction already mentioned it is only by inference that a builder assesses the quality which he will give: we all know that he would expect to have to produce the best possible workmanship for a concert hall or an embassy, whereas he would not do so for a housing estate or a farm building—yet in the past specifications have often failed to make any clear distinction.

BRITISH STANDARDS

In spite of there being no system of grading there is now—for joinery—one official attempt to define quality of both workmanship and materials: namely the British Standard Specification 1186. *Quality of Timber and Workmanship in Joinery (Part I: Quality of Timber; Part II: Quality of Workmanship).* * These are very useful documents but the standard set is in its own words a 'standard of workmanship which is considered acceptable for general housing'. It provides 'a more precise alternative to such time-honoured expressions as "in a workmanlike manner" and "to the architect's satisfaction" which in practice depend entirely upon the judgment of an individual'. It is not in fact of a high enough standard for all purposes, and furthermore, of course, it is one of the dangers of British Standards that adherence to them is often demanded without proper knowledge of what they contain. To say that all joinery shall be in accordance with BS 1186, Parts I and II, would be satisfactory if no other contradictory clauses were added, as is so often done, and if the architect fully realized what he was asking for. He must also, of course, see to it that the builder or manufacturer obtains a copy of the BS and adheres to it. So often specifications, even when clearly set out, are not read by builders, and whilst it ought not to be so, it is more than likely that a reference to a British Standard contained in a general specification will be totally ignored. In our view it would be better to extract the clauses of the British Standard relevant to the particular job and write them out in full in the specification.

Even if a higher quality of joinery should be required than laid down by the British Standard, the documents referred to are undoubtedly a sound basis for compiling one's own specification. We shall refer to them in greater detail below.

* See relevant extracts reproduced in Appendix II, pages 200–4.

ENFORCEMENT

As we have already said, there is a danger that builders do not read specifications because they so often contain little but old standard clauses, and it does not necessarily follow that even if the specification is prepared with great care, much attention will be paid to it, particularly to any variations from old-established practice, unless the joiner's attention is specially drawn to them. Also, it is possible that joinery of a different quality will be produced by different manufacturers even though each is working to the same specification unless the architect sees to it by frequent inspections that his requirements are carried out.

THE CONTENTS OF A JOINERY SPECIFICATION

The object of a joinery specification—which is usually part of a general specification which itself contains such contractual and legal clauses as are considered necessary—is to convey to the builder the kind of materials he is to use, the way the components, of which he will have a drawing, are to be made and finished, and where, when and how they are to be fixed. More precisely the specification can conveniently be divided into sections dealing with:

1. Scope of the work.
2. Materials, timber.
3. Moisture content.
4. Other materials.
5. Workmanship and manufacture.
6. Procedure.
7. Description of particular components to be made and schedules.

We ought to mention that in building specifications the clauses dealing with joinery are generally grouped with carpentry and ironmongery. This is because the 'tradesmen' are titled 'carpenters and joiners', although not all carpenters are capable of doing joinery! Ironmongery is included because it is fixed by carpenters and joiners. We discuss in this chapter only the joinery clauses, which we think should be collected into a separate specification.

The clauses which follow—set in italics and placed in the margin— embody and illustrate the various points made: many of them show alternative ways of dealing with particular problems, and, as explained, not all are equally good. Together they do not, and are not intended to, form a type specification. In particular the clauses dealing with materials are given only to illustrate method and we do not necessarily recommend the materials described. A check list of items which usually require specifying is given on page 185.

The principle has been followed of dealing first with the materials, then with the workmanship and finally with the procedure for carrying out the work. Whilst it is suggested that this is the best method it is perhaps over elaborate for minor items unless a very full specification is being written. Thus in the sample clauses, priming paint is described under Materials, the method of application is given under Workmanship, and the time when it is to be applied is given under Procedure. These clauses and clauses relating to other finishes could possibly be grouped together in briefer specifications.

SECTION 1: SCOPE OF THE WORK

The purpose of this clause is to make quite clear what work is to be done and estimated for. It would be necessary only if the specification were addressed to a manufacturer who is not the general contractor.

The work shall consist of the manufacture, delivery to the site and fixing in the building of all joinery described in the Specification and shown on drawings Nos. ———: including the supply and fixing of:
*(a) metal, straps, lugs and dowels,** *
(b) priming, preservatives and polishing,
(c) all ironmongery specified or shown on the drawings.

* Rough grounds, pallets and slips would normally be fixed by the general contractors' carpenter and should be included in the section of the general contractor's specification dealing with carpentry.

SECTION 2: MATERIALS: TIMBER

It has been the custom to specify the quality of timber required in a building under a general clause which might read as follows: 'all timber shall be bright, dry and reasonably free from waney edges, sap and shakes. It must be free from rot, worm, beetle, vermin, splits, large loose or dead knots or other defects.'

Now if one pauses to think of the implications of this clause one will realize first of all that it makes no differentiation between timber for carpentry and timber for joinery; also that many of the requirements are open to very different interpretations and some may well be almost impossible to satisfy.

It would seem, too, that it is concerned more with softwoods and that it was written with them in mind. It is true that most of the requirements are applicable to hardwoods, but it is usually in work done with softwood that it is necessary to take particular care to see that they are carried out.

In our opinion it is probably best to specify hardwoods separately from softwoods, and we suggest below several methods of specifying each.

SPECIFICATION OF HARDWOODS

1. *Selection by British Standard* 1186, *Part I: Quality of Timber* (see extract, Appendix II, page 200). This is to date the most detailed and precise specification we have come across, and although designed to set a standard suitable for general housing and similar structures it does provide a very satisfactory lower limit for all work. It includes detailed standards for the quality of timber under the headings given below (it also deals with moisture content, plywood and the selection of species suitable for particular uses):

(a) Rate of growth. (b) Straightness of grain. (c) Character of grain. (d) Boxed heart and exposed pith. (e) Sapwood. (f) Checks, splits and shakes (g) Knots. (h) Plugs and inserts. (i) Pitch pockets. (j) Decay and insect attack.

166

Unfortunately the average builder does not possess and know all the British Standards to which architects are nowadays prone to refer. They are indeed quite expensive, which discourages builders from buying them, and being so exact are not readily absorbed and understood except by those who specialize in the subject matter of each particular specification.

It would be reasonable to specify one's timber 'in accordance with BS 1186' when addressing joinery factories: for most average builders, until the British Standards are more widely known, a specification is likely to be more effective if it is written out by the architect in more or less detail according to the size of the job and the type of contractor—the financial consequences of the replacement of sub-standard work being more serious on the larger job.

2. *Selection by species and grade.* The most practical way for an architect to specify timber, if he does not refer to the British Standard, is to specify the species and the commercial grades which will be acceptable and to state as an added precaution what particular defects are to be rejected should they occur in the grade chosen.

It may generally be assumed that in certain respects hardwood used in joinery is likely to be free from some of the defects which are associated with softwoods, because it seems to be accepted by importers and manufacturers that a higher standard will be required of work for which the former is specified and in any case the trunks of hardwoods are very much bigger than softwoods and are free from branches which cause knots. On the other hand, whilst there are relatively few species of softwood used in joinery, there are literally hundreds of hardwoods, whose characteristics and appearance differ widely. When using hardwoods it is therefore of great importance to name the species which it is proposed shall be used, but there may be difficulty, as discussed later, in doing so at the time of writing the specification.

Naturally the choice will depend upon the suitability of the timber for the purpose required, but it will also be dependent to a great extent upon the appearance of the timber.

As far as its suitability is concerned, the architect must rely on his own and others' experience and upon the data given in books and also in the British Standard. We give a list of joinery timbers in Appendix I, page 188.

We would always advocate that a choice be made at the time of writing the specification, but to do so involves making sure that the price of the timber is what can be afforded, that the timber will be available when required, and that the client is unlikely to change his mind halfway through the job.

If, therefore, it should happen that it was not essential to have one particular kind of timber, some means of specifying alternatives must be arrived at. It may be possible to include the names of several timbers, so that it is then up to the contractor to select when pricing the lowest priced timber which he can be sure of obtaining. It often happens that even if the species of timber is specified a different timber is eventually used for some reason or other, and it is therefore advisable to ask those who are tendering to state in their quotation the basic prices of the timbers included.

In practice a particular grade for hardwood is seldom specified, the assumption being that for joinery the wood will always be of the best quality, or chosen to be suitable for the purpose required. Nevertheless, hardwood is graded commercially. The difficulty is that there is no universally recognized system of grading, and even the names for the grades vary from country to country. However, certain terms are generally recognized in the trade and could reasonably be used in specifications.

FAS (FIRSTS AND SECONDS) OR EQUIVALENT would require the best quality and SELECTS AND NO. 1 COMMON, OR EQUIVALENT, the next lower quality. Lower qualities than these would not often be suitable for joinery.

The grading rules mentioned above apply to square-edged boards exported from the countries of origin. Where hardwood logs are imported to this country they are usually graded A, B and C, but on conversion by the timber merchant the planks are graded again FAS, Selects, etc.

A small joinery concern would usually buy square-edged boards from a timber merchant. Large concerns can buy whole logs (possibly cut through-and-through) and find a use for such parts of them as may not be suitable for the joinery in question. This would probably prove more economic and would provide a greater choice of timber.

The requirements for the qualities FAS and Selects cannot be accurately defined since they vary from country to country. The best known systems of grading are the American National Hardwood Lumber Grading Rules, which are in fact applied as a minimum standard for most African timbers, and the recently revised Malayan Grading Rules.

FAS should theoretically provide clear timber free from the defects applicable to hardwood—knots, sapwood, waney edge, warping, pith, brittle heart, rot, stain and beetle attack. In *Selects* the defects should be of a minor nature, but in either case it is advisable to state as a precaution which of these defects would quite definitely not be accepted.

3. *Selection by species to sample*. In hardwoods the selection of the timber is often dealt with by specifying a particular species and stating that it is to be of a quality not less good than a sample which the architect has previously obtained from the manufacturer (or from several manufacturers if the works are being tendered for in competition).

This system is the only practicable one if special importance is attached to the figuring and character of grain, and indeed in these circumstances it may be necessary to examine and approve all the timber to be used after the work has been let.

4. *Selection by cost*. If for any reason the architect cannot choose the timber at the time of writing the specification, he can get over the difficulty by inserting a prime cost sum for the wood. This arrangement excludes the cost of the timber from the competition and does not give the joiner sufficient indication of the amount of labour which may be involved, which varies according to the kind of wood chosen. If only for these reasons, we feel that this system should be avoided if possible.

168

A. To comply with BS 1186, *Part I. Species to be chosen for each use from the medium hardwoods marked 'Suitable' in Table* 3.

B. Hardwood to be African mahogany, to comply with BS 1186, *Part I, except that no knots will be permitted in joints. The wood is to comply with the* BS *requirements for wood 'selected for staining'.*

C. Hardwood to be Iroko, grade FAS *or equivalent. None of the following will be permitted: sapwood, pith, splits, stain or any evidence of beetle attack or rot. Isolated sound tight knots less than* ½ *in. diameter will be permitted provided they do not occur in joints or on visible faces. The estimate is to include the basic price of the wood (kilned and square sawn).*

D. Hardwood to be one of the following species, grade FAS *or equivalent: iroko, afzelia, afrormosia, makoré.*

E. Hardwood to be guarea to match a sample already approved by the architect.

F. Include the sum of 40s. *per ft. cube (sawn square to required sizes and kilned) for hardwood to be selected by the architect.*

SPECIFICATION OF SOFTWOODS

1. *Selection by British Standard.* As in hardwoods described above.

2. *Selection by species and grade.* The species of softwoods are far less in number than those of hardwoods, though possibly more difficult to distinguish: we describe seven of them which are commonly used in joinery in our list of recommended woods printed in Appendix I. The *grades* in which the timbers are at present obtainable in this country are those described in the first chapter.

In general terms the Scandinavian timbers suitable for joinery are graded as '*unsorted*' (that is, a mixture of grades of seconds, thirds and fourths, and sometimes including some 'firsts': the exclusive grade of firsts being still unavailable. The next grade down, 'fifths', is not considered good enough for joinery). American timber is graded differently. The first quality is known as 'clears and door stock' and this is equivalent to Scandinavian 'firsts' and is obtainable. The second quality, equivalent to unsorted, is 'select merchantable'. It should be noted in passing that 'clears' may cost as much as 50 per cent more than 'select merchantable'.

3. *Defects in softwood.* The defects in softwoods are likely to be more commonly encountered than in hardwoods and it will be important in one's specification to say what limits shall be set upon them. We suggest that to do this the architect should refer to the clauses of the British Standard and modify them to suit his particular requirements.

ALTERNATIVE CLAUSES

A. To comply with BS 1186, *Part I.*

B. To be Douglas fir, grade select merchantable. The following defects will not be permitted: pith showing on the surface, sloping grain exceeding one in eight, checks, splits and shakes, knots, excepting isolated sound tight knots of less than ¾ *in. diameter, any evidence of beetle attack or rot.*

(Add if required: Timber for door styles (and other positions if required) to be 100 *per cent quarter-sawn.)*

SECTION 3: MOISTURE CONTENT

We have stated throughout how important it is to ensure that the timber in joinery has an appropriate moisture content at the time the building is taken into use, and we have discussed the subject in detail in Chapter 2.

In order to avoid shrinkage and warping, the timber must be purchased from the merchant at the correct moisture content or be kilned by the joinery manufacturer himself and must thereafter be maintained in that condition.

To make sure that this is done the specification may (a) require the moisture content to accord with BS 1186, Part I *; (b) state an actual figure for the moisture content, or (c) describe the anticipated conditions of heat and humidity to which the joinery will be subjected, and require the contractor himself to select an appropriate moisture content.

Whichever method is used it is customary for the specification to require the contractor to make good any shrinkage or warping at the end of the 'maintenance period' of the contract. This requirement is usually covered in most contracts by a general clause but is also often restated in that part of the specification dealing with the joinery.

If an architect specifies a species of wood and a particular moisture content and the wood subsequently warps and shrinks, the question arises whether the contractor can still be held responsible. Although it might appear that if the builder can prove that he has abided strictly by the instructions he is absolved from responsibility, under the present conditions of most contracts this would not be so, although the architect would have little grounds for argument if the moisture content he specified did not accord with the figures which are included in the British Standard and which can be taken as accepted practice.

In Chapter 2 we showed that since the hygroscopicity of wood varies, it would be more accurate to specify the moisture content for each purpose according to the species of wood to be used. We have classified the most common joinery timbers into three groups of hygroscopicity, and have given a table of moisture contents for each group. This table indicates for example that for external frames the correct moisture contents for teak (Group A) would be 13 per cent, for Douglas fir (Group B) would be 17 per cent, and

* The moisture content of the timber, when the joinery is manufactured and dispatched from the factory, shall be within the following limits:

	Moisture content	
	Minimum %	Maximum %
(a) Internal joinery, including doors, when specially ordered for buildings with central heating or other forms of continuous heating	10	12
(b) All other internal doors	12	15
(c) All other internal joinery	14	17
(d) All external doors	15	18
(e) All other external joinery	17	20

170

for gedu nohor (Group C) would be 19 per cent. At present the British Standard figures are generally accepted but for very special work our own table should give even greater reliability.

Unless the British Standard is quoted, therefore, the choice lies in making a precise requirement for the moisture content (possibly requiring to see evidence of this) with the risk of there being some argument as to responsibility; or in leaving the choice of moisture content to the builder, with the risk that he will not take proper care, hoping that nothing will go wrong. Whilst it is easy to say that the architect shall insist on defects being replaced, it is difficult in practice, because amongst other reasons it often involves delays which are unacceptable to one's client. Also, it is one thing to condemn, say, a really bad example of shrinkage, but it is not so easy to condemn work on account of an accumulation of minor defects due to bad seasoning, although these defects might very much detract from the appearance of the work. In our opinion, therefore, the British Standard, or better still the precise moisture content required for each item of work, should be stated in the specification.

It may be objected that architects cannot easily ensure that their instructions are carried out. Certainly at the time of writing it is not usual for architects to have tests made to determine the moisture content of joinery. It is established practice, however, to order regular tests of concrete, and there seems no reason why tests should not also be made of timber.

In the first place it should not be difficult to obtain copies of certificates issued by the kiln owner relating to the timber used. Whilst this is obviously not a complete safeguard it at least ensures that the timber is at the correct moisture content before manufacture. Properly, of course, the test should be made at the time the joinery is taken into use.

This can be done in two ways: either by using a battery-operated electronic moisture meter or by sending a sample for a laboratory test. Meters usually work by measuring the resistance to an electric current between two needles which are driven a short way into the wood—not more than $\frac{3}{16}$ in. Only the moisture content at the surface therefore can be obtained by this type of instrument. At least one meter is available having electrodes to be screwed into the wood up to a depth of $2\frac{3}{4}$ in., thus overcoming this difficulty. It is claimed, however, that with the relatively small sections encountered in joinery, a surface reading gives a sufficiently good indication of the general condition of the wood for practical purposes. The Inspectors for the Ministry of Works, whose duty it is to examine joinery and furniture being manufactured, use moisture meters as a first check. In case of doubt an accurate laboratory test can be ordered. A portable moisture meter which would be suitable for architects' use costs about £30.*

---

* *Marconi moisture meter:* covers range 7 per cent to 25 per cent (margin of error $\frac{1}{2}$ per cent). Weight 10 lb. Size approximately 9 in. by 9 in. by 9 in. £35. *Gann Hydromat KL20-02* (German meter sold by Messrs Interwood Ltd). This is illustrated and described on p. 173.

The laboratory test consists of drying the sample in an oven until all moisture is driven off, and then comparing its dry weight with its original weight. The Forest Products Research Laboratory will carry out tests for architects where they do not have laboratories available to them. The charge is 15s. for one or two samples and 5s. for each additional sample in the batch. The results are given in a day or two. Samples should be protected by waterproof wrapping or by a sealed container. If possible the full section should be sent 6 in. to 9 in. long.

ALTERNATIVE CLAUSES

A. *The moisture content of the timber when the joinery is manufactured and delivered to the site shall come within the limits given in* BS 1186, *Part* I, *for each use, and shall be maintained until the building is completed.*

B. *The moisture content of the timber used for internal joinery is to be* 10 *per cent and that used for external doors and frames is to be* 16 *per cent when the joinery is delivered to the site, and these moisture contents are to be maintained until the building is finished. The architect will require evidence of correct moisture content to be submitted to him before the joinery is fixed.*

C. *The attention of the contractor is drawn to the fact that the building will be centrally heated. All timber for joinery is to be properly kilned. The moisture content is to be between* 9 *per cent and* 16 *per cent according to the position of the timber.*

D. *The joinery manufacturer is to ensure that the moisture contents of the various items of joinery delivered to the site are appropriate to the conditions of use to which the components are to be put. In particular the following conditions are to be taken into account:*

(1) *Central heating during the heating season in all parts of the building excepting the following rooms:* . . .

(2) *The proximity of window boards and casings to radiators.*

(3) *High relative humidity to be expected in* . . .

SECTION 4: OTHER MATERIALS

As will be evident, natural timber is by no means the only material used in joinery. The specification may need to include requirements for the following:
Plywood

Blockboard

Laminboard

Wood veneers

Plastic veneers

These have been dealt with at some length in Chapter 6 and since there is not the same difficulty in specifying them as solid timber, we refer readers to this chapter.

Plywood for exterior use: *To be British made to comply with* BS 1455 *bonding WBP, Grade* 1 *where varnished and Grade* 2 *where painted; or foreign made plywood of equivalent bonding and grade.*
Plywood to be painted to be gaboon, birch or other wood approved by the architect. Plywood to be varnished to be Douglas fir.
Plywood for interior use: *To be British made to comply with* BS 1455 *bonding INT, Grade* 2 *where painted, and Grade* 3 *where hidden; or foreign made plywood of equivalent bonding and grade.*

172

Fig. 264

Fig. 264. THE GANN HYDROMAT. *This German moisture meter covers a range 5 per cent to 30 per cent (margin of error 5–15 per cent =1 per cent; 15–30 per cent = 2 per cent). It weighs 3 lb., and its size is approximately 8 in. by 6 in. by 3 in., and it costs £30 including case. (Type KLB is supplied with screw-in electrodes.)*

Fig. 265. A SPECIMEN OF DRY ROT. *The bottom of a window board removed during alterations to a house. The window wood is badly affected by dry rot although it did not show on the surface. The house was built about thirty years ago and the back of the frame had not been protected.*

Fig. 265

SCHEDULE OF DOORS.

Position	Size	Specification	Frame or Lining	Furniture & Locks (See list of Provisional Sums)
Front Door	6'9" x 3'0" x 2"	Framed and battened and ledged in oak.	ex 4" x 3" softwood painted.	Night latch. Mortice lock. Pr. bronze knobs. Special letter plate.
Living Room, Study, Dining Room	6'6" x 2'6" x 1⅝"	Flush painted.	ex 5½" x 1½" softwood painted.	Mortice lock. Pr. lever handles.
Kitchen	6'6" x 2'6" x 1⅝"	Flush painted.	ex 4" x 1½" painted softwood.	Mortice lock. Pr. lever handles.
Cloaks	6'6" x 2'3" x 1⅝"	Flush painted.	ex 4" x 1½" painted softwood.	Mortice latch. Pr. lever handles. C.P. bathroom bolt.
Larder	6'6" x 2'6" x 1⅝"	Flush painted.	ex 4" x 1½" painted softwood.	6" 'D' handle. Adjustable roller bolt.
Back door	6'6" x 2'6" x 1¾"	Softwood framed ledged braced battened.	ex 4¼" x 3"	Mortice lock. Pr. knobs. Pr. 6" barrel bolts.

Fig. 266. A typical schedule of doors.

Furniture for sliding sashes in wood.

Roller	2 per window	Item 57	To be brass roller 9/16" diameter with curved bearing surface ⅜" wide, cast brass body with 1½" x ⅝" face plate drilled with 2 holes for ⅝" x 5 countersunk sherardised screws.
Bearing plate	1 per window	Item 58	To be standard brass T-section ¾" x 3/16" x 1/16" thick flanges drilled at each end and at 6" staggered centres on alternate flanges, for No.5 size ⅝" long countersunk head wood screws.
Bolts	1 per window	Item 59	To be 3" silver anodised satin finished aluminium alloy straight barrel bolt and two sockets and screws to match.
Pull handle	1 per window	Item 60	To be 4" aluminium alloy extruded section grip handle with all exposed surfaces silver anodised satin finished with face plate drilled with 2 holes for 1" x 8 countersunk sherardised screws.

VENTILATORS

Larders in Blocks Nos. 2 and 3	1 per Larder	Item 62	To be approved 4" diameter Kitchen Cabinet Ventilator with gauze, silver anodized satin-finish with screws.

Fig. 267. An extract from a typical schedule of ironmongery.

Plywood to be polished to be gaboon.

Plywood to be painted to be gaboon, birch or other wood approved by the architect.

Blockboard: *To be best quality British manufacture finished with gaboon plies.*

Wood veneer: *To be prime quality French walnut not inferior to the samples already submitted and approved. The architect is to be informed when the whole of the stock is ready for his inspection and approval, before the work is commenced.*

Plastic veneers: *To be Messrs XXXXX decorative veneer ORANGE colour MATT finish applied to $\frac{3}{4}$ in. blockboard strictly according to the manufacturer's instructions. Doors are to receive a backing of $\frac{1}{16}$ in. brown plastic veneer made for this purpose.*

Glues, Screws and Nails

These are described in Chapter 5 and *preservatives, paints and finishes* in Chapter 7. Ironmongery must also be specified in detail—it is not sufficient to put in a prime cost sum without description since the joiner must know what work is entailed in fixing.

Nails: *To be oval lost head wire nails to comply with* BS 1202.

Screws: *To be countersunk wood screws to comply with* BS 1210. *Steel screws are to be used in concealed positions. Brass screws (with brass cups where specified) are to be used on exposed faces where indicated on the drawings. Screws for fixing ironmongery are to be of the same metal as the hardware except that aluminium alloy hardware is to be fixed with brass screws finished satin chrome. No steel screws are to be used in positions subject to dampness.*

Hinges: *Casement hinges are to be rust proofed steel hinges to comply with* BS 1227 *reference* [7]. *Door hinges are to be brass with steel pins and washers.*

Metal dowels, straps and other fastenings: *To be galvanized mild steel.*

Ironmongery: *To be to materials and designs set out in the Schedules.*

Glues: *For joinery to be exposed externally to be synthetic resin adhesive to* BS 1204 *type* WBP, *e.g. 'XXXXX' applied strictly according to the manufacturers' instructions. For internal joinery to be 'XXXXX' as above (or where expressly indicated animal glue to comply with* BS 745).

Preservative: *To be 'XXXXX' Clear wood preservative made by Messrs 'XXXXX'.*

Priming paints: Either:

To be of the same manufacture as the finishing paints specified, i.e. first quality wood primer made by Messrs 'XXXXX', or:

To be white lead wood primer to comply with BS 2521/54 *Lead Based Priming Paints.*

Knotting: *To comply with* BS 1336.

Varnishes: *To be standard oil varnishes to British Standards as below:*

BS 256 *Interior oil varnish.*

BS 258 *Flatting or rubbing varnish.*

BS 257 *Exterior oil varnish.*

BS 274 *Extra hard drying varnish.*

Synthetic varnish *or* Plastic polish (Synthetic resin finish) *or* Cellulose lacquer: *To be 'XXXXX' undercoats and finishing coats for brushing (or spraying) to be supplied by Messrs 'XXXXX' with full instructions for application.*

Wax polish: *To be made from genuine beeswax and turpentine.*

Fillers for polishing: *To be paste fillers consisting of whitening or china clay in methylated spirits or turpentine, tinted to match the wood.*

Stains: *To be spirit stains of approved colour.*

French polishes: *To be white or transparent polish (to preserve as far as possible the natural colour of the wood).*

The specification of priming paint is important for two reasons. Firstly, if it is not of good quality (some 'pink primers' are little better than distemper) it will cause the coats of paint applied on top of it to peel off; and secondly, if for any reason at all the paint fails, the painter and paint manufacturer may put the blame on the primer. The second danger can be overcome either by specifying the primer to be of the same manufacture as the paint which is to be used on top of it, or by specifying the primer to be one of the types covered by BS 2521/4 (2521 lead based). The latter is the more convenient for the joiner, since he can probably continue with a brand he has in stock, but if it is intended that the finish is to be a 'synthetic' paint, or of unusual formulation, it would be advisable to find out whether the BS primer will be satisfactory.

Schedules of doors, windows and cupboards incorporated in specifications, or set out separately as drawings, are of great assistance in visualizing the ironmongery required for each item and in remembering to specify the materials and finishes, kinds of screw and so on. The complexity of this part of the architect's work can be judged from the schedule of doors and the schedule of hardware on p. 174.

SECTION 5: WORKMANSHIP AND MANUFACTURE

The average joinery specification says very little about the interpretation of architects' drawings, method of manufacture, quality of workmanship: that is, about the kinds of joints to be used and their design and degree of accuracy.

The items traditionally included in specifications deal with allowances for planing; with the work being 'framed up in a workmanlike manner', and with 'the work being prepared and framed as soon as possible after the contract is signed, but not glued and wedged until the joinery is needed for fixing'.

We think that this part of the specification should give a clearer indication of exactly what is required.

Drawings

The degree to which joints and detailed methods of construction are shown on architects' drawings varies considerably, and whether they are shown or not, the manufacturer frequently alters them, either to suit his particular machine technique or preferences, or because he does not approve the methods shown.

Whilst it may be reasonable for him to do this, and indeed the architect may allow in the specification for him to suggest alterations, the specification should state that the architect requires to see the joiner's full-size setting-out drawings before the work is begun, so that he may have an opportunity of approving any modifications which are being proposed. We suggest that a clause dealing with this should be included under 'procedure'.

Conversely, if a component has been carefully worked out and the architect does not wish *any* alterations to be made, he would do well to say so clearly.

176

If the architect shows nothing but profiles, he has no option but to make use of some general clause asking for the work to be done according to 'the best traditions of the trade'.

ALTERNATIVE CLAUSES

A. *The joinery is to be constructed exactly as shown on the architect's details. Where joints are not specifically indicated, they are to be the same as joints shown on the drawings for similar positions of use.*

B. *The manufacturer is to be responsible for the sound construction of the components, using the recognized forms of joints in appropriate positions. The architect's drawings are intended to show the final appearance of the work rather than the complete construction.*

C. *The work is to be manufactured according to the best traditions of the trade, to the satisfaction of the architect.*

D. *The components are to be constructed with joints as set out in the Schedule below: e.g. 'Double-hung sashes'*: Jambs, heads and sills shall be scribed and framed together with combed joints of not less than two laminations per member to provide four glued joints. Dowels shall be not less than $\frac{3}{4}$ in. diameter wood dowels.*

Jambs and heads shall be provided with parting beads as shown.

External and internal linings shall be securely nailed to jambs and heads, and be mitred at intersections and scribed and shaped at junctions with sills.

Sills shall be sunk, weathered and rebated all as shown.

Sashes shall be scribed and framed together with either morticed and tenoned joints or combed joints, glued and nailed together with rustproofed nails of the lost-head type. Sashes shall be grooved at back as shown for sash balances.

The meeting faces of the meeting rails shall be recessed as detailed.

Sash bars shall be scribed and tenoned into mortices in the sashes. Vertical bars through-tenoned and wedged.

All frames and sashes shall be assembled accurately and cramped together so as to be square and flat and all surfaces exposed to view shall be true, clean and smooth finished from the machine.

* Description taken from British Standard 644, Part II.

Dimensions

It is an accepted practice, which we suggest should be followed, that the members are referred to in specifications by their nominal sizes, preferably with the prefix 'ex', and the specification should state what allowance can be made for planing. The architect's full-size drawings indicate the *finished size*, the reduction for planing having been made.

The overall dimensions shown on the architect's drawings for joinery, other than that which is to be built in as the work proceeds, are usually considered to be subject to verification by measurement on the site, since traditional building is often not accurate. This invariably causes delays because in fact by the time the measurements can be taken the joinery is required on site: furthermore, it makes nonsense of the clause asking for 'the work to be framed up at the commencement of the job'.

It is not common practice, but there does not seem to be any reason why the joinery should not be made without checking on site but allowing a tolerance in the overall dimensions of $\frac{1}{16}$ in. or $\frac{1}{8}$ in. either way. This would not be difficult for the joiner, but it would be necessary to impress on the general contractor the importance of building accurately.

A. All dimensions are to be checked on site before manufacture is commenced.
B. No dimensions are to be taken on site. The components are to be manufactured strictly to the overall dimensions given on the architect's drawings. A tolerance of plus or minus $\frac{1}{16}$ in. will be permitted.
Allowance for planing and finishing
In softwood $\frac{3}{32}$ in. will be allowed for each wrought face, from the nominal size of the section specified. In hardwood $\frac{3}{32}$ in. (or $\frac{1}{16}$ in.) will be allowed on two faces from the nominal thickness of the board specified. The architect's full-size details indicate finished sizes and are to be adhered to.

Design and quality of Workmanship in Joints

Part II of BS 1186 lists the most important joints and gives precise requirements for their design and accuracy of manufacture. It also gives requirements for gluing of joints (giving a choice of four different types of glue) and surface finish for the completed joinery. Since it would be impracticable to set out in full such requirements in a normal specification, this is a valuable standard for use where there is any doubt about the quality of manufacture to be expected. It must be emphasized, however, that the standard does not say which joint is to be used in any particular position because that information is covered in other standards dealing with the design of individual components.

Joints are to be designed and executed to comply with the requirements of BS 1186, Part II. All glued joints for both external and internal use are to be put together in synthetic resin adhesive.
(Add if required: all edge-to-edge joints to be joined with cross-grained tongues.)

Finish

The requirements for the finish of joinery in BS 1186, Part II, read as follows:

'Unless otherwise specified, surfaces of joinery intended to receive the final decoration shall be such that, if properly finished with a matt paint, imperfections in manufacture will not be apparent.' This formula can obviously be adapted to give a reasonable indication of the quality of surface finish which is required.

A. All joinery to be finished with a clean wrought face. Surfaces of softwood intended for painting or clear finish shall be such that if properly finished with matt paint, imperfections in manufacture will not be apparent. Surfaces of hardwood for a gloss or matt transparent finish shall be such that, when so finished, imperfections in manufacture shall not be apparent.
B. The surfaces to be treated with a gloss transparent finish are to be scraped and sanded in such a way that after the filling and polishing specified, the texture of the surface of the wood will not be apparent.

Fixing on Site

The division of the old 'Carpenter and Joiner' trade specification into its two

178

parts presents the problem of deciding which is to include site fixing. As mentioned previously, the tradesman in the factory has different talents from his namesake on the site. In fact such work is usually done by the rare tradesmen who are actually carpenters *and* joiners, having had experience in both sides of the trade. Since bad fixing can do much harm to joinery, we suggest that it should be included in joinery rather than the carpentry section.

> *Joinery intended to be painted is to be fixed by nails. Nail heads are to be punched below the surface and filled with lead paste filler in external work and a leadless paste filler in internal work. Joinery intended for polishing is to be secretly fixed. Heads of screws are to be let in and pelleted in the same wood and with matching grain.*

Preservative Treatment

It is now common practice to treat structural timbers with preservative; at least where built into walls. As discussed in Chapter 7, it is desirable to treat joinery in the same way. Creosote or other highly coloured liquids cannot be used because they would discolour the paint or finish, even if only used on backs of frames. However, there are many clear preservatives on the market which do not have this disadvantage. One manufacturer has introduced a variety of a well-known preservative (available both coloured and clear) containing waxes and resins which are claimed to seal the wood and to reduce considerably the absorption of moisture before the joinery is fixed and painted.

> *Unless the timber is impregnated with preservative, or unless otherwise specified, the backs of frames to be fixed in walls and all other bedding surfaces are to be painted with two coats of preservative before priming.*

Knotting, Priming and Transparent Finishes and Polishes

It is generally accepted that joinery to be painted should be primed on all faces before fixing and that it should be brushed on rather than sprayed. There are, however, two schools of thought as to where it should be done— that which requires the work primed before dispatch from the factory to give it as much protection as possible against the absorption of water (although priming is known to be little value in giving this protection), and that which requires it to be done on site after inspection by the architect or clerk of works. The latter gives a better chance of inspection before any defects are covered by priming and possibly gives the architect more control over the priming used. Our opinion is that unless some other protection against moisture is used, such as the preservative mentioned above, priming should be applied in the factory to give some resistance to moisture during transit and temporary storage on site. Good priming in fact is not opaque and does not cover defects except perhaps very minor ones.

Good priming paint is very important.

179

All work shown on the Schedules to be painted is to be treated with knotting as necessary and given one brush coat of priming to all faces. Surfaces to be joined are not to be primed.

(Add if required: In addition to priming, all bedding surfaces are to be given two coats of oil paint.)

N.B. *The number of coats and methods of application of each finish are to be specified.*

SECTION 6: PROCEDURE

This heading is not one that is normally found in specifications, but in our view it is useful to collect together under it all the clauses dealing with the order in which various operations are to take place, and such administrative points as the protection of work during transit, and the making good of defects.

We have discussed the procedure for the interpretation of the architect's drawings: we have also made reference to the clause which is often inserted about framing up work loose at an early stage. There is, however, an argument in its favour for 'traditional' framed and panelled doors, which need not await measurement on site and where the wide boards used in their construction are liable to shrinkage and warping, especially since the door as a whole is unrestrained when hung. The object, of course, is to be able to replace any defective members before the door is glued up, but in our view it is not a requirement which is applicable to other kinds of joinery.

A note should be included under 'Procedure' which makes it clear when and where priming, painting, polishing and preservative treatment are to be carried out.

Too often good joinery is spoilt by being brought to the site too soon—when it suffers from the damp and from mechanical damage. It is most important to see that this does not happen, and it is also important for the architect to be quite clear in his own mind which parts of the joinery are expected to be built in and which are to be brought to the site after plastering is complete. It is no good instructing the builder to keep the joinery off the site if in fact he cannot fit it in after plastering. In this connection architects should be acquainted with the trade expressions 'first fixings', which comprise work that is 'built in', and 'second fixings', the bulk of the joinery work which is fixed later.

The specification should always include a clause pointing out the necessity for protecting the joinery, particularly against dampness, in transit and on the site, and clear directions should be given as to what is considered adequate. The examples, Fig. 271, of the rate of absorption of moisture, taken from figures obtained by the FPRL, show how very important this matter is, particularly with any joinery having a low moisture content.

Drawings

ALTERNATIVE CLAUSES

A. Work is not to commence until the architect has approved the manufacturer's full-size setting-out drawings. Suggestions which the manufacturer may wish to make for modifying the construction and joints shown on the architect's drawings will be considered when the shop drawings are examined.

180

B. No deviation is to be made from the architect's details without his written approval.
Inspection
Facilities are to be given for the architect to inspect all work in progress in shops and on the site.
Framed doors
Framed and panelled doors are to be prepared as soon as practicable after the work is ordered, put together loose and stored in conditions of heat and humidity similar to that of the completed building. When required for fixing, any warped members are to be replaced and any shrinkage is to be made good before gluing up.

Preservative treatment
ALTERNATIVE CLAUSES
A. The treatment is to be carried out after machining and before the components are assembled.
B. The treatment is to be carried out after the components are assembled and before priming.
Priming
Joinery which is prepared for painting is to be knotted and primed before the work is dispatched to the site. Where adjustments are made on site the priming is to be made good.
Painting
The bottoms of doors are to be painted the full number of coats specified before the doors are hung.
Transparent finishes
The joinery is to be given the first coat of finish before being dispatched to the site.
Add if required: The panels of framed doors to be french polished are to be polished before the doors are assembled.
Time for delivery
None of the joinery is to be delivered until it is required for fixing in the building. Joinery which does not require to be built in as the work proceeds is not to be brought to the site and fixed until the building is enclosed, and the heating is in operation.
Transport and protection
The joinery is to be kept under a waterproof cover during transit and is to be similarly covered and kept clear of the ground on the site.
It is to be handled and stacked carefully to avoid damage.*
Make good defective work
Should any shrinkage or warping occur or any other defects appear in the joiner's work before the end of the defects liability period, such defective work is to be taken down and renewed to the architect's satisfaction and any work disturbed in consequence must be made good at the contractor's expense.

* When the joinery is taken in charge by the general contractor he will be expected to provide boxing and other temporary coverings to protect the joinery from damage and a suitable clause should be included in the general contractor's specification.

SECTION 7: DESCRIPTION OF PARTICULAR COMPONENTS
TO BE MADE
This should include schedules of doors, windows and cupboards.

SUMMARY OF ARCHITECT'S PROCEDURE
To summarize what we have said throughout this chapter about the various stages in the architect's work in the production of joinery, we give overleaf a table which also shows the four main ways of approaching the problem.

System 1: *Indicate joinery required on small-scale plan* (*probably* $\frac{1}{8}$ *in. scale*). Write list of components to BS sizes and designs and quote BS for each component, e.g. storage fitments, draining boards, wood windows and doors, stairs, skirtings and mouldings, etc. Submit for tender to manufacturer specializing in this kind of work. Applicable to housing and similar work.

System 2: *Prepare drawings as in System* 1. Write brief notes with sketches showing any details which influence the architectural character and send them to a trusted specialist manufacturer to whom you are prepared to give freedom in interpreting the design, without doing any detailed drawings or specification. It is presumed that the manufacturer would then discuss the work with you at various stages so that you would benefit from his knowledge and craftsmanship. Although you would be able to obtain a firm price before committing yourself, there would be no element of competition.

System 3: *Prepare* $\frac{1}{8}$ *in. scale drawings and draft* $\frac{1}{2}$ *in. and* FS *details together with a draft specification and schedules. Consider the kinds of timber to be used and, if necessary, visit a timber yard.* Assuming that the work is to be put out to tender to joinery firms for inclusion as a prime cost in the main contract, the architect can take the opportunity of discussing the work before tender with the technical representative of one of the firms he is asking to quote, so as to ensure that the details are workable, and the sizes chosen are appropriate and the method of construction economical. This may seem unfair but it has become a common practice in this and other trades where the degree of technical knowledge required for design has become such that architects cannot be expected to keep abreast of it. Submit to tender.

System 4: *Prepare drawings and draft specification as in System* 3. If the joinery is to be included in the work to be tendered for by the general contractors who might in any event sublet it, the architect will not have the same opportunity for consultation, and he will have to complete his detailing and submit his drawings with specification notes to his quantity surveyor, for measurement and incorporation in the Bill of Quantities.

Notes on Tendering

Common with invitations to all subcontractors and suppliers to tender, it is important to make clear:

(*a*) whether the work is to be supplied, or supplied and fixed;

(*b*) what form of contract will be entered into: architects wanting a particular form of contract such as the RIBA form to apply to subcontractors should say so and should beware of large areas of pale type on the backs of quotations laying down quite other conditions!;

(*c*) the appropriate discount for cash to be included for the general contractors (under RIBA contract 5 per cent for suppliers, $2\frac{1}{2}$ per cent for subcontractors);

(*d*) by what date the tender is required;

(*e*) what period for delivery is required from the date of order.

It cannot be emphasized too much that on receipt of tenders the architect should read them and study them carefully, checking them against his

Fig. 268

Fig. 269

Fig. 270

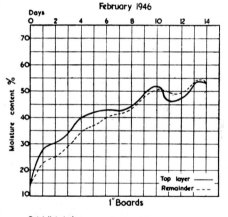

Fig. 271

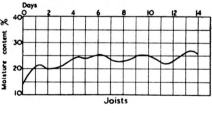

Fig. 268. *Simple framing for a 'built in' cupboard fixed before the plastering is done.*

Fig. 269. *The appearance of a hardwood window before delivery to the site. The hinges are fixed but not the fastenings. The diagonal brace is a temporary means of keeping the frame square before fixing.*

Fig. 270. *Corner of window frame 'built in' to an external wall. A slate sill is to be inserted under the bottom member. This emphasizes the need to protect the backs of such frames which cannot of course be inspected or repainted once fixed.*

Fig. 271. *Graph showing variation in the moisture content of Scots pine stored in the open.* [*From* Moisture Changes in Timber Exposed to Normal Weather Conditions *by* W. C. Stevens *and* R. E. Hodge (FPRL), Timber News.]

Fig. 272. 'Framed up loose at the commencement of the work': a time-honoured specification clause which we consider is applicable nowadays only to framed and panelled doors, as discussed on pp. 180–1.
Fig. 273. Part of a joinery manufacturer's machine shop. The machine in the foreground is a double-ended tenoner. Sections are being conveyed through the shop on trolleys during the course of their preparation before putting together.

specification. It frequently happens that, without drawing one's attention to it, the firm quotes for something different from what one has asked for. For large jobs one should send tender forms to be quoted on so as to avoid this possibility. The RIBA issue a special printed tender form.

Inspection

As many inspections and visits should be made as possible, and during the course of the work the architect should have: approved the timber in the shop; examined the shop drawings; seen samples of polishes and veneers; examined and approved the ironmongery; inspected the work under construction to see that it complies with the drawings; inspected the building-in; and we confess that, even if all the recommendations in this book have been adopted, it will undoubtedly be necessary to list the defects at the end of the defects liability period!

Joinery Specification Check List

SCOPE OF THE WORK
Supply or supply and fix.
Inclusion of fixings, finishes and ironmongery.

MATERIALS—TIMBER
Hardwoods species to BS or commercial grade.
Softwoods species to BS or commercial grade.
Quarter-sawn or flat-sawn.
Samples for approval.

MOISTURE CONTENT OF WOOD
According to BS or to figure quoted.
Conditions of use.

OTHER MATERIALS
Plywood, blockboard, chipboard.
Wood veneers, plastic veneers.
Nails, screws, hinges, dowels and straps.
Ironmongery.
Glues.
Preservatives and paints.
Knotting, cellulose, varnish, plastic polish, french polish, wax polish.

Dimensions and tolerances.
Allowance for planing and finishing.
Method of construction.
Design of joints.
Standard of finish.
Fixing to grounds and plugs.
Preservative treatment.
Knotting and priming.
Transparent finishes and polishes.

PROCEDURE
Drawings.
Inspection.
Framing of doors, i.e. putting together loose.
Treatment with preservative, priming, etc., at workshop or on site.
Delivery after heat on.
Protection during transit.
Make good defects.

DESCRIPTION OF PARTICULAR COMPONENTS TO BE MADE
Include schedules of doors, windows, cupboards and ironmongery.

PARTICULAR ITEMS
windows and skylights
sills and window boards
glazing beads
draught stripping
doors
folding and sliding doors
door frames and linings, architraves
shoes or dowels for door frames
cupboards and sink units
draining boards
staircases and balustrades and handrails
skirtings, picture rails and trim
pipe casing, duct covers, access panels and trap doors
fascias
mat well linings
mantelpieces and fire surrounds
hatches
shelving
work tops
fuel store boards
bath panels
boxing to tanks

battens for coat hooks
pelmet boards
fixing blocks for cabin hooks, brackets, etc.
notice boards
weather boarding
panelling
insulating board linings.

Appendix 1. Selection of timbers suitable for joinery

The timbers in the list on pages 190 to 199 have been selected on the basis of general availability in this country and for general use in joinery: highly decorative woods have not been included, nor those used primarily in veneers.

NOTES ON THE FOLLOWING LIST

Column 1   *Name.* There is much confusion about the names of timbers. The only safe course is to use names given in BS 881 and 589:1955 *Nomenclature of Commercial Timbers.*

   2   *Weight.* This is the average weight of the timber at 15 per cent moisture content. In general terms strengths of timbers are in proportion to their weights. Fuller information on strengths (bending, stiffness, crushing, etc.) is given in *A Handbook of Hardwoods* and *A Handbook of Softwoods* published by HMSO 17s. 6d. and 8s. 6d. respectively.

   3   *Colour.* ⎫ These are difficult to describe. Small wood samples may be obtained from
   4   *Grain.* ⎭ the Timber Development Association (price 1s. 3d. each). It is suggested that one side should be polished to show the effect of applying a clear finish which is usually to darken the wood and to emphasize its colour.

   5   *Natural durability.* This applies to heartwood only. It is the measure of *resistance to fungal decay* of timbers exposed externally and buried in the ground. Five grades are given:

P   =Perishable (less than 5 years)
ND =Not durable (5–10 years)
MD=Moderately durable (10–15 years)
D   =Durable (15–25 years)
VD =Very durable (more than 25 years)

It should be noted that many woods which are not naturally durable may be made more resistant to fungal decay by impregnating with preservatives. However, some hardwoods are impenetrable and cannot be so treated. Detailed information on this subject is also provided in the two handbooks mentioned above. The consideration of natural durability applies to timbers to be used externally. No timber is liable to fungal decay if used internally and kept dry, i.e. below about 20 per cent moisture content.

Resistance to insect attack. The grades of durability do *not* include resistance to insect attack. Practically all timbers are susceptible to attack by one or more timber beetles, and the only safeguard is to treat with preservative. Generally, sapwood is more prone to attack than a heartwood.

   6   *Moisture movement in service.* Timbers are graded according to the amount of radial and tangential movement which would be experienced when subjected to a change from 90 per cent to 60 per cent relative humidity in the surrounding atmosphere. This roughly corresponds to normal conditions of use in this country, although central heating may produce lower relative humidity percentages.

   7   *Availability* 1957. This and the following three columns give commercial information current at the time of writing. The position is bound to fluctuate but it is hoped that the comparisons which can be made will remain valid for several years. The information will also provide a starting point for detailed inquiries to the trade for

particular items of work. The supply position is complicated by the fact that some importers specialize in certain woods which may be readily obtainable from them but very scarce elsewhere. Three grades are given for availability:

I   =Plentiful
II   =Moderate supplies
III =Intermittent or limited supplies

Sizes. In making the selection of timbers suitable for joinery only those that are usually available in reasonable sizes have been chosen. Where hardwood logs are imported and can be converted for particular work, sizes are of course only limited by the size of the tree. Otherwise the average hardwood board is about 8 in. wide by 12 ft. long. Standard thicknesses are 1 in., $1\frac{1}{4}$ in., $1\frac{1}{2}$ in., 2 in., $2\frac{1}{2}$ in. and 3 in. Notes are given of exceptions to this general rule.

Costs 1957. Hardwoods are graded according to the average price per cubic foot for common sizes (e.g. $1\frac{1}{2}$-in. boards) already kilned. A good joinery quality is assumed. It should be noted that prices vary according to the sizes required as well as to the quality.

Cost of hardwood:

A =Over 50s. per cu. ft.
B =40s. to 50s. per cu. ft.
C =30s. to 40s. per cu. ft.
D =20s. to 30s. per cu. ft.

Softwoods: Although normally quoted *per standard* (165 cu. ft.) prices are here given *per cu. ft.* for comparison with hardwood. Prices are for *unkilned* sawn battens (e.g. 2 in. by 7 in., 3 in. by 7 in.). Boards are generally more expensive. Where two prices are given the higher is for the best quality (e.g. Scandinavian 'Firsts' and Canadian 'Clears and Door Stock') and the lower is for normal joinery quality (e.g. Scandinavian 'Unsorted' and Canadian 'Select Merchantable').

E =18s. to 22s. (say £165 per standard)
F =16s. to 18s. (say £140 per standard)
G =14s. to 16s. (say £125 per standard)
H =12s. to 14s. (say £105 per standard)
I =10s. to 12s. (say £90 per standard)

Whether available as veneer. This is important, when veneered work is to match solid wood. Conversely, there are many well-known decorative veneers available which cannot be obtained in the solid.

Suggested positions of use. The notes given are based on general practice. Unless stated it is assumed that external work would be painted or finished with a weather-proof transparent finish such as varnish. As mentioned in connection with 'Durability', certain woods of naturally poor durability may be used externally after impregnation with preservative.

Column 8
9
10
11

189

KEY TO COLUMNS. 1. BS name and country of origin. Other common names given in brackets. 2. Average weight per cu. ft. in lbs. 3. Colour. 4. Grain and texture. 5. Natural durability. 6. Degree of moisture movement. 7. Availability in this country. 8. Special notes on sizes. 9. Comparative costs. 10. Availability as veneer. 11. Suggested positions of use. 12. Remarks.

HARDWOODS

1	2	3	4	5	6	7	8	9	10	11	12
ABURA Tropical Africa	36	Uniform light pinkish brown	Moderately straight grain and even texture	ND	Small	I	Average (i.e. boards approx. 8 in. wide by 12 ft. long)	D	Yes	Internal	Popular medium strength wood. Works well and takes good finish. Requires care in nailing to avoid splits
AFARA/LIMBA Tropical Africa	35	Light yellowish brown with grey markings	Close straight grain sometimes wavy	ND	Small	II	Good lengths and widths	C	Yes	Internal	Easy to work, finish and polish. Requires care in nailing to avoid splits. Prone to brittle heart. The light coloured wood is called in the trade Light Afara or Limba
'AFRICAN WALNUT'	34	Brown with dark streaks. Light coloured sapwood	Interlocking grain producing ribbon figure when quarter sawn. Medium texture	MD	Small	II	Average	C/D	Yes	Internal and external	Closely related and similar in appearance to African Mahogany
AFRORMOSIA Gold Coast (Kokrodua)	44	Brownish yellow with darker streaks	Grain straight to interlocking. Fine texture	VD	Small	II	Good lengths and widths	B	Yes	Internal and external including sills. Could be used externally without finish	Very strong hard wood resembling teak, though it is not oily like teak. Useful for superior joinery where durability and stability combined with good appearance are desired. Stains when in contact with ferrous metals under damp conditions
AFZELIA Tropical Africa (Apa, Doussie)	52	Light reddish brown: sapwood pale straw	Irregular grain often interlocking. Coarse even texture	VD	Very small	II	Good widths	B/C	No	Internal and external including sills. Could be used externally without finish	Hard, strong, durable and stable. Somewhat hard to work but finishes well and is of good appearance

1	2	3	4	5	6	7	8	9	10	11	12
AGBA Tropical Africa (Tola Branca)	32	Yellowish to pink	Resembles mahogany in grain. Fine texture	D	Small	I	Good widths	C/D	Yes	Internal and external including sills. Could be used externally without finish	A good all-round timber suitable for a wide range of purposes. Works easily. Brittle heart liable in large logs and gum exudation is sometimes troublesome during seasoning
ASH, EUROPEAN	44	White to light brown and very clean	Straight grain. Coarse texture	P	Med.	II	Average	C/D	Yes	Internal	A tough elastic wood which bends easily when steamed. Works well and takes excellent polish. Ash burrs valued for veneers
BEECH, EUROPEAN	45	White to light brown	Straight grain. Fine texture	P	Large	I	Average	D	Yes	Internal	A strong tough wood used for interior joinery, furniture and cabinet making. Works well and can be stained and polished. Bends easily when steamed
BIRCH, YELLOW (Canadian Yellow Birch, American Birch)	44	Light to dark reddish brown. Sapwood lighter	Straight grain. Even texture	P	Large	II	Average	B/C	Yes	Internal	Strong hardwearing general purpose hardwood. Moderately easy to work and machines to smooth finish. Gives excellent results with transparent finishes. Bends easily when steamed
'CENTRAL AMERICAN CEDAR' AND 'SOUTH AMERICAN CEDAR' (Honduras Cedar)	30	Pale pinkish brown to dark reddish brown	Straight grain. Moderately coarse texture	R	Small	III	Average	C	Yes	Internal and external	A mild easily worked timber characterized by a fragrant scent. Used for interior fittings, panelling and furniture. Also boat building and cigar boxes. No botanical relationship with the true Cedar (Cedar of Lebanon) which is a softwood

KEY TO COLUMNS. 1. BS name and country of origin. Other common names given in brackets. 2. Average weight per cu. ft. in lbs. 3. Colour. 4. Grain and texture. 5. Natural durability. 6. Degree of moisture movement. 7. Availability in this country. 8. Special notes on sizes. 9. Comparative costs. 10. Availability as veneer. 11. Suggested positions of use. 12. Remarks.

1	2	3	4	5	6	7	8	9	10	11	12
CHESTNUT, SWEET UK, Southern Europe, N. Africa (Spanish Chestnut)	35	Similar to oak but without silver grain	Variable	D	Small	II	Average	C/D	Yes	Internal and external including sills	A wood similar to oak though softer and not so strong. Works well but is inclined to split. Takes a good finish
DANTA West Africa	46	Reddish brown with light brown sapwood	Interlocked grain. Even texture	MD	Med.	III	Average	D	No	Internal and external	A strong durable timber, very tough and elastic. The interlocked grain produces a striped appearance rather like sapele. Works with moderate ease. Takes a good finish and polishes well. Is used mainly for constructional purposes and floors
ELM, EUROPEAN	35	Dull brown with light brown sapwood	Coarse wavy grain	ND	Med.	II	Good widths	D	Yes	Internal and external	A wood of fine appearance but because of its tendency to warp is safer to use in veneer form. It is, however, used in solid form in furniture (chair seats), weather boarding, and for boat building, since it is very durable in water. It is difficult to saw but otherwise works well
GUAREA West Africa	57	Pinkish brown. Darkens on exposure. Sapwood whitish	Straight or wavy grain. Fine texture	D	Small	II	Good widths	D	Yes	Internal and external	Similar to Honduras Mahogany but harder. Fairly easy to work and finish though gum exudation may cause difficulty. A variety called Scented Guarea has more resistance to splitting. A good looking wood

1	2	3	4	5	6	7	8	9	10	11	12
GURJUN/KERUING YANG India and Burma	46	Dull greyish brown. Yang may have a pinkish tone	Fairly straight but often interlocked. Coarse even texture	MD	Large	I	Good lengths	D	No	Internal and external including sills and drainers	A very strong wood but rather difficult to work. Resin is sometimes troublesome. Besides joinery, is used for floors and constructional work
IDIGBO West Africa (Framire, Emeri, Black Afara)	35	Pale yellow with occasional brown stripes	Straight or slightly irregular. Coarse uneven texture	D	Very small	II	Average	C/D	Yes	Internal and external including sills	Good all round timber. Works fairly easily though liable to splitting and finishes well. Subject to brittle heart which should not be used. The name 'Black Afara' is misleading since this wood is not a variety of Afara
IROKO E. and W. Africa (Myule)	41	Light to dark brown. Clearly defined sapwood. Darkening with exposure	Interlocking grain well figured. Coarse even texture	VD	Very small	I	Good widths	B/C	Yes	Internal and external including sills and drainers. Could be used externally without finish	Valued for its stability and resistance to decay and is much used as an alternative for Teak. About as strong as Oak. Works with moderate ease but requires grain filling before finishing
MAHOGANY, AFRICAN West Africa	35	Light pink brown to deep red brown	Straight to interlocking grain. Texture varies	MD	Small	I	Good lengths and widths	C/D	Yes	Internal and external use	Cheapest and most readily obtained of the mahoganies. Very suitable and popular for general joinery and fittings. Working quality fairly easy but variable. Grain sometimes picks up and very sharp cutters are essential. Finishes satisfactorily

KEY TO COLUMNS. 1. BS name and country of origin. Other common names given in brackets. 2. Average weight per cu. ft. in lbs. 3. Colour. 4. Grain and texture. 5. Natural durability. 6. Degree of moisture movement. 7. Availability in this country. 8. Special notes on sizes. 9. Comparative costs. 10. Availability as veneer. 11. Suggested positions of use. 12. Remarks.

1	2	3	4	5	6	7	8	9	10	11	12
MAHOGANY, AMERICAN (British Honduras Mahogany)	34	Light yellowish brown to deep red orange brown	Some interlocked grain but good proportion straight plain grain. Finer texture than African Mahogany	D	Small		Average	A	Yes	Internal and external use	Closely related to the highly reputed Cuban or Spanish Mahogany which is no longer generally available. It is lighter and softer than Cuban Mahogany. Irregularities in the grain produce a variety of figure. Works and finishes excellently though some grades liable to be woolly and sharp tools essential
MAKORÉ West Africa (Baku, Cherry Mahogany)	40	Pale pinkish brown to dark purplish brown	Straight grain. Fine texture with lustrous surface	VD	Small	II	Good lengths and widths when cut from log	C	Yes	Internal and external including sills. Could be used externally without finish	Comparable with the mahoganies but heavier, harder and with greater resistance to splitting. Useful for furniture and when figured for decorative work. Works with moderate ease, but blunts tools quickly
MANSONIA West Africa	38	Dark greyish brown with light and dark bands. Sapwood whitish	Straight grained. Smooth fine texture	VD	Small	II	Good lengths	C	Yes	Internal and external use including drainers	Similar in appearance to American Black Walnut. Has been used for joinery and pianos, shop fittings and furniture. Works easily and produces a good finish
MERANTI, RED AND YELLOW Malaya SERAYA, RED Borneo LAUAN, RED Philippines	35	Pale straw to deep reddish brown	Slightly interlocking. Rather coarse texture	MD	Med.	II	Good lengths	D	No	Internal and external use including sills. Weather boarding without finish	These are a group of similar timbers sold as Red and Yellow Meranti, Red and White Seraya according to the colour and country of origin of the particular species. Useful for general joinery and furniture. Works fairly easily

1	2	3	4	5	6	7	8	9	10	11	12
MUNINGA East Africa	40	Golden brown with streaks of dark red brown	Straight and irregular interlocked grain	VD	Very small	III	Average	B	No	Internal and external use	Very handsome wood but in limited supply. Similar in appearance to Padauk but softer and lighter. Eminently suitable for high class decorative joinery, panelling and furniture. Works and finishes readily
NIANGON West Africa (Nyankom)	40	Light red brown. Sapwood greyish	Interlocking grain. Coarse texture	MD	Med.	I	Average	D	No	Internal and external use	Similar to African mahogany. Quarter-sawn boards have attractive figure. Resins sometimes give the wood a sticky or greasy surface. Fairly easy to work but difficult to glue or finish because of resinous nature
OAK, EUROPEAN	45	Light yellow brown to deep warm brown with silver grain	Variable grain. Medium texture	D	Med. to large	I	Average	C/B	Yes	Internal and external including sills. Could be used externally without finish but is liable to stain in contact with ferrous metals	Imported from various European countries and home grown. The latter is probably the strongest and most durable. Although heartwood is extremely durable, sapwood is liable to insect attack. Suitable for wide range of uses from gate posts to high-class joinery. Working qualities generally satisfactory but vary. Gives exceptionally fine finish
OBECHE West Africa (Wawa)	24	White to pale straw	Interlocking grain. Open texture	ND	Small	I	Good widths	D	Yes	Internal	A rather soft easily worked lightweight wood. Very suitable for internal joinery. Although its natural light yellow colour is not very attractive it takes stain well and, since the grain is similar to mahogany, it is sometimes stained and used as a substitute for this wood. The sapwood is very prone to insect attack

195

KEY TO COLUMNS. 1. BS name and country of origin. Other common names given in brackets. 2. Average weight per cu. ft. in lbs. 3. Colour. 4. Grain and texture. 5. Natural durability. 6. Degree of moisture movement. 7. Availability in this country. 8. Special notes on sizes. 9. Comparative costs. 10. Availability as veneer. 11. Suggested positions of use. 12. Remarks.

1	2	3	4	5	6	7	8	9	10	11	12
OKWEN West Africa	40	Fawn to dark brown ir light and dark stripes	Close texture	ND	Med.	III	Average	D	No	Internal	A wood of distinctive appearance which is mostly used for furniture, turnery and carving, and in veneer form. Works fairly easily
OPEPE West Africa (Bilinga, Kusia)	47	Uniform yellow or orange brown	Interlocking grain. Open texture	VD	Small	II	Average	D	Yes	Internal and external including sills. Could be used externally without finish	A heavy strong timber primarily useful for constructional work and flooring. The better grades are suitable for joinery. Works with moderate ease and takes stain and polish but requires filling
RAMIN Malaya, Sarawak (Melawis)	42	White to pale straw	Straight grain. Fine texture	ND	Med.	I	Good lengths but narrow widths	D	No	Internal	Recommended for superior joinery, doors and furniture. Works fairly easily and finishes cleanly
SAPELE Tropical Africa (Sapele Mahogany)	40	Dark reddish brown	Interlocking grain giving regular striped figure when quarter-sawn. Medium texture	MD	Med.	I	Good lengths and widths	D	Yes	Internal	Generally used for interior joinery and fittings, panelling and furniture. It is rather more difficult to work than Honduras mahogany but takes a clean finish if properly machined and polishes excellently. Gedu Nohor is similar to this wood
SYCAMORE UK and Europe (Same genus as Maple)	58	Creamy white. Darkens on exposure to golden yellow	Straight grain. Fine texture	P	Med. to large	II	Average	B/C	Yes	Internal	Mainly used in veneer form. In the solid it works easily and finishes well, being particularly good for staining. Sometimes it is treated by dyeing to produce a grey colour known as 'Harewood'

1	2	3	4	5	6	7	8	9	10	11	12
'TASMANIAN OAK' Australia	45	Light brown. Superficially resembling English oak	Generally straight grain. Medium texture	MD	Large	III	Average	B/C	Yes	Internal	Three species are grouped under this name but none has any botanical relationship with oak. It sometimes suffers collapse in kiln-ing and needs special reconditioning. Works with moderate ease and finishes cleanly. Suitable for joinery, furniture and flooring
TEAK Burma, India, Siam, Indo-China, Java	41	Golden brown. Darkens on exposure	Straight grained	VD	Small	II	Average	A	Yes	Internal and external including sills and drainers. Could be used externally without finish	Well known for its outstanding qualities of durability (it has a naturally oily nature), stability, high strength in relation to weight, resistance to fire and corrosion by acids. It is of very good appearance. It is undoubtedly the best wood for draining boards and is specially suitable for laboratory and other work tops. Where cost permits it is no less suitable for general joinery, but it is not exceptionally good for floors or stair treads since the grain rubs up under abrasive wear. Works with moderate ease but dulls tools
UTILE West Africa (Closely related to Sapele)	40	Dark reddish brown	Interlocking grain more irregular than Sapele. Medium texture	D	Small	I	Good widths and lengths	D	Yes	Internal and external	A wood similar in appearance to Sapele although it is less highly figured. It is useful for joinery and fittings

KEY TO COLUMNS. 1. BS name and country of origin. Other common names given in brackets. 2. Average weight per cu. ft. in lbs. 3. Colour. 4. Grain and texture. 5. Natural durability. 6. Degree of moisture movement. 7. Availability in this country. 8. Special notes on sizes. 9. Comparative costs. 10. Availability as veneer. 11. Suggested positions of use. 12. Remarks.

1	2	3	4	5	6	7	8	9	10	11	12
WALNUT, EUROPEAN	45	Grey with reddish brown markings. Sapwood pale straw	Well figured, particularly English. Fine texture	MD	Small	II	Average	A	Yes	Internal	Very popular for furniture fittings and panelling but mainly used in veneer form. Suitable for use in the solid, but expensive. The wood should not be confused with African Walnut which is not a true walnut but in fact more like African Mahogany

SOFTWOODS

1	2	3	4	5	6	7	8	9	10	11	12
'DOUGLAS FIR' 'Pseudotsuga taxifolia' British Columbia, Western USA and UK (BC Pine, Oregon Pine, Columbian Pine)	57	Pale reddish yellow to deep orange brown	Straight grain varying in texture. Relatively free from knots	MD	Small	I	Available in very large sizes	E to H		Internal and external including sills	Employed generally for carpentry and joinery especially where large sizes or high strength are wanted. A little more difficult to work and finish than Redwood, and tends to split on nailing, but produces a good finish. Sometimes very resinous. The use of blunt tools produces raised grain, and this also has to be overcome in finishing
HEMLOCK, WESTERN 'Tsuga heterophylla' British Columbia, Alaska and Western USA	31	Pale greyish yellow with well marked growth rings	Straight grain. Even texture	ND	Med.	I	Large sizes	F to I		Internal	A lightweight wood, better for joinery than carpentry since it tends to split in nailing. Works readily but not so easily as Redwood. Free from resin and therefore finishes very well
'PARANA PINE' 'Araucaria angustifolia' South America	34	Pale to dark brown with red streaks. Sapwood white	Mostly straight grained. Close texture	MD	No data: assumed large	II	Good lengths	F		Internal	Easy to work though less mild than Redwood, and tends to split. Takes a very smooth finish and can be stained, polished or painted without difficulty

1	2	3	4	5	6	7	8	9 10	11	12
PINE, YELLOW 'Pinus Strobus' East of North America (White Pine, Quebec Pine, Weymouth Pine)	26	Pale straw to light reddish brown	Straight grain. Even texture	ND	Small	III		As Hard-wood Group C	Internal	Finest of high quality softwoods, both durable and stable. Works very easily and takes excellent finish. Used for high class joinery and pattern making. Western White Pine and Sugar Pine are only slightly inferior to this wood
REDWOOD 'Pinus sylvestris' Northern Asia and Europe (Fir, Red or Yellow Deal, Scots Pine)	51	Yellowish to reddish brown with cream sapwood	Texture varies	ND	Med.	I		F to H	Internal and external including sills	Used for all building work from carcassing to joinery. Easy to work and finish. Contains frequent knots but these are normally small and solid. Sapwood not durable and requires preservative treatment if used externally
'WESTERN RED CEDAR' 'Thuja plicata' British Columbia and USA (Giant Arborvitae)	24	Variable reddish brown with lighter sapwood	Straight grain. Soft texture	D	Small	II		E to H	Internal and external including sills. Need not be treated for external use	Easy to work but rather too soft for normal joinery. Contact with un-protected iron causes stains and corrosion. Specially suitable for weatherboarding or positions where its exceptional resistance to decay is an advantage. No botanical relationship with the Cedar (Cedar of Lebanon). Cheaper grades not very useful for joinery
WHITEWOOD 'Picea Abies' Northern and Central Europe (White Deal, European Spruce)	29	White to light yellow	Small knots common	ND	No data: as-sumed med-ium	I		G to I	Internal	Strength properties not as high as Redwood but adequate for most internal joinery. Used generally in Scotland in place of Redwood. This is not to be confused with American Whitewood which is a light hardwood imported in large quantities before the war for in-terior joinery

199

Appendix 2. An Extract from BS 1186, Part 1, 1952

The following paragraphs are quoted, with the permission of the British Standards Institution, from BS 1186, Part I, 1952: *Quality of Timber and Workmanship in Joinery: Quality of Timber.*

RATE OF GROWTH

6. Timber shall not be used for joinery if there are at any point on any cross-section less than eight growth rings to the inch, measured as the average number of growth rings to the inch intersected by a straight line 3 in. long normal to the growth rings, passing through the centre of the section and commencing not less than 1 in. from the pith. When a line 3 in. in length is unobtainable the measurement shall be made on the longest possible line normal to the growth rings and passing through the centre of the member (see Fig. 1).

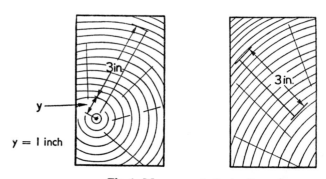

Fig. 1. Measurement of rate of growth

STRAIGHTNESS OF GRAIN

7. The slope of grain, as distinct from figure or surface marking, but ignoring local deviation in grain due to the presence of knots, shall generally be not greater than:

(*a*) One in eight in hardwoods.

(*b*) One in ten in softwoods.

A method of measuring the slope of grain is described in Appendix A of BS 1860, *Structural softwood: measurement of characteristics affecting strength.*

CHARACTER OF GRAIN

8. In jointed panels the component pieces of each panel shall be of the same

200

species of timber. In joinery which is ordered as 'selected for staining' all the surfaces of each article which are intended to receive the final decoration shall be of the same species of timber and have the same character of grain, which should as far as possible be matched.

BOXED HEART AND EXPOSED PITH
9. Boxed heart shall be permissible provided always that there is no shake on the exposed surfaces. No soft pith shall appear on any surface which is intended to receive the final decoration.

SAPWOOD
10. (a) Sapwood shall not be permitted in hardwood thresholds and projecting window sills.

(b) Sapwood shall not be permitted in hardwood joinery unless properly treated against *Lyctus* attack with a suitable preservative, except that sound untreated sapwood shall be permitted in the case of beech* and birch*.

(c) In softwood joinery which is ordered as 'selected for staining' discoloured sapwood shall not be permitted in surfaces which are intended to receive the final decoration.

(d) In other types of joinery sapwood, including discoloured sapwood, shall be permitted.

CHECKS, SPLITS AND SHAKES
11. (a) Neither splits (extending through the piece from one surface to another) nor ring shakes shall be permitted in any joinery.

(b) In external joinery all surfaces intended to receive the final decoration shall be free from checks and shakes (other than ring shakes), more than $\frac{3}{64}$ in. wide.

(c) In internal joinery which is ordered as 'selected for staining', surfaces which are intended to receive the final decoration shall be free from checks and shakes more than $0 \cdot 01$ in. wide.

(d) In internal joinery not ordered as 'selected for staining', surfaces which are intended to receive the final decoration may include checks and shakes, other than ring shakes, provided that:
- (i) They are neither more than 12 in. long nor more than $\frac{1}{16}$ in. wide.
- (ii) They do not exceed in depth one-quarter of the thickness of the piece.
- (iii) If over $0 \cdot 01$ in. wide they are suitably filled with either timber inserts or hard stopping.

(e) All surfaces not intended to receive the final decoration may include checks and shakes provided that they do not exceed in depth one-half of the thickness of the piece.

* The sapwood of most hardwoods is susceptible to *Lyctus* attack; beech and birch are exceptions. Where there is a distinct colour difference between sapwood and heartwood (e.g. in oak and mahogany), there is usually no difficulty in recognizing sapwood. In certain light-coloured timbers (e.g. sycamore, obeche and agba) special precautions may be necessary to determine the limits of the susceptible sapwood.

(*f*) For the purpose of this clause, the depth of a check or shake shall be the distance to which a feeler gauge 0·005 in. thick can be inserted into it at any point.

KNOTS

12. (*a*) Exposed surfaces of hardwood sills shall be free from knots other than isolated sound tight knots not exceeding $\frac{3}{4}$ in. in diameter.

NOTE: The usual sill grades of home grown oak will not comply with this clause.

(*b*) In joinery which is ordered as 'selected for staining', all surfaces intended to receive the final decoration shall be free from knots.

(*c*) Glazing bars shall be free from all knots other than sound knots appearing on one surface only and not exceeding $\frac{1}{4}$ in. diameter in the web and $\frac{1}{2}$ in. diameter elsewhere.

(*d*) In all other cases sound and tight knots, including knot clusters, which appear on any surface and do not break into an adjacent surface shall be permitted provided that:

(i) the mean of the largest and smallest diameters, or in the case of knot clusters the sum of the means of the largest and smallest diameters of the separate knots forming the cluster, does not exceed $1\frac{1}{2}$ in. and

(ii) the knot or knot cluster does not at any point occupy more than half the width of the surface in which it appears.

(*e*) In cases covered by (*d*) sound and tight splay or corner knots shall be permitted provided that when measured on their ends as shown in Fig. 2 neither dimension X nor dimension Y exceeds $1\frac{1}{2}$ in. and dimension X does not exceed half the width of the surface in which it appears.

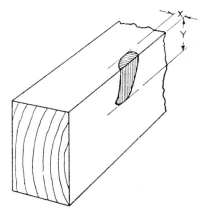

Fig. 2. Size of splay or arris knot

(*f*) Decayed or dead knots shall not be permitted in any joinery but may be cut out and plugged in accordance with Clause 13. Loose knots and knot holes shall not be permitted in any surface intended to receive the final decoration but may be cut out and plugged in accordance with Clause 13.

202

PLUGS AND INSERTS

13. Defects arising from manufacture, and knots and other defects by reason of which the timber does not comply with the requirements of the preceding Clauses 9, 11 and 12, may be bored out or cut out and replaced with a plug or insert of similar species well glued in position. The width of any plug or insert shall not exceed $1\frac{1}{2}$ in. or half the width of the surface in which it appears whichever is the less. The plug or insert shall be the full depth of the hole. The grain of the plug or insert shall run in the direction of the grain of the piece.

In joinery which is ordered as 'selected for staining', all repairs shall be permitted only if carried out so that they will not be conspicuous when the decoration is completed.

PITCH-POCKETS

14. Pitch-pockets shall not be permitted, but may be cut out and replaced as described in Clause 13.

DECAY AND INSECT ATTACK

15. All timber for joinery shall be free from all signs of decay and insect attack other than pinworm holes. Pinworm holes are permissible except where timber is required for decorative purposes or where it will be required for staining, but such holes shall be filled with hard stopping.

NOTE: Great care should be taken to ensure that any worm holes which are included are in fact those of pinhole borer (*ambrosia*) beetles and of no other insect: the size of the hole alone is not a reliable guide. Diagnostic features of pinhole borer damage are described in Forest Products Research Leaflet No. 17, and further information on the subject can be obtained from the Director, Forest Products Research Laboratory, Princes Risborough, Bucks, or The Chief Scientific Officer, Timber Development Association Ltd, 21 College Hill, London, EC4.

PLYWOOD

16. (*a*) *Moisture content*. The moisture content of all plywood at the time of manufacture of the joinery and its dispatch from the factory shall be between 10 and 15 per cent.

(*b*) The adhesives in plywood used for external purposes shall be such as will withstand the tests prescribed for Grade A70 in BS 1203, *Synthetic resin adhesives for wood*. All plywood shall be such that there is proper adhesion between the plies. A method of testing adhesion between plies is described in Appendix D of BS 1455, *British-made plywood for building and general purposes*. The face veneers shall be of such texture as to be capable of being finished with a smooth surface.

(*c*) In joinery which is ordered as 'selected for staining', plywood surfaces which are fully exposed shall comply with the following:

End joints, including scarf joints, in veneers: Not permitted.

Edge joints in veneers: Permitted only if the adjoining veneers are of the same species of timber and have the same character of grain, which should as far as possible be matched.

Overlaps in core veneers: Not permitted.

Dead knots: Not permitted.

Patches and plugs: Not permitted.

Open defects: Not permitted.

Depressions due to defects in the core: Not permitted.

Isolated pinworm holes: Permitted, provided they do not run in the plane of the veneer and the depth of any hole does not exceed the thickness of the face veneer.

Other insect attack: Not permitted.

Fungal attack: Not permitted.

Discoloration: Not permitted if differing from that normally associated with the species.

(d) All other plywood surfaces which are fully exposed, and plywood surfaces whether to be stained or not which are only occasionally exposed or seen through glass (e.g. the inside of a cupboard with glazed doors), shall comply with the above requirements except that scarf joints, edge joints and discoloration shall be permitted, and patches and plugs shall be permitted provided they are well fitted and similar in texture to the surrounding wood.

(e) Plywood surfaces which are not exposed shall not contain dead knots or knot holes whose greater dimension exceeds $1\frac{1}{2}$ in., or insect attack other than isolated pinworm holes, and the depth of any pinworm hole shall not exceed the thickness of the face veneer.

Appendix 3. British Standard Specifications Applicable to Joinery

BS 256:	1936	⎫
BS 257:	1936	⎬ *Standard Oil Varnishes.*
BS 258:	1936	⎬
BS 274:	1936	⎭
BS 455:	1957	*Schedule of sizes for locks and latches for doors.*
BS 459:		
Part 1:	1954	*Panelled and glazed wood doors.*
Part 2:	1956	*Flush wood doors (with plywood faces).*
Part 3:	1951	*Fire-check flush doors and frames.*
Part 4:	1951	*Match-boarded doors.*
BS 476:	1953	*Definitions for fire-resistance.*
BS 565:	1949	*Glossary of terms applicable to timber, plywood and joinery.*
BS 583:	1934	*Wooden gates.*
BS 584:	1956	*Wood trim.*
BS 585:	1956	*Wood stairs with close strings.*
BS 588:	1935	*Grading for plywood veneered in oak, mahogany, walnut, teak and other ornamental woods.*
BS 589: *see* BS 881.		
BS 606:	1954	*Planted sash cords made from hemp.*
BS 644:		
Part 1:	1951	*Wood casement windows.*
Part 2:	1946	*Wood windows (double-hung sashes with cased and solid frames).*
Part 3:	1951	*Wood double-hung sash and casement windows— Scottish type.*
BS 745:	1949	*Animal glue for wood.*
BS 881 & 589:	1955	*Nomenclature of commercial timbers.*
BS 952:	1953	*Glass for glazing.*
BS 973:	1945	*The glazing and fixing of glass in buildings.*
BS 1142:	1953	*Fibre building boards.*
BS 1186:		*Quality of timber and workmanship in joinery:*
Part 1:	1952	*Quality of timber.*
Part 2:	1955	*Quality of workmanship.*
BS 1195:	1948	*Kitchen fitments and equipment.*
BS 1202:	1944	*Wire nails and cut nails for building purposes.*
BS 1203:	1954	*Synthetic resin adhesives for plywood*
BS 1204:	1956	*Synthetic resin (phenolic and aminoplastic) adhesives for constructional work in wood.*

BS 1210:	1952	*Wood screws (dimensions).*
BS 1226:	1945	*Draining boards.*
BS 1227:	1945	*Hinges.*
BS 1228:	1945	*Iron, steel and non-ferrous door bolts.*
BS 1282:	1945	*Classification of wood preservatives.*
BS 1285:	1955	*Wood surrounds for metal windows.*
BS 1292:	1945	*Storage fitments for living-rooms and bedrooms.*
BS 1331:	1954	*Builders' hardware for housing.*
BS 1336:	1946	*Knotting.*
BS 1444:	1948	*Cold-setting casein glue for wood.*
BS 1455:	1956	*British-made plywood for general purposes.*
BS 1567:	1953	*Wood door frames and linings.*
BS 1722:		
Parts 5, 6 & 7:	1951	*Wooden fences.*
BS 1860:	1952	*Structural softwood: measurement of characteristics affecting strength*
BS 1960:		
Part 2:	1953	*Cabinet goods for storage purposes.*
BS 2015:	1953	*Glossary of paint terms.*
BS 2521/4:	1954	*Ready mixed oil-based priming paints.*
BS 2525/32:	1954	*Ready mixed oil-based undercoating and finishing paints (exterior quality).*
BS 2604:	1955	*Medium-density resin-bonded wood chipboard.*

BSI HANDBOOK NO. 3: *British Standards for building materials and components for housing.*

BRITISH STANDARD CODES OF PRACTICE APPLICABLE TO JOINERY

CP 112:	1952	*The structural use of timber in buildings.*
CP 151:		*Doors and windows including frames and linings.*
Part 1:	1957	*Wooden doors.*
CP 201:	1951	*Timber flooring.*
CP 231:	1952	*Painting—*
		Sub-code 231.100: *The painting of wood.*
		Sub-code 231.200: *The painting of building boards, sheets and slabs.*

Appendix 4: Traditional Joinery Components Showing Typical Sizes of Sections

The following drawings have been included in order to establish a reference for the sizes of section appropriate for certain typical components. All but three of the examples are 'traditional' in design and detail and from them one may learn the dimensions which from experience were found to be satisfactory.

These dimensions must naturally be related to the overall size of the component and we suggest limiting sizes on our drawings. Knowledge of the sizes used in these and other basic components will help the architect provide appropriate sizes for new design.

The three non-traditional examples are included for comparison and show that frequently it is possible to reduce the sizes of sections for the sake of economy.

The drawings are not to be regarded as working drawings since it is not the intention to provide copy-book patterns, but merely references to typical sizes.

The drawings have been reproduced so that the scales are as follows:

Elevations $\frac{1}{2}''$ to 1' 0''
Details $\quad$ $1\frac{1}{2}''$ to 1' 0''

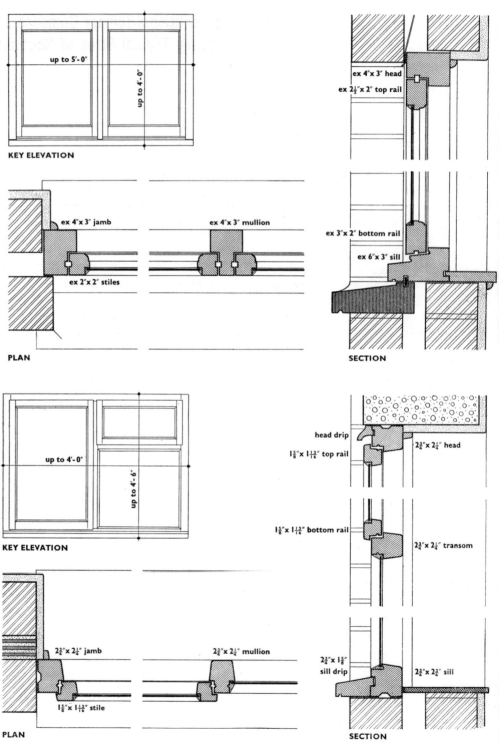

KEY ELEVATION

up to 5'- 0"

up to 4'- 0"

PLAN

ex 4"x 3" jamb

ex 4"x 3" mullion

ex 2"x 2" stiles

SECTION

ex 4"x 3" head

ex 2½"x 2" top rail

ex 3"x 2" bottom rail

ex 6"x 3" sill

KEY ELEVATION

up to 4'- 0"

up to 4'- 6"

PLAN

2¾"x 2¼" jamb

2¾"x 2¼" mullion

1⅝"x 1¹³⁄₁₆" stile

SECTION

head drip

1⅝"x 1¹³⁄₁₆" top rail

2¾"x 2¼" head

1⅝"x 1¹³⁄₁₆" bottom rail

2¾"x 2¼" transom

2¾"x 1⅝" sill drip

2¾"x 2¾" sill

208

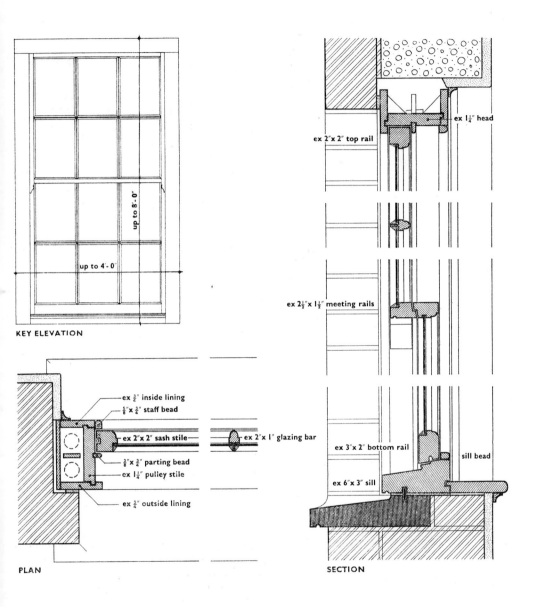

KEY ELEVATION

up to 8'-0"

up to 4'-0"

ex 1¼" head

ex 2"x 2" top rail

ex 2½"x 1½" meeting rails

ex 3"x 2" bottom rail

ex 6"x 3" sill

sill bead

PLAN

— ex ¾" inside lining
— ⅛"x ¾" staff bead
— ex 2"x 2" sash stile
— ⅜"x ¾" parting bead
— ex 1¼" pulley stile
— ex ¾" outside lining

ex 2"x 1" glazing bar

SECTION

WINDOWS (Facing page, above): *A traditional casement window with two opening lights.*

(Facing page, below): *An* EJMA *casement window with side opening casement and top hung ventilator. The differences in size and shape of the sections should be noted.*

(This page): *A traditional double hung sash designed for weights. Although complex in design its construction is well understood by joiners: however by comparison the* BS *includes a design for use with spiral metal spring balances permitting solid stiles which are less complicated and are more economical in timber.*

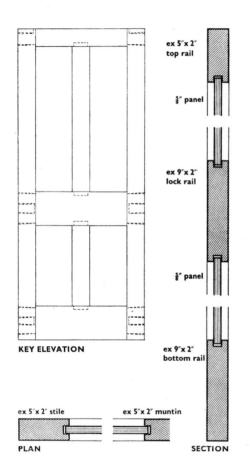

ex 5″x 2″
top rail

⅝″ panel

ex 9″x 2″
lock rail

⅝″ panel

ex 9″x 2″
bottom rail

KEY ELEVATION

SECTION

ex 5″x 2″ stile

ex 5″x 2″ muntin

PLAN

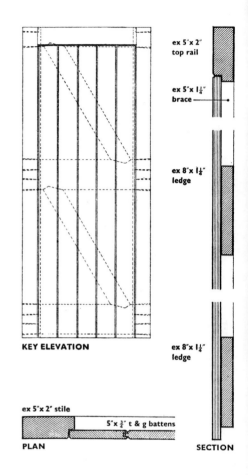

ex 5″x 2″
top rail

ex 5″x 1¼″
brace

ex 8″x 1¼″
ledge

ex 8″x 1¼″
ledge

KEY ELEVATION

SECTION

ex 5″x 2″ stile

5″x ¾″ t & g battens

PLAN

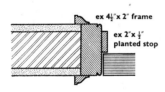

ex 4½″x 2″ frame

ex 2″x ½″
planted stop

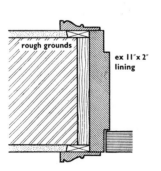

rough grounds

ex 11″x 2″
lining

DOORS (Above and left): *Traditional 4-panelled and framed, ledged and braced doors, each 2′ 9″ × 6′ 6″. By comparison the stiles and top rails in BS doors (external) are ex 4″ × 2″ and the bottom rails ex 8″ × 2″. Although not shown on the drawing, the usual practice is for the vertical battens in the framed, ledged, and braced door to be tongued into the head. Similarly the thickness of the internal frame and lining shown might nowadays be reduced to ex 1½″ and the width increased to master the plaster and thus to avoid architraves.*

STAIRCASE (Facing page): *A 'cottage' staircase say 2′ 10″ over strings. The stair has been reduced to its simplest form to show the principle of traditional construction. Strings and handrail span between newels and the balusters provide an infilling for safety. For staircases of greater width, one or more bearers would be necessary. These are usually 4″ × 2″ members running under the flight to give support to the centre of the treads and risers. They also provide a convenient fixing for plaster or other lining to the soffit.*

210

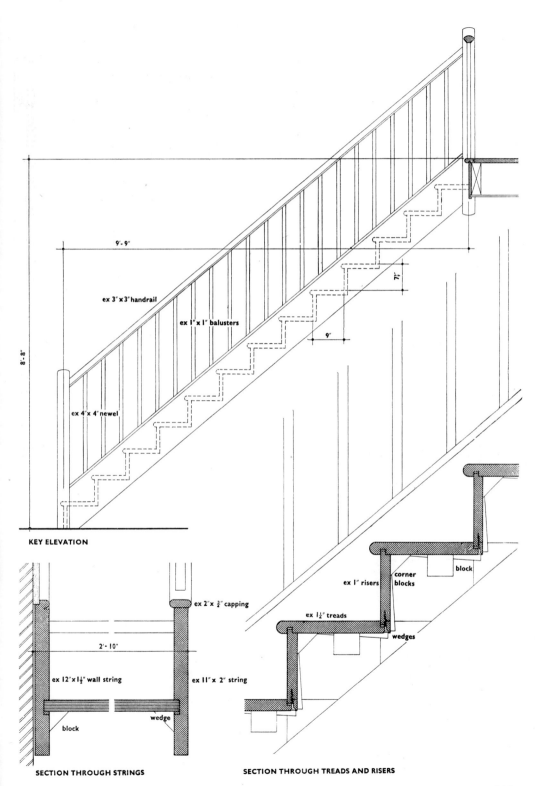

KEY ELEVATION

ex 3″ x 3″ handrail

ex 1″ x 1″ balusters

ex 4″ x 4″ newel

9′- 9″

7½″

9″

8′- 8″

ex 2″ x ¾″ capping

2′- 10″

ex 12″ x 1½″ wall string

ex 11″ x 2″ string

block

wedge

SECTION THROUGH STRINGS

block

corner blocks

ex 1″ risers

ex 1½″ treads

wedges

SECTION THROUGH TREADS AND RISERS

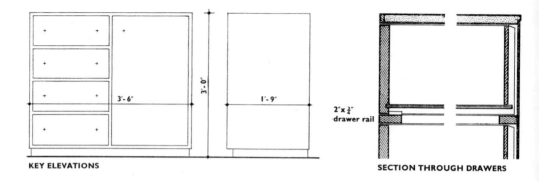

KEY ELEVATIONS

3'- 6"

3'- 0"

1'- 9"

2" x ¾"
drawer rail

SECTION THROUGH DRAWERS

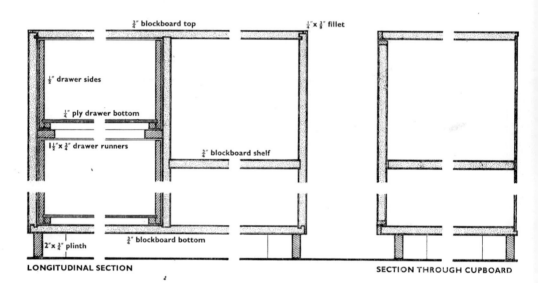

¾" blockboard top

¼" x ⅜" fillet

½" drawer sides

¼" ply drawer bottom

1½" x ¾" drawer runners

¾" blockboard shelf

2" x ¾" plinth

¾" blockboard bottom

LONGITUDINAL SECTION

SECTION THROUGH CUPBOARD

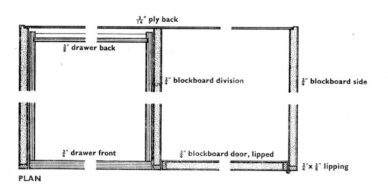

3/16" ply back

⅜" drawer back

¾" blockboard division

¾" blockboard side

⅜" drawer front

¾" blockboard door, lipped

¼" x ⅜" lipping

PLAN

CUPBOARDS *A modern version of carcass construction (sides, top and bottom in the solid). Blockboard is shown in the examples but glued-up solid timber would have been used traditionally—with a panelled door to the cupboard.*

212

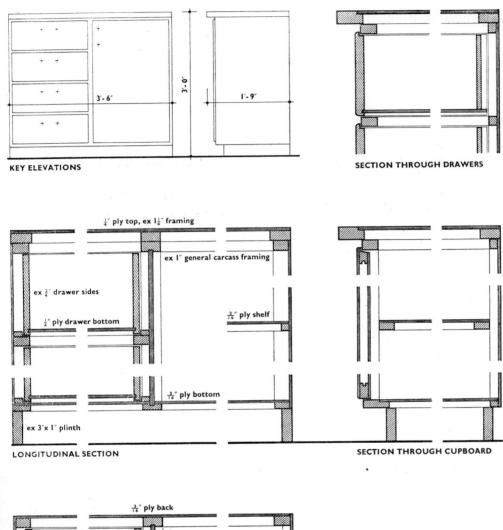

KEY ELEVATIONS

3'- 6"

3'- 0"

1'- 9"

SECTION THROUGH DRAWERS

¼" ply top, ex 1¼" framing

ex 1" general carcass framing

ex ¾" drawer sides

¼" ply drawer bottom

³⁄₁₆" ply shelf

³⁄₁₆" ply bottom

ex 3"x 1" plinth

LONGITUDINAL SECTION

SECTION THROUGH CUPBOARD

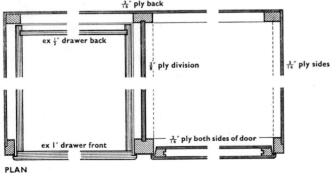

³⁄₁₆" ply back

ex ½" drawer back

³⁄₈" ply division

³⁄₁₆" ply sides

ex 1" drawer front

³⁄₁₆" ply both sides of door

PLAN

CUPBOARDS *A typical cheap modern cupboard framed up and covered with plywood. The lipped fronts to the cupboard drawers conceal inaccuracies in fitting, so reducing production costs.*

213

Appendix 5: Bibliography

OLD BOOKS

James Newland. *The Carpenter and Joiner's Assistant* (Blackie and Son, 1860 and 1869)

Peter Nicholson, revised by Thomas Tredgold. *Practical Carpentry, Joinery and Cabinet Making* (Thomas Kelly, 1845, and several other editions)
The basis of many later books—illustrated with beautiful drawings

FOREIGN BOOKS

Geoffrey Baker and Bruno Funaro. *Windows in Modern Architecture* (Architectural Book Publishing Company, New York, 1948)
Profusely illustrated with detail and photographs of American windows

H. Guyer and E. Kettiger. *Mobel und Wohnraum* (Verlag für Architektur, Erlenbach/Zurich, 1946)
Picture book with drawings showing some construction of post-war Swiss furniture

Adolf G. Schneck. *Fenster aus Holz und Metall* (Julius Hoffmann Verlag, Stuttgart, 1953, 5th edition)

Adolf G. Schneck. *Türen aus Holz und Metall* (Julius Hoffmann Verlag, Stuttgart, 1956, 5th edition)
Exhaustive studies in German with photographs and details

Fritz Spannagel. *Der Mobelbau* (Otto Maier Verlag, Ravensburg, 1954, 10th edition)
Comprehensive treatise on furniture and fitments with notes on techniques, timbers and finishes

Antonio Vallardi. *Documenti di Architettura, Serie 0, Fasc. 1, No. 2: Porte* (Vallardi, Milano, 1946)

Antonio Vallardi. *Documenti, Serie 0, Fasc. 2, No. 5: Finestre* (Vallardi, Milano, 1946)
A series of detail sheets of examples of continental work. A fairly useful library reference

MATERIALS

N. C. E. Clifford, *Timber Identification for the Builder and Architect* (Leonard Hill Ltd, 1957)
A useful set of notes on timbers giving their characteristics and uses with emphasis on identification

H. A. Cox. *Wood Specimens* (100 reproductions in colour) (Nema Press, 1949)

Wood Specimens (A second collection of 100 reproductions in colour) (Tothill Press Ltd, 1957)
Reproductions in colour of different woods with descriptive notes on their characteristics and uses

H. E. Desch. *Timber: its Structure and Properties* (Macmillan, 1953, 3rd edition)
  A readable and authentic work on the subject
W. P. K. Findlay. *Dry Rot and other Timber Troubles* (Hutchinson, 1953)
  A standard work
A. L. Howard. *Trees in Britain and Their Timbers* (Country Life, 1947)
  Of general interest, well illustrated
R. A. G. Knight. *Adhesives for Wood* (Chapman and Hall, 1952)
A. D. Wood and T. G. Linn. *Plywoods* (W. and A. K. Johnston, 1950, 2nd edition)
  A useful and complete reference book
Timber Development Association. *Plywood* (TDA, 1957)
  A concise and thoroughly practical guide to plywoods and their uses

GENERAL JOINERY
D. A. C. A. Boyne and Lance Wright (editors). *Architects' Working Details*, Volumes 1, 2, 3, 4, continuing series (Architectural Press, 1953, 1954, 1955, 1957)
  Source of illustrated examples of contemporary joinery detail.
A. E. and T. R. Bridgwood. *Carpentry and Joinery (Advanced)* (George Newnes Ltd, 1952)
  Addressed to advanced students of joinery and covers the subject of the geometry of staircases and handrails
George Ellis. *Modern Practical Joinery* (Batsford, 5th edition, 1924)
  A standard work on traditional joinery
T. O. Howard. *Teach Yourself Joinery* (English Universities Press Ltd, 1951)
  A useful introduction addressed to amateurs and apprentices.
W. E. Kelsey. *Carpentry, Joinery and Woodcutting Machinery* (Macmillan, 1954)
  A thorough textbook addressed primarily to craftsmen
W. B. McKay. *Building Construction*, Volume III (Longmans, 1957, 2nd revised edition)
W. B. McKay. *Joinery* (Longmans, 1946)
  A good handbook with clear illustrations of joinery construction
Edward D. Mills (editor). *Architects' Detail Sheets*, Volumes 1, 2 and 3, continuing series (Iliffe and Sons Ltd, 1953, 1954, 1956)

FURNITURE AND FITMENTS
Denise Bonnett. *Contemporary Cabinet Design and Construction* (Batsford, 1956)
  A collection of contributions on the various aspects of the problem. Examples modern in character
John Hooper. *Modern Cabinet Work, Furniture and Fitments* (Batsford, 1952, 6th revised edition)
John and Rodney Hooper. *Modern Furniture and Fittings* (Batsford, 1949)
  Standard works illustrated with photographs and working drawings. Most examples traditional in character
Gordon Logie. *Furniture from Machines* (Allen and Unwin, 1948)
  An account of the application of machine production to modern furniture; includes metal and plastic as well as timber and plywoods

SPECIFICATION

H. T. Davey. *Wood Finishing* (Pitman, 1940)
   A concise and helpful description of the subject

F. R. S. Yorke and Penelope Whiting. *Specification* (Architectural Press, annually)

RESEARCH ORGANIZATIONS

Building Research Station Digests:
   The Design of Timber Floors to Prevent Dry Rot, No. 1 (HMSO, 1948)
   Painting Woodwork, No. 30 (HMSO, 1951)
   Use of Hardwoods in Building, No. 59 (HMSO, 1953)

K. St. G. Cartwright and W. P. K. Findlay. *Decay of Timber and its Prevention* (HMSO, 1947)

Department of Scientific and Industrial Research. *A Handbook of Softwoods* (HMSO, 1957)

Department of Scientific and Industrial Research. *A Handbook of Hardwoods* (HMSO, 1956)

Forest Products Research Laboratory. *Bulletins* (HMSO)

Timber Development Association. *Red Books* (TDA)

Research Association of British Paint, Colour and Varnish Manufacturers. *Bulletins* (RABPCVM)

JOURNAL

Wood, issued monthly by the Tothill Press Ltd

Index

217